DALTONS!

DALTONS!

THE RAID ON COFFEYVILLE, KANSAS

by
Robert Barr Smith

University of Oklahoma Press : Norman and London

Books by Robert Barr Smith

Literate Lawyer: Legal Writing and Oral Advocacy (Austin, 1986, 1991)
To the Last Cartridge (New York, 1994)
Daltons! The Raid on Coffeyville, Kansas (Norman, 1996)

Library of Congress Cataloging-in-Publication Data

Smith, Robert B. (Robert Barr), 1933–
    Daltons!: the raid on Coffeyville, Kansas / by Robert Barr
    Smith.
      p. cm.
    Includes bibliographical references and index.
    ISBN 0–8061–2795–3 (alk. paper)
    1. Coffeyville (Kan.)—History. 2. Dalton family. 3. Outlaws—
    Kansas—Coffeyville—History—19th century. 4. Frontier and
    pioneer life—Kansas—Coffeyville. I. Title.
    F689.C6S64   1996
    364.1′552′0978193—dc20   95–41645
                                             CIP

The paper in this book meets the guidelines for permanence and durability of the Committee on Production Guidelines for Book Longevity of the Council on Library Resources, Inc. ∞

1 2 3 4 5 6 7 8 9 10

This book is respectfully dedicated to the defenders of Coffeyville, Kansas, in the Year of Our Lord 1892, to all the men who rose up to shoot it out with a bunch of hoodlums intent on terrorizing their quiet country town.

It is dedicated especially to the men who died defending their town, ordinary people who got involved in their neighbors' troubles and came to help in spite of danger:

Lucius M. Baldwin
Charles Brown
Charles T. Connelly
George B. Cubine

CONTENTS

List of Illustrations   **ix**
Preface   **xi**

Chapters
1. A Fair City and a Smiling Land   **3**
2. No God West of Fort Smith   **19**
3. Horsemen from the South   **34**
4. A Scene of Peace and Splendor   **83**
5. A Flash of Lightning from a Clear Sky   **116**
6. Men Who Did Their Duty Well   **135**
7. When the Smoke Cleared   **149**
8. The Sixth Man, and Other Mythology   **183**

Afterword   **208**
Notes   **211**
Bibliography   **223**
Index   **229**

ILLUSTRATIONS

following page 105

1. Downtown Coffeyville in the autumn of 1892
2. Coffeyville, Kansas, about 1880
3. Walnut Street about 1892
4. The west side of Walnut Street about 1895
5. Frank Dalton
6. Bob Dalton with unidentified woman
7. Grat Dalton
8. William Todd ("Bill") Power, or Powers
9. The Condon Bank at Coffeyville, Kansas, 1892
10. Bullet holes in the Condon windows
11. Death Alley after the raid
12. First National Bank Lobby, 1892
13. The Dalton Gang after the raid
14. Lucius Baldwin
15. Marshal Charles T. Connelly
16. George B. Cubine
17. Charles Brown
18. John J. Kloehr
19. William M. Dalton

PREFACE

THIS BOOK IS ABOUT a bandit raid on a little town in southeast Kansas. It is also about the wild frontier times that produced the raid, and about the gang that planned it and carried it out, the famous—or infamous—Daltons. And, with great respect, it is about the men who defended the town, ordinary citizens who rallied without command or plan and pitched in to fight a band of heavily armed criminals.

Some of these citizens died in the fight against the Dalton gang. Others were hurt. The wonder of what they did is not that they won their fight—they did—but that they risked their lives at all. Most of them had no especially good reason to fight, except that they didn't like hoodlums coming into their town and stealing things and pushing people around.

The abiding sadness of the present century is the tragic disappearance of the public spirit and courage that moved the defenders of that little Kansas town. These days, in most places anyway, people "don't want to get involved." And that, more than any other reason, is why evil people do monstrous things today without any real fear of resistance. It is pleasant, therefore, to read for a little about a time when and town where people believed in standing up for their neighbors, even at the risk of their lives.

A preliminary word about the invaders. Throughout this book, it is important to keep in mind just who the Daltons and their followers actually were. As it has with the James and Younger brothers, popular fiction—especially film—has tended to cast the Daltons in something of a heroic light. Even O. Henry got into the act, with a wildly inaccurate story called "Holding Up a Train." Long years later, a batch of made-up movies and reams of purple prose have transmogrified the Daltons into hybrids of Robin Hood and honest-cowboy-avenging-ancient-wrongs.

Neither image even approaches the truth. For the Daltons and those who followed them were not Robin Hood, nor were they Pepe le Moko or Zorro or Raffles. They were simply criminals who found it easier to steal from other people than to work.

The James boys had some claim to the mantle of Robin Hood. At least they could shelter in the mythology of the vicious border war between free-soil man and slave-state supporter. In the last century many people believed—some still do—that the Jameses and Youngers were just good boys driven to the owlhoot trail by an implacable enemy, giving to the poor and being nice to old ladies. Although this image was unadulterated moonshine, there was at least some reason to idealize the Jameses and Youngers.

Not so the Daltons. They were not Civil War veterans, bushwhackers, and guerrillas as the James boys were. The eldest of the Daltons at Coffeyville, Grat, was born the year the great war ended.

To do further violence to the legend of the Daltons, there is ample evidence that the Dalton boys were not, with the possible exception of Bob, very bright. No doubt I will get all sorts of angry letters about that statement from folks who revere the myth of the noble outlaw. Still, it is hard to characterize the Daltons' lack of planning and caution at Coffeyville as anything but just plain stupid. I shall make what case I can for the gang's incompetence, and the reader may judge as he or she will.

The *Daily Oklahoman*, Oklahoma City's venerable newspaper, summed up the Dalton gang pretty well in a 1939 story. Its language may overstate the case a little, but it surely scrubs the sheen of romance from the image of a bunch of common outlaws. "They were lousy loafers ... who refused to do their share of the backbreaking labor of pioneering, scum of the civilization that came ... to tame the wilderness. They lived by stealing from those who did the real work, murdering them if they resisted."[1]

In spite of reality, and with the aid of a bevy of mostly fictional movies, the Daltons nevertheless won an astonishing measure of fame. Even today they ride perpetually on into the sunset, and their notoriety is not limited to the United States. The Daltons—four of them—are the villains of a popular European comic strip called "Lucky Luke," in which Luke, with his faithful horse and dog, endlessly pursues the Daltons. Perhaps by device, in this comic strip the Daltons, who come in four sizes like stair-steps, all look very much like Adolf Hitler. They run about muttering, in German and twenty-four other languages, things like "Wir brauchen jetzt schnellstens Pferde!" (We need horses *fast*). Coffeyville appears in the strip as the peaceful town of Rightful Bend, forever menaced by the gang.[2]

I have used a great number of sources in writing this book. The wellspring, the starting place for everybody who has written anything about the Coffeyville raid, is a long newspaper article in the *Coffeyville Journal* of Friday, October 7, 1892. It was written by a remarkable man, Captain David Stewart Elliott, who both edited and published the *Journal*. Later in 1892, Elliott also produced a little book called *Last Raid of the Daltons*, an expansion of his newspaper article using much of the same prose.

The *Journal* article and the *Last Raid* book are the only full accounts of the raid written at the time. They have the added virtue of being written by an experienced journalist who was also a man of intelligence and unchallenged integrity. Making some small allowance for Captain Elliott's understandable pride in his town and its courageous citizens, it is safe to take Elliott's writings as the most accurate—as well as the most contemporary— accounts of the raid.

The bandit side of the Coffeyville fight is largely undocumented; four of the five gang members were killed during the raid. Long years afterward, the sole survivor, much-wounded Emmett Dalton, produced a couple of books in which he wrote about Coffeyville. Sadly, *When the Daltons Rode* and *Beyond the Law*, though they make stirring reading, do not adhere overmuch to the truth. They are fun to read but they have been rejected as reliable sources by most historians, and I concur in that judgment. From time to time I refer to both volumes in this book, but I place no reliance on them.

There are numerous other accounts of the raid, including what purport to be eyewitness histories. Some of them are the real thing, others are fantasy, others one cannot be sure about. There have been all manner of books about the Dalton gang, as well, many of which contain demonstrable inaccuracies, not to say downright inventions. With these sources, too, it is hard to sort out the real from the imaginary across the shadows of a hundred years.

I want especially to mention another source that I found particularly useful in writing this book. It is an interesting adventure in indefatigable scholarship, and I relied heavily on its fine collection of newspaper clippings. The book is Nancy B. Samuelson's *The Dalton Gang Story*. Another excellent book, written with integrity, is Frank Latta's *Dalton Gang Days*. I relied on it as well, making allowances for the fact that much of the material came from a Dalton brother then much advanced in years, whose only knowledge of many events was necessarily secondhand.

I also enjoyed, and relied on, a fine little book published by the Coffeyville Historical Society, Professor Lue Barndollar's

What Really Happened on October 5, 1892. Barndollar did an admirable job of pulling together the story of the raid from a variety of sources, and included in *What Really Happened* a marvelous assortment of pictures, some of which appear here. I recommend *What Really Happened* as the best short account of the raid since Colonel Elliott's report, and that is high praise indeed.

Finally, nobody can write about the outlaw days in early Oklahoma without relying heavily on the works of Glenn Shirley, the dean of western writers. I strongly recommend his *West of Hell's Fringe.* Nobody ever caught the flavor of those wild days better than Shirley has. His books are a delight the first time through—and better still on second reading.

There are many other useful sources for anybody interested in the Daltons and the attack on Coffeyville. They are set out in the bibliography. A series of pieces in the *Coffeyville Journal* have been especially helpful, reflections of a fine little town that remains proud of its history and honest about it.

I am profoundly grateful to the Coffeyville Defenders' Museum staff and its curator, Woody De Pontier, for their unfailingly courteous assistance. They were remarkably patient in answering a number of dumb and sometimes repetitive questions. I owe a particular debt to J. B. Kloehr and Lue Barndollar, and above all to Jackie Isham Barrett, who cheerfully provided an immense amount of useful material and her own time, insight, and good advice about the Dalton raid.

My thanks also to the *Coffeyville Journal* and its publisher, Mike Thornberry, and to the Coffeyville Historical Society, especially Gary Misch. Many of the illustrations in this book are reprinted through their courtesy. I am grateful to Pat Waddle of Vinita, Oklahoma, for the rare photo of Bill Powers and for information about him.

Out of respect for their privacy, I have not named all the Coffeyville defenders' descendants who were kind enough to write to me and share clippings, pictures, and family memories. I am, nevertheless, grateful for their gracious assistance.

I also owe a huge debt to the Western History Library at the University of Oklahoma and to its able staff, especially Kristina Southwell. I am particularly grateful to Dr. John Lovett, the librarian, who knows everything there is to know about the West and is never too busy to share it. Thanks also to the public libraries of Coffeyville and Bartlesville for their help and courtesy.

Coffeyville remembers and celebrates the Dalton raid. But it does so for the right reasons. Its annual remembrance of the raid is called Defenders' Days, and its excellent little museum is called the Defenders' Museum. In short, the citizens of Coffeyville honor not the hoodlums who came to terrorize their town but the townsmen who rallied round and fought them off.

It is, to borrow words from a very great man, altogether fitting and proper that they do this, and I have tried to approach this book in the way in which Coffeyville approaches its history. I have therefore written as much as I can find about the men who fought back, who laid their lives on the line rather than let a gaggle of hoodlums steal and intimidate in their town.

They were ordinary people, the men who risked their lives against the Daltons. Not one of the citizens killed in the fight owned even a small piece of either of the banks the bandits raided. The dedication in this book reflects my feelings about those citizens, the winners and the real heroes of the Coffeyville fight.

This, then, is the story of a bunch of bad men, a group of good men, and a vicious, close-range firefight that burst, as Captain Elliott wrote, "upon the peaceful city like a flash of lightning from a clear sky."[3]

ROBERT BARR SMITH

Norman, Oklahoma

DALTONS!

1

A FAIR CITY AND A SMILING LAND

Today's Kansas, "the Sunflower State," strikes Americans as a place of prosperity, of solid old-fashioned values, of peace and quiet. And so it is, today. But Kansas wasn't always that way. For a long time Kansas was, as the hellfire preachers said, a way-station on the turnpike to hell. The state's rich earth was watered with the blood of a lot of men and women, good and bad, and the bleeding started long before the rifles roared in Coffeyville.

The modern history of southern Kansas really begins about 1825, for in that year the United States made a solemn compact with the Osage and the Kanza, a treaty that granted the tribes certain illusory rights in return for most of their traditional land. Other tribes, displaced from their own ancestral lands by treaty, moved into the vacuum left by the departure of the Osage and Kanza—until, in 1854, the white government moved the Indians of Kansas again, this time shunting most of them south into the wild Indian Territory, today's Oklahoma. And by 1854 another trouble deeply vexed settlers in the Kansas Territory: the ugly spectre of slavery.

The problem had been alleviated a little in 1820, when the Missouri Compromise admitted that state as slave territory but guaranteed freedom north of the Missouri line. But nobody, proslavery or free-stater, would accept the compromise as a final answer. After passage of the Kansas-Nebraska Bill of 1854, those favoring slavery became convinced that Nebraska would enter the Union as free soil. That being so, they were determined to bring in Kansas as a slave state and thereby preserve their precious free/slave balance in the United States Senate.

Free-soil people were just as determined that the horror of slavery would never befoul the fair land of Kansas. Colonies of abolitionist immigrants appeared, grew, and prospered—and were ready to fight for their beliefs if they had to. New England abolitionist clergyman Henry Ward Beecher thoughtfully sent his disciples not only Testaments but also Sharps rifles—"Beecher's Bibles" they were called—the better to do the Lord's work in Kansas. More free-soil settlers trekked out to Kansas, and more rifle money was raised in the East.

Colonies of southerners grew as well. Organized groups like "Buford's Men" out of Georgia arrived to swell the ranks of the proslavery forces. Partisans of both sides were not particular about how they advanced their political peculiarities. As one Kansas newspaper bitterly commented, "I have seen thousands of armed Missourians cross the river ... to vote in an election, and return home the next day."[1] It was only a short step from stuffing ballot boxes to shooting folks who disagreed with you. The rifles were at hand; so was the anger. The time for killing had arrived.

And so Kansas the Eden of the West became Bleeding Kansas, as men began to fight to see whether Kansas would be a place in which one human being could own another. It was not an organized war. It was something much worse. It was murder from ambush and wanton cattle killing, barn burning, and kidnapping and screams in the night, and the level of hatred steadily rose. Both sides recruited more settlers, men and women who believed deeply in slavery or in abolition and were quite willing to kill people with views of which they disapproved.

People had begun to hate so deeply that in May of 1856, in the hallowed chamber of the United States Senate, a slave-state man beat Massachusetts Senator Charles Sumner almost to death with a heavy cane. "Bully" Brooks was a South Carolinian who resented abolitionist Sumner's remarks attacking slavery and one of its chief partisans, Brooks's kinsman Senator Andrew Butler.

Just the day before Brooks splashed Sumner's blood across the desks of the Senate, a rowdy mob of Missouri proslavers had made their own brutal statement about slavery. This band of border ruffians terrorized thriving Lawrence, Kansas, a staunch free-soil town on the Kansas River not far west of the Missouri line. The ruffians, many of them drunk, beat, burned, and looted, and generally brutalized Lawrence's citizens.

The ferocious, unforgiving spirit of the times is clearly reflected in the words of one of the ruffians' leaders, sometime United States Senator David Atchison, who egged on his drunken supporters with these temperate words: "Be brave, be orderly, and if any man or woman stands in your way, blow them to hell with a chunk of cold lead."[2] Atchison's ominous language just about summed up the ugly temper along both sides of the border.

About the same time, a fanatic, shiftless failure of a man crept through the warm May night along Pottawatomie Creek with murder in his heart. Backed up by some of his sons, this terrible old man called proslavery settlers out from their homes to hack them to death with war-surplus artillery swords. Grim old John Brown had already started on the road to Harper's Ferry, killing unarmed men in the name of God and rejoicing in the blood. He even cut off his victims' hands, did old Brown, an especially ugly Old Testament kind of postscript to murder in the dark.

In those days Brown held forth at Osawatomie, only about eighty miles northeast of Coffeyville on the Marais des Cygnes River. Before long proslavery men did bloody murder in revenge. At Easton, Kansas, a free-soil man named Captain E. P. Brown was foully murdered—not just killed but, like old Brown's victims, butchered, "literally chopped to pieces with hatchets . . . and his bleeding corpse flung before his young wife."[3] And the free-soilers burned John Brown's home and killed one of his sons, and the ugly cycle of escalating hatred rolled on unbroken. Blood spilled begat more blood and malice repaid malice manyfold.

It might have gotten even worse. Armed bands were on the move, and the summer of 1856 looked like being the start of an all-out war along the Kansas-Missouri border. Fortunately, a detachment of the minuscule regular army came out from Fort Leavenworth and flexed its blue-clad muscle; both free-soil and slave state men went home to mutter and glower and bide their time.

The fire was not out, however, not by a long shot. It would smolder, ready to burst into flame, and the time for that was not long in coming. In 1858, on the quiet river called the Marais des Cygnes, eleven free-soil men were murdered by a band of slave-staters from both Kansas and Missouri. With every killing, hate and ill will swelled and festered, a bloated boil on the face of Kansas. The ugliest kind of rupture was on the way.

At the end of January, 1861, Kansas entered a tortured Union which several southern states had just abandoned. With the coming of formal war, even more men took up arms, and bushwhackers and redlegs killed and burned and raped and brutalized. If you belonged to the wrong side you suffered, and sometimes people died just because they tried to stay out of this dirty backroad struggle.

For four weary years the vicious guerrilla war dragged on and Kansas continued to bleed. Poor old Lawrence was sacked again in the summer of 1863, this time by William Quantrill and his bushwhackers. There was no resistance but the guerrillas left more than 150 civilians dead behind them—two people were burned alive—and over a million dollars' damage in burned houses, barns, and stores.

The bushwhacker bands of Quantrill and Bloody Bill Anderson and other guerrilla leaders were hunted down in time, chased to destruction by regular troops and by other irregulars very like themselves, pro-Union men who called themselves jayhawkers. The jayhawkers did their own share of wanton burning and killing. They even took their name, as one of them said, from "a bird in Ireland that catches small birds and bullyrags the life out of them like cats do mice. I'm in the same business meself."[4] Both Quantrill and Anderson, the worst of the lot, were exterminated by Union forces before the great war ended. Even so, the long four years of guerrilla struggle left an ugly legacy.

Most of the bushwhackers who survived the war went home and picked up more or less where they had left off. Once the killing was done they lived lives of reasonable respectability, very much like their neighbors who had not ridden with the guerrilla bands. But some did not; hard-bitten, unforgiving men with names like James and Younger, they found peace too dull to abide, or found honest work beneath them, or maybe both.

After the war settlers flocked west and Kansas began to bloom. At first there were cattle, the great bawling herds out of Texas, bound for the new railheads and the voracious appetites of the eastern United States. The formidable longhorn roamed Texas in millions after the Civil War, perhaps as many as ten million animals, money on the hoof. The railroad reefer car had come into its own, a thick-walled carriage insulated with packed sawdust, the way icehouses were built. Texas beef appeared on eastern menus, and the demand was enormous.

Some of the toughest towns in the country sprang up along the railroad rights-of-way: Wichita, Dodge City and Caldwell, Hays, Ellsworth and Abilene. These wild trail towns attracted most of the preeminent gunfighters of the day, men like the Masterson boys, Luke Short, Rowdy Joe Lowe, Mysterious Dave Mather, Doc Holliday, Wyatt Earp, and Bill Hickok. Many men went armed as a rule in those times and places, and everybody knew how to handle a weapon.

Most of the trail towns boomed and blossomed with the coming of the railroad, then wilted a little as the railhead moved on and the herds and the whores and the gamblers and the gunfighters moved on with it. But while the boom was on, in the mushroom Kansas cow towns hell was constantly in session, as the cowboys said.

Violence was the order of the day. Some of it was relatively harmless, food for amusement rather than fear. Take, for example, an encounter between two well-known "soiled doves" in old Dodge City. Thus spake the *Ford County Globe*, in an article aptly entitled "Scarlet Sluggers": "A desperate fight occurred at the boarding house of Mrs. W., on 'Tin Pot Alley' ... between two of the most fascinating doves of the roost.... [I]t was a magnificent sight to see. Tufts of hair, calico, snuff and gravel flew like fir [sic] in a cat fight.... [T]he vanquished virgin was carried to her parlors."[5]

Often, however, nobody laughed. Mr. Winchester and Mr. Colt's sons and daughters were widely used to arbitrate personal disagreements summarily, along with divers kinds of knives, broken bottles, axhandles, shotguns, and poolcues. The story of a single night in a single town will set the tone of the Kansas cow towns after the war. It happened in raw, railhead Newton where, the Texans said, more bad whiskey was sold than anyplace else in all of Kansas.

One hot summer night in 1871 there was a falling out between a bellicose Texan called Bailey and special policeman Mike McCluskie, a cement-fisted ex–section boss for the railroad. One thing led to another and Bailey, full of prime coffin varnish, made his first mistake of the evening: he went after McCluskie with his fists in the Red Front Saloon. McCluskie promptly flattened the Texan, knocking him clean through the saloon doors. As McCluskie followed Bailey into the street, the Texan reached for his gun, which was his second mistake. He was a little slow here too, and McCluskie permanently ventilated him.

Bailey died but the quarrel did not, and a week later a band of Texican cowboys sought out Mike McCluskie at Perry Tuttle's saloon down in "Hide Park," the aptly named red-light district of Newton. In the fight that followed McCluskie was mortally wounded by a belligerent Texan, a Salado cowman called Anderson. Firing became general and when the smoke cleared McCluskie and four other men were dead or dying and at least four others were wounded.

So, even with the war behind it, Kansas was not yet the peaceful Sunflower State, and if anybody needed proof of that, they got it two summers later. Into Medicine Lodge, a wide spot in the road, rode McCluskie's brother. He had spent a long time looking for Anderson, his sibling's killer, and he found the Texan tending bar in this dinky settlement. The two men shot it out by appointment later that day, slamming slugs into one another until both were down. Soaked with blood, they kept on clawing away, finally slashing one another to death with Bowie knives as they groveled on the ground.

But if Kansas was not the quiet, settled East, there were still lots of hard working, respectable people coming out to till the soil and open stores and raise families, more and more of them every year. And there were schools and churches built in plenty. Still, the state retained much of the rawness and self-sufficiency of the frontier. And if in time violence usually hid its face from civilization, the beast was still alive; it was wary of the light of day, but it was never very far away.

The shining steel of the railroad meant vitality and long life in the last century. The citizens of Liberty, Kansas, off the right-of-way, jacked up their whole town and moved it two and a half miles to the main line. Served by three railroads, Coffeyville had bright prospects indeed. At first that future depended on cattle, a share of the great trail herds pushing up out of Texas. Coffeyville was far enough east to miss the worst of the wild doings associated with the trail herds. Most of the longhorns came north over the fabulous Chisholm trail and other established tracks west of Coffeyville.

But some cattle were driven north over what was variously called the Osage or Shawnee trail, to meet the railroad at Coffeyville and nearby Baxter Springs. In the drives of 1873, for example, Texas trail crews pushed perhaps half a million head north to the Kansas railheads. Of these, about a tenth ended up in the Coffeyville–Baxter Springs area. A lot of the dogies boarded the eastbound trains from a loading pen in South Coffeyville, in those days called Stevens Switch.

Little Coffeyville was served by the Missouri Pacific, the Kansas and Arkansas Valley—commonly called the Iron Mountain—and the Leavenworth, Lawrence and Galveston, later to be the Santa Fe. There was also the Katy—the Missouri, Kansas and Texas—which extended on south toward the border with Indian Territory, and tied into the Kansas and Arkansas Valley, meandering up through the Osage country from Fort Smith.

And for a little while burgeoning Coffeyville looked a lot like the other bawdy, raucous Kansas cow towns, with the obligatory contingent of saloon owners, gamblers, and con men. With them came the standard company of Dulcineas, nymphs du prairie, fancies, and calico queens—whores, that is—to service the Texas cowboys who pushed the herds north. Twelfth Street was called "Red Hot Street," a clutter of shanties, shacks, and tents, and it qualified fully as the sin strip of Coffeyville.

Red Hot Street echoed nightly to the roistering and quarreling of the young cowpunchers, mixed in with a goodly number of teamsters, soldiers, and Indians, all of them out to paint the town red. Faro, poker, and monte games ran wide open, and dance halls were "run by men who were equal to any crime, and filled with females tough enough to delight the toughest cowboy who ever threw a gentleman cow.... [G]amblers, desperadoes and dissolute women made almost every night hideous by their carousals.... [F]or many mornings in succession there was a 'man for breakfast,' and death was so familiar that it no longer inspired the customary awe or horror."[6] Most of the hell-raising was good natured, but some of it was not. On Christmas night, 1871, for example, a dance at the Big Tent Saloon ended in gunfire, with three of the celebrants down and bleeding on the barroom floor.

Things continued wild and woolly at least through 1872. In the summer of that year, the whole county thrilled to the saga of Ollie Davis, a wonderfully comely nymph of the night, at least according to the story. A newspaper account waxed poetic over her beauty and elite background: "[W]e can easily picture her a beautiful young girl who gave every promise of being a credit to her parents, a joy to her friends an ornament to society."[7] Alas! Ollie turned out to be an ornament all right, but not at all in the way her friends and parents might have wished. Instead, she was by way of being the queen of Red Hot Street, attractive indeed, but a termagant in her cups.

And her lust for John Barleycorn proved to be her nemesis. Having imbibed too much of the grape one memorable evening, Ollie was moved to draw her handgun and clear a whole saloon, after some misunderstanding with the bartenders there. Some spoilsport called the law and marshal Pete Flynn came down to the saloon to fix things. Ollie didn't like that, so she opened up on Flynn with her pistol. Even with a bullet in the groin, however, Flynn was a tough cop. He took shelter behind a door and banged away, while Ollie poured more lead at him from behind the bar until one of Flynn's slugs hit Ollie in the head, ending at once the fight and Ollie's career.

It's said that Ollie was much mourned in Coffeyville. She was certainly much talked about, and even the *Journal* could not resist a last sanctimonious speech: "She was only a fallen woman, but somebody's heart bled because of her fall, and who knows what the circumstances were which led to her downfall? Mayhap she was more sinned against than sinning."[8]

In the days after Ollie's sad demise, the cowboys still called Coffeyville "Cow Town" and their end-of-trail celebrations reigned pretty well unrestrained. Even in those wild early days, however, there were signs of civilization. The *Coffeyville Journal* had begun publishing, run by a bearded gentleman politician named Peffer, sometime United States Senator and firebrand populist orator. Three doctors practiced in town, the Reed Brothers had opened a grocery store, and the town grew steadily as other businesses appeared.

If the town was growing more civilized, there were also more sinister happenings. Not far north of Coffeyville lived a family called Bender, father, mother, son, and daughter Kate. They ran a sort of rooming house on a well-traveled road, a house with one serious defect. From it, travelers were apt to disappear without a trace.

It seems the Benders sat their lodgers down to eat with their backs to a curtain, through which, as opportunity offered, one of the family bashed the victim in the head with the traditional blunt instrument. The traveler then descended into the nether regions of the house through a trapdoor—a little like Sweeney Todd's arrangement in old London. Down below, bloodthirsty Kate cut the lodger's throat, rejoicing all the while, as legend has it.

In time, the local gentry got together, formed a vigilante group, and dealt with the deadly Benders. There may have been some shooting when the vigilantes collected the Benders, especially from the pugnacious Kate. However the deed was done, nobody ever talked much about what happened afterward. Persistent rumor had it that the family disappeared in the Arkansas River quicksand. "Just put the whole thing in," one vigilante said afterward, "horses, wagon and all."[9]

In those days, there wasn't a great deal of law in southeastern Kansas, and good citizens had to deal with evil themselves. It was a responsibility of citizenship, like dealing fairly with your neighbors. One of the Bender vigilantes is said to have been the dignified editor and politician, W. A. Peffer. Vigilante groups also dealt with a rash of claim jumping around the end of the 1860s. They called themselves "claim protection clubs" and decided disputes over ownership in a summary but effective way. Without a whole lot of due process of law, claim stealing quickly became a lost art in this area.

In 1870 there were as many as a dozen murders, and the lawlessness only began to decline when another band of citizens enforced some law on their own. They made quite an example, too. In fact, they hung three murderers together, decorating a tree on the claim owned by their victim. A fourth murderer, who had betrayed the other three, simply disappeared. A persistent rumor indicated he had gone for a dip in the nearby Verdigris River—with some help—and had not been seen to emerge.

Coffeyville got its start on the trail herds, but what made it finally prosper and grow was not beef. The key to the town's future was wheat, an unusual, hardy strain that flourished in the heat of the Kansas prairie and stuck out dry spells that killed other kinds of grain. It was called Turkey Red, and it came to the heartland of America by way of Russia. Turkey Red seed arrived in large quantities, shipped in from Russia by a visionary called Bernard Warkentin, who settled on the Little Arkansas in 1873.

So, as the heyday of the cattle drives passed away, the prairie turned literally to amber waves of grain. Farmers the world over tend to be steady, substantial people, with both fists sunk deep in the soil, and as plows turned the earth around Coffeyville, respectability and peace came to the growing little town. Turkey Red wheat and solid, industrious farmers replaced bawling steers and wild young cowhands.

Much Turkey Red came to Kansas carefully stashed in the dunnage of thrifty Mennonite farmers. Most of these tough farmers were of German stock, exiles who had lived long in the black-earth regions of Russia. Military service cut against the Mennonites' religious beliefs, and so, when in 1874 Czar Alexander II removed their army service exemption, thousands of Mennonites began to look for another, friendlier, home. Europe heard much about the great new land of America in those days, some of it from propaganda produced by the hot competition between the Kansas Pacific and the Santa Fe for immigrant traffic.

The first lot of Mennonites arrived about 1874, and began to buy acreage in large chunks. One group bought a hundred thousand acres in four Kansas counties. These Mennonites knew good farmland when they saw it, and were undeterred even by a plague of grasshoppers. "Grasshoppers go to none but a good country," they said, and proceeded to prove the truth of that adage.[10] More Russian Germans followed and other Mennonites came from Switzerland and Germany, and even Illinois and Pennsylvania.

The Mennonites brought their whole lives with them, great loads of gear which included threshing equipment and stoves. They had come to stay, they knew how to make things grow, and they cannily reasoned that what had thrived on the steppe would thrive on the prairie. And it did.

Coffeyville was not an old town, as Kansas hamlets went. There had been a settlement of sorts on the placid Verdigris River by the late 1860s. Louis Scott, an ex-slave, had come up from Texas with his family, a pair of oxen, a cow, and his blacksmith tools, becoming at once the first settler and the first businessman of the area. Scott settled north of Onion Creek, west of the Verdigris, in 1867. In the next year, tough widow Susan Powell arrived, pushing two yoke of oxen and a wagon filled with her nine children.

Illinois-born Colonel James A. Coffey had arrived that same year and built a trading post about where Maple Avenue and Fifteenth Street meet in present-day Coffeyville. He bought the land for fifty dollars in gold. Coffey's post, like others he had founded before the Civil War, bartered with the Osage tribe, in this case with the Black Dog band.

In the summer of 1869, with an eye to a settled future, Coffey and some other men had laid out a town around the post. Coffey himself became the first postmaster. About the same time, Montgomery County was organized, named according to one story for General Richard Montgomery, an ex-British officer killed leading American Revolutionary soldiers against Quebec in 1775. The tiny settlement was already getting competition from a hamlet called Parker, just across the Verdigris.

Not much later the Leavenworth, Lawrence and Galveston Railroad, which Colonel Coffey had courted for his town, reached and passed Coffeyville. The railroad laid out its own settlement north of Colonel Coffey's so-called Old Town, even stealing away its post office, the traditional symbol of civilization. The Old Town responded with litigation. The twin villages competed commercially for a while, but in 1873 they amalgamated to meet the threat from Parker, their neighbor to the southeast.

Unified Coffeyville pretty well wiped out Parker, luring away some of its leading merchants with what the county history quaintly called "liberal inducements."[11] And Coffeyville slowly grew, in spite of two bank failures and the persistent curse of malaria.[12]

Coffeyville acquired both Catholic and Methodist churches in 1870 (the Baptists and Presbyterians came along in the next decade), and a public school was opened the next year. The same year the town staged a "jamboree" to honor the first LL&G passenger train to reach the city. A newspaper also opened for business in 1871, a short-lived sheet founded by, of all people, ex-Senator E. G. Ross, who not long before had cast the swing vote that defeated the impeachment of Andrew Johnson. His paper was called, logically enough, *Ross' Paper*, and did not publish for long before it simply blew away in a tornado. Perhaps Ross took his disaster as a heavenly mandate; perhaps he was just uninsured. Whatever the reason, he ceased publication and moved on.

The *Journal* began publishing as a weekly in 1875.

Five years later Coffeyville voted—as did the rest of Kansas—for prohibition. Kansas was to be the chief stomping ground of the formidable Carry Nation, ax-wielding scourge of John Barleycorn in all his guises. A Texas import, Nation began her memorable booze-smashing career in Medicine Lodge. Kansas's vote for temperance bespoke a retreat from the wild old days, a yen for respectability and the quiet life. Kansas had come a long way since the days of the Texas herds and rowdy Red Hot Street.

Colonel Coffey moved on in 1878. Leaving a thriving town in place of the desolate trading post he had started, Coffey moved to Dodge City, where he died a few years later. The colonel's place was taken by a new generation of hardy tradesmen, among them J. J. Barndollar, a Pennsylvanian who had opened the Star Grocery in 1872 and built his little business into Barndollar Brothers, with satellite stores down in Indian Territory to the south. A few doors away J. T. Isham was building his hardware business (you can still buy a pound of ten-penny nails at Isham's, to this very day).

Adamson and Wells Brothers did a land-office business packing quail and prairie chickens to satisfy eastern appetites. The Kloehr brothers ran both a bustling livery business and the Southern Hotel. One of their regular visitors was a Kansan named Clem Rogers, who sometimes brought along his son, a bright youngster called Will.

Tom Ayres began a banking company in 1880, a thriving concern that five years later became the First National Bank of Coffeyville. In 1886 Ayers got some competition. C. M. Condon, already a successful banker in Oswego, Kansas, opened for business just a few feet away. In the next year Coffeyville could boast a population of two thousand.

The streets were still dirt in 1891 and there were only two streetlights in town, both of them privately owned. Doctors made their night calls with lantern and pistol. Even so, the town kept growing: a roller-skating rink opened for business in 1884.

While some folks skated for fun, others indulged in trap-shooting at the local target club. The pigeons these citizens pulled down on were not the tame old clay variety; when somebody yelled "Pull!" a club member jerked a string that collapsed a cage and released a flock of real, live pigeons. One of the best shots on the range was liveryman John Kloehr. It was as well that he honed his shooting skills. One fall day not far off, he would need them desperately.

Natural gas drilling started in 1892, the year of the Great Raid, and in May of that year, at 650 feet, drillers brought in the biggest well thus far in the big Mid-Continent Field. The strike meant not only more jobs and prosperity but also light and heat for Coffeyville's stores and homes, and cheap light and heat at that. Coffeyville built its waterworks in 1895 and founded its own library, a civic enterprise supported by the sweat and charity of its citizens.

Life was simple and good. A dollar was harder to come by in those far-off days, but then you could buy more with it once you got it. In the fertile country ten miles west of Coffeyville, for example, in 1892 you could buy 178 acres, including "good orchard, 3 room frame house, Kansas barn and crib ... cheap as dirt at $2000." Or, for a mere $800, you could invest in "80 acres, 55 under cultivation, two room house, stone barn, all fenced and cross fenced, 25 acres pasture, well watered by both spring and well."

With the departure of the trail herds, cowboys, gamblers, and whores, Coffeyville became a peaceful town. There was some disturbance during the hectic election year of 1888—an alleged bomb plot by members of the upstart Labor Party—but Coffeyville was becoming a town where people lived quietly and trusted their neighbors.

The town had risen to the eminence of a third-class city in 1872, and in that year spent fifteen hundred dollars—a lot of money for the day—on a brand-new brick schoolhouse. Coffeyville was on its way. In time, it absorbed the neighboring villages of Westralia, Claymore, and Verdigris City, as well as its old rival Parker.

Thus by the autumn of 1892, Coffeyville, Kansas, was rather as it is today, the very core of America's heartland. In that far-away year the town boasted a population of about thirty-five hundred souls. All around Coffeyville rolled the rich farmland of southeast Kansas, the Verdigris River meandering through it southeast into Oklahoma and in time flowing into the mighty Arkansas. As the country around the town grew and prospered, so did its citizens thrive and multiply. They took pride in their town and they worked hard so that their progeny would inherit and enjoy the good things they had built.

And so they would. But first, the citizens of Coffeyville would have to face a dreadful trial. It came in 1892 and it came from the south, from the Indian Territory, which began just a mile and a half south of the town.

2

NO GOD WEST OF FORT SMITH

"No SUNDAY west of St. Louis," the old saying went, "and no God west of Fort Smith." The Indian Territory west of the Arkansas line was a wilderness crawling with bootleggers, horsethieves, cattle rustlers, robbers, and murderers on the run. Nobody stirred without a weapon and neighbors were few and far between. At one point, there were fifteen murders in just a few weeks at Muskogee and Fort Gibson. The whole area teemed with stock thieves; and horses and cattle disappearing in Kansas and Texas regularly reappeared in the Territory. Here, as an old-time deputy marshal said, "the laws were only rumors."[1]

Policing this hive of criminals and human flotsam was the task of the federal authority at Fort Smith, just across the border in Arkansas. In the 1880s and '90s this authority was "hanging judge" Isaac Parker, a tough and tireless district judge. Parker held forth on the Fort Smith bench for twenty-one years, during which time he tried well over thirteen thousand cases. Parker sentenced 160 men to execution for a variety of foul crimes, and seventy-nine of them actually died on the gallows, sixty at the end of ace hangman George Maledon's manicured ropes.

Maledon, a slight, quiet deputy, prided himself on his expertise. Men called him the "prince of hangmen" because of his ability to break a condemned man's neck instead of strangling him. Maledon was also a bad man to cross away from the scaffold. Altogether, four prisoners tried to escape him: none of them outran his pistols.

Of the men sentenced to the gallows but not put to death, two had been pardoned and forty-six received presidential sentence commutations. The rest had died in jail, gone crazy, or been granted new trials that ended in acquittal or conviction of a noncapital crime. One man, as western writer Homer Croy put it, had been "released on bond ... and neglected to come back."[2] The bail jumper had probably been well advised. He and the other bad men west of Fort Smith were afraid of the judge, and they had good reason to be. If Judge Parker had not stamped out crime in the Territory, he had certainly permanently disposed of some of its worst offenders.

Parker was a devout Christian and a decent man, but he had no use for killers. He preceded sentencing with a long sermon on the vile things the defendant had done, glowering at the criminal, as another author wrote, "like an avenging angel."[3] Parker saw himself simply as an instrument of justice, although no doubt the hangings weighed on his decent soul. At the end of his road, and dying, he murmured, "I never hanged a man. The law hanged them. I was only its instrument."[4]

The law may have done the hanging but the judge surely helped out. He sent his deputy United States marshals west into the wilderness to clean house. "Bring them in alive," the judge said, "or dead," and the marshals rode out into no-man's-land to do his bidding. They had something like seventy-four thousand square miles to police and not nearly enough men to do it.

Still, the lethal judge and his tough marshals made their mark. Far out in Indian Territory, today's Oklahoma, on the banks of the Canadian River, a sign marked the trail east: "500 Miles to Fort Smith." Along the way somebody had shot the sign full of holes and somebody else had scratched an addition to it—whoever it was spoke for every criminal in the badlands: "500 Miles to Fort Smith—and Hell."

Judge Parker's court processed the trash of the whole Indian Territory, a constant stream of hoodlums dragged in by Parker's hard-riding cadre of deputy marshals. There were never more than two hundred of these men to cover some seventy thousand square miles. They were paid always poorly and usually late to enforce the law in the most dangerous country in the whole United States. Sixty-five of them died in the line of duty, died as Deputy Marshal Frank Dalton did in a blazing shoot-out with a band of outlaws. Some were simply cut down from ambush in the wild country west of the Arkansas. Often in outlaw country for weeks at a time, the marshals braved weevily food, constant peril, and terrible isolation for the privilege of running down some of the most dangerous men in the world.

Much of the trouble revolved around whiskey, which was prohibited in the Indian Territory and accordingly imported in great quantities. Most of the illegal booze was pure rotgut, and the "good stuff" wasn't much better. When store-bought firewater or white lightning was not available, the people of Indian Territory could make do with a patent medicine called Perana. "It came in three grades, 1, 2, and 3, number 1 having the highest percentage of alcohol, while number 3 had the highest percentage of medicinal ingredients." And if you were out of both booze and snake oil, there were always morphine and opium: "Opium was in a form resembling putty and was chewed instead of being smoked. Morphine also was taken internally, the consumer often measuring off a quantity on the end of his pocket knife and swallowing it in the presence of everyone in the store."[5] It was bad enough for a lawman to go up against a hoodlum crazy with bad whiskey or a bellyful of Perana. A gunman off in his own world on narcotics might be deadlier still.

The Indian Nations created their own police, the Lighthorse, tough tribal lawmen who controlled their own people and did what they could to root out the white riffraff that came to steal and to sell whiskey in the Nations. The Lighthorse rode hard and shot without hesitation. Down in the Nations men said the Lighthorse were sometimes executioners as well as policemen. If they were, they had reason, for they, like the marshals, dealt daily with some of the toughest hard cases in the West.

Enforcing the law was always dangerous, and especially so when the marshals went after the worst desperadoes. Ned Christie, for example, killed one lawman and wounded at least twelve others over the years between 1885 and 1892. Deputy Marshal Heck Thomas wounded Christie terribly in 1889 but the outlaw escaped and stayed on the loose until 1892. In that year, a party of lawmen surrounded Christie's lair, a place called Ned's Fort Mountain.

This time, the lawmen brought with them a little three-pounder cannon, dragged all the way from, of all places, Coffeyville, Kansas. The little gun had been built by a Coffeyville blacksmith and was used to celebrate the Glorious Fourth and for other civic occasions. This time, it was due for more serious employment.

The lawmen got their artillery loaded and banged away for a while, at least until the breech of the piece split, but the tiny projectiles could not dent the thick logs of Christie's fortress. Finally, however, the posse built a timber shelter and pushed it close enough to dynamite the fort. In smoke and flame Christie ran for it, until a Winchester slug reached out to pull him down for keeps.

Fortunately, most of the bravos down in the Nations were nowhere near as venomous as Christie. Even so, a deputy marshal's life expectancy was strictly limited. It took brave and dedicated men to stay in the marshaling business and survive, men like Bill Tilghman, Heck Thomas, and Chris Madsen, known in time as the "three guardsmen," after Dumas's fabulous musketeer officers. In later years, both Madsen and Thomas—especially Thomas—trailed the Dalton boys for weeks on end. As we'll see, that relentless pursuit played a substantial part in the tragedy at Coffeyville.

The generality of criminal was bad enough. There was Blue Duck, the murderous paramour of much-overrated Belle Starr. Blue Duck, in addition to a long list of other offenses, shot a man to death just for fun and got the inevitable sentence from Judge Parker. Belle hired the best legal help she could find and Blue Duck ultimately got a presidential commutation to life in prison.

Belle herself had started life as plain old Myra Belle Shirley—wife and mistress to various hoodlums, but never the "bandit queen" of legend. Belle got her start in the outlaw business in Texas, where, in about 1866, she fell in with Cole Younger and his brothers. She also fell for Cole, and legend says he left her pregnant when he and the boys rode back north. Cole's autobiography denies Belle's child was his.[6]

One thing led to another, and Belle in time took up with one Jim Reed, a small-time horsethief who broadened his activities to include murder and robbery. She had at least one more child by Reed, and may have ridden along on a job or two. Jim got himself killed by a deputy in Paris, Texas, in 1874, and Belle was fancy-free.

This time she turned to Sam Starr, son of the dangerous and disreputable Tom Starr, perennial irritation and disgrace to the Cherokee nation. Belle farmed out the kids and joined the outlaw gang Sam ran with, helping to plan operations and get rid of the loot profitably. They operated out of the Starr ranch, deep in wild country in a bend of the Canadian. The place was called Younger's Bend—legend says Belle named it in honor of her first love.

In the fullness of time, Belle herself had an audience with
Judge Parker after she and Sam were caught purloining somebody
else's horses. In 1883 Parker gave Belle two six-month terms in
the Detroit House of Corrections. She made a lot of newspapers
as a result of the trial, and from this time dates lots of the hogwash
about the "lady desperado."

Back at Younger's Bend, Sam and Belle seem to have had
a parting of the ways. One tale says that Belle began entertaining
other men and Sam was on the dodge again. Belle was tried and ac-
quitted for a couple of minor offenses. Sam ultimately surrendered,
got out on bail, and then picked a fight with a Cherokee policeman
who had captured him once before. The officer died with Starr's
bullet in his neck, but his own slug tore through Starr's heart.

Belle lost no time in marrying a twenty-four-year-old Creek
called Jim July, who even then was facing charges of horse stealing
at Fort Smith. While July was off at court in 1889, Belle got herself
ambushed and killed with a couple of shotgun blasts. It might
have been a disgruntled tenant of Belle's who killed her but more
probably it was July himself, or somebody he hired. We'll never
know, for July lost a fight with Deputy Marshal J. R. Hutchins.
Dying, he said he wanted to confess something to Hutchins, but
the devil got him before Hutchins could reach his bedside.

For many years, before and after the Daltons' heyday, Indian Territory swarmed with lowlifes like Belle and her string of
husbands and lovers. There was gang leader Bill Cook (Parker gave
him forty-five years); the repulsive Rufus Buck gang, rapists and
murderers (the good judge hanged 'em all); and multiple murderer
Cherokee Bill—alias Crawford Goldsby (well and truly swung in
1896 for several brutal killings, some of them done for pure sport).

One of the worst of the bunch was young Bob Rogers, who
idolized the Daltons in spite of their bloody, bungled end. Judge
Parker made a mistake with Rogers, putting him on probation for
horsetheft because he was only nineteen. Parker gave the young

tough good advice: "This is your first offense, lad. If you continue in this path of life, death may be the penalty."[7] Tragically Rogers did, and death was, not just for Rogers but for others who deserved a better end.

Rogers specialized in minor crimes for a while, then graduated to the big time by wantonly cutting the throat of a man with whom he'd had a minor quarrel. After that Rogers led four other hoodlums—one of them colorfully called Dynamite Jack—in a series of train and bank robberies in Oklahoma and Kansas. They cut quite a swath, these desperadoes, but they didn't cut it long.

On January 24, 1894, a party of deputies blew Rogers's henchmen into the next world, and a little more than a year later they surrounded Rogers at a house about twenty miles south of Coffeyville. After a bloody fight in which a lawman was killed, young Rogers left the house, but not to surrender. He "came smokin'," as the saying went, and the posse shot him to pieces at close range.

Thus concluded the careers of a few of the more memorable criminal denizens of the Indian Territory. This was Dalton country, full of stories of swashbuckling outlaws, rich robberies, and famous fights. It was frontier country still, in which a young man could find as many bad examples as good ones. In the land rush of 1889, part of the central Indian Territory was opened to settlement. This area became the Oklahoma Territory and it expanded to include more and more of the old Indian Territory. Even with widespread settlement south of the Kansas line, Oklahoma remained a rough-and-ready, raw new land, thick with new people, honest and otherwise, farmers and outlaws, preachers and gunmen, conmen and businessmen, peace officers and fugitives, whores and temperance ladies.

Justice, when there was any, was frequently improvised on the spot and tended to fit the crime. Murdering somebody usually got you strung up, as did stealing livestock or assaulting a woman. Other pecadillos were treated more leniently, but usually painfully, and justice was often administered by unlikely parties. In the early days of Oklahoma City, for example, a Texan rejoicing in the handle of "Satan" Shields got word that a gang of hoodlums were lounging around a saloon, waiting to kill a friend of his. Arming himself with a hickory ax handle, Satan invaded the saloon and laid about him, leaving all six of his opponents bloodied and prostrate on the floor. Hauled before Police Judge Bent Miller, the aching and chastened would-be killers were fined a hundred dollars each, the humiliating charge being "attempted suicide."[8] At that, the defendants were lucky; offenses such as lying in wait with murder in your heart were generally dealt with by Colonel Colt or a handy length of rope.

All things considered, this brand-new country was the promised land, not only for God-fearing, hardworking pioneers but for grifters, professional thieves, and misfits of every description. It was rough country, too, with few roads, a natural refuge for men "on the scout." A man who knew the terrain had every chance of staying at least one jump ahead of a posse, particularly if he had friends on the shady side of the law.

It was probably natural that a good deal of train robbing went on here and hereabouts. The Katy was especially vulnerable, as its wood-burning locomotives chugged lustily through the Indian Territory. It was held up over and over again, beginning in the 1870s and continuing into the twentieth century. The first recorded stickup was pulled in the summer of '73, when a band of Cherokee outlaws collected a hatful of cash and some watches and rings down close to the Red River.

Almost exactly a half-century later, a certain Al Spencer held up a train in the Osage country below the Kansas line. Al wasn't very bright but he achieved some minor fame for two accomplishments: he thought of wearing rubber finger stalls on the job, to frustrate the rising art of fingerprint identification, and he was the last bandit to stick up a Katy train. Al didn't live to enjoy his achievements, however. He was filled full of holes by a band of Katy detectives, who had thoughtfully inquired around to see who had been buying lots of finger stalls.

In between, a good number of others held up the poor old Katy, including the Daltons and their successor mob, the Doolin gang. Train holdups were easier and more attractive than they might seem. Railway express cars were the primary transport for money in those days, hard gold and silver, currency, bearer bills, and notes. The express cars were not armored—at least, not till much later—and no railway or express company could afford to protect every train with an army of guards. And trains were easy to hold up, a whole lot easier than a bank, which generally was in the middle of town, close to sheriffs and pugnacious armed citizens. A train could be attacked at night—a bank couldn't—and stopped at all kinds of deserted places where the crew could not hope for assistance.

People had been robbing trains for a generation by the time the Daltons got into the act—the first peacetime railroad holdup we know about was pulled in Seymour, Indiana, in 1866. The James-Younger gang, among others, were leading exponents of the art, and their first strike at the railroads should have destroyed forever the phony noble-outlaw image of the James-Younger gang. It happened at Adair, Iowa, in July of 1873. The James-Younger bandits simply pulled up a rail ahead of the train and wrecked the whole outfit. The engineer died in the scalding steam and twisted metal. The crew's frantic efforts to reach the engineer apparently failed to distract the bandits, who simply went on robbing the express car and the passengers.

The next time out, the James-Younger gang turned to simpler methods, probably not for any humane reason but because it was easier than prying up rails. They boarded the train at a station—in this case Gad's Hill, Missouri—in January of 1874. Once on board, they got the drop on the crew and relieved both the express car and the passengers of anything of value. This technique, the station robbery, became the norm in later years. This is the way the Daltons did it, choosing mostly tiny, isolated stops where the crew and express messenger were on their own, far from bothersome sheriffs and marshals and outraged citizenry.

The tools of the trade were the common weapons of the frontier. Out here, many men went armed, perhaps most, except for residents of the most settled towns. A homesteader might keep a rifle or a shotgun or both. The gambler or conman might carry a sneak gun in his vest pocket—Henry Deringer (yes, one r) built the first tiny, heavy caliber handgun, and his imitators' weapons came to be called derringers.

But the weapons of choice for most men in the 1880s and '90s were about the same on both sides of the law. The rifle was the dominant arm, whatever you see on the silver screen. A rifle made it possible to shoot your enemy at long range, before your enemy got anywhere close to being able to use a handgun. With it, you could hold off hostile Indians or kill game for meat; most horsemen carried one in a leather saddle scabbard.

The omnipresent Winchester saddle gun was the standard weapon on the frontier, and the arm of decision in the Coffeyville fight. It had been in production for many years, in one version or another, and in a wide variety of calibers. It was a lever-action rifle—that is, the firer cocked the weapon by shoving down and pulling back a looped lever with the right hand. The lever was just behind the trigger guard and part of it, so that when the firer worked the lever his hand ended up conveniently close to the trigger, ready to fire again.

The cocking action not only pushed back the exposed hammer of the rifle but ejected any spent cartridge in the breech and loaded another from the tubular magazine that extended forward under the barrel. The weapon had iron sights, which was really all it needed, for its effective range was relatively short. That was because its action was not strong enough to stand the pressures of a really high-powered cartridge. However, since a western firefight or game shot generally did not require shooting farther than two hundred yards, the Model 73 and its successors were plenty good enough for the average man, or for the average outlaw or peace officer, for that matter.

You could get the Winchester into action quickly and its tube magazine and lever action gave it high volume of fire. It was easy to reload, too—you just shoved cartridges into a slot on the right side of the receiver, just above and forward of the trigger. If the Dalton gang bought new Winchesters for the Coffeyville foray, as a couple of stories say they did, those rifles would have been the 1886 or 1892 models.[9]

A word about cartridges. They were made of brass, of course, just a cylinder with a little detonating cap in the base, grains of powder inside, and a lead bullet firmly seated in the business end. By the 1890s cartridge manufacture was well advanced. One seldom had trouble such as a ruptured case that might jam in the breach of a weapon. Over time, carrying brass cartridges in the loops of a leather belt induced corrosion—the military went to canvas cartridge belts as a result—but careful shooters cleaned their shells regularly and were not troubled by corrosion.

A favorite Winchester round was the .44-40, so named to convey that the diameter of the bullet was 44 one-hundredths of an inch and its brass case held 40 grains of powder. It was not a particularly powerful cartridge but it had one outstanding virtue, especially for men who lived on horseback. The same cartridge fit the .44 caliber revolver, manufactured by both Remington and Colt.

At the time of the Coffeyville raid, all western hand-guns were revolvers. The first useful semiautomatic pistol, the

German-made Mauser self-loader, did not appear until 1898. It was a couple of years later that small numbers of Mausers had made their way west.

The westerner's favorite handgun was the famous 1873 Colt Peacemaker, also called the Frontier Model, and officially known as the Single Action Army Model. The weapon was an instant success, sturdy, simple, and hard-hitting. An excellent, rugged, dependable weapon, it became the staple handgun of the West. As one frontiersman commented, "It wasn't God or the Declaration of Independence that made all men free and equal, it was Colonel Sam'l Colt."[10]

The Peacemaker was Colt's first large revolver designed for brass cartridges. It was commonly found in both .44 and .45 caliber (45/100ths of an inch) and fired a 235-grain lead bullet pushed along by 40 grains of black powder. Colt made the New Model Army in a wide variety of barrel lengths and several calibers, all the way from monstrous .476 to tiny .22 Short. The barrel of its civilian model was 4 $\frac{3}{4}$ inches long; the military models had longer barrels. The Peacemaker continued in production into the 1920s, and more than seven hundred thousand of them were made. Other makers build similar revolvers to this very day.

The Colt Army was single action; that is, you had to cock the hammer with your thumb before each shot. You loaded it through a little swing-out gate in the shield that covered the back of the cylinder. Colt fixed a spring-loaded rod to the barrel. With the loading gate swung open, you poked the rod back through each cylinder to push out expended cases. The favorite Peacemaker calibers were .45 and .44-40, the .44-40 because it was interchangeable with the Winchester saddle-gun of the same caliber.

All you ever see in potboiler western movies is the Peacemaker, as though that was the only handgun westerners carried. In fact, there was a bewildering variety of revolvers in use in 1892 and the 1873 Army was only one of them, albeit a very popular gun. Some of the Dalton gang packed Colt Armys when they rode into peaceful Coffeyville, but not all.

Emmett, for example, carried a Colt 1878 Army and Frontier Model, chambered in .45. Although this revolver was not as strongly built as the Peacemaker, it had the advantage of a double action. That is, it cocked itself when you pulled the trigger and fired in the same action. Thus, it was easier to handle quickly one-handed, as by a mounted man shooting while trying to control a frightened horse. And it was easier to get off your first shot quickly—all you had to do was pull the weapon and squeeze the trigger.

As already noted, a good deal of myth and misinformation surround the whole history of the Daltons. Uncertainty extends even to the weapons the robbers packed on that fair October morning. According to one writer, Bob Dalton was equipped with a .38 Smith and Wesson revolver and a .45 "Bisley Colt." The Bisley was a Peacemaker variant developed for target shooting, named for the English range where international pistol matches were held. The Colt displayed today in the Coffeyville museum, said to have been Bob's, is certainly not a Bisley, and for good reason. Colt did not begin building Bisleys—basically a target weapon—until almost two years after the raid.[11]

Some sources say that altogether Bob carried three handguns: the .38 S & W, an ordinary Colt Army, and his favorite backup, a British Bulldog made by Webley, longtime purveyor of rugged service revolvers to the British Army. The Bulldog was chambered in .38 caliber and was popular as a concealed weapon, a "hideout gun," convenient for a shoulder holster or the inside pocket of a coat. Bob carried his out of sight when he rode into Coffeyville. The Smith and Wesson was stashed in his boot.

Frontiersmen took good care of their revolvers. A "cutter" or "hawglaig" (you have to say it right)—a sidearm—was a tool

to most men, just like a rope or saddle. Some men, of liking or
necessity or both, lavished a great deal of time in pistol practice,
for good or evil. These men were the shootists, men whose lives
and livings depended on their skill with a gun.

Good marksmen in the frontier days fired their weapons
much like good marksmen before and since. They pointed the
weapon at their target, and used some care in doing it. We've all
seen movie cowboys "fanning" a six-shooter, holding the trigger
back, elbow braced against the side, the edge of the left hand
slamming down across the hammer to fire the revolver.

Indeed, it can be done that way, and you can get a lot of
lead out of the gun in a hurry. But you had better be darned near
belly-to-belly with your target, because nobody fanning a pistol
at more than a few yards has more than a general idea where the
slugs may end up. The impact of the left hand slamming against
the hammer has to move the muzzle off line, a little or a lot. No,
the gunfighter—outlaw and lawman alike—knew he'd better make
that first round count. He could do that in either one of two ways.

First, he could draw his revolver, rock back the hammer,
aim, and shoot. That, I'm convinced, is how he did it when he
was any distance at all away from his opponent. If the range was
very short, he could draw his weapon, thumb over the hammer,
cocking it as the weapon came level. Then he fired from the hip
and kept on blasting away as long as he needed to or as long as he
could.[12]

At very short range—say, in a saloon—the first shot was
crucial, for a couple of reasons. Obviously, if you pointed the Colt
straight, you put a bullet in the middle of your man, and he forthwith lost much of his interest in fighting. Less obviously, even if
you missed, you got the substantial shock advantage of the muzzle-
blast from your piece. The Colt Army shot out a fierce burst of
flame and powder particles and pieces of wad—later on we'll meet
Black-faced Charlie Bryant, a living example of the effects of a

muzzle-blast so ferocious that it could even set your opponent's clothing afire. If you were close enough that blast could shake your enemy enough to throw off his aim.

Much has been written about gunfighting techniques and special holsters and the like. There were gunfighters who carried their revolvers in specially made lined trouser pockets. Others carried a Colt attached to a swivel on their belt, without a holster, so all they had to do was grab it, cock it, and swivel it to the horizontal. And then there was a variety of shoulder holsters, some real scabbards, others a collection of custom-made springs.

All these bizarre killing rigs existed. All of them were used. The average outlaw or peace officer, however, generally carried his piece or pieces in an ordinary holster, slung to a belt lined with cartridge loops and filled with spare ammunition. Some carried two revolvers in this fashion, like Hopalong Cassidy. Most carried a single weapon only, although, like Bob Dalton, they might also carry a hideout gun in addition. Such a "stingy-gun," was a small, lighter weapon stashed in a pocket, shoulder holster or waistband, or tucked away up a sleeve.

Make no mistake. A professional criminal who lasted any length of time was generally a pretty fair shot. But outlaws were not alone in being dangerous. Ordinary citizens could be deadly too.

3

HORSEMEN FROM THE SOUTH

NOBODY KNOWS EXACTLY when planning began for the Coffeyville raid. It probably was first discussed by the gang members at least a week or so before the raid itself. Not long before his death, Emmett Dalton told a reporter they had been "planning for months."[1] Years before that, however, Emmett had written that he first heard about the raid when he rejoined the gang south of Tulsa about the first of October, 1892. Brother Bob was "unusually quiet and taciturn" for a day, until he suddenly turned and said to the others, "Come on, we're going to Coffeyville."

According to Emmett, he objected immediately, "Why there? What's the use? They all know us there and they are watching those trains too closely now anyway."[2] And then Bob dropped his bombshell. This was to be no ordinary holdup, no nighttime express car raid at some lonely hamlet. This would be a daylight strike at a substantial town, a bank robbery, the most daring of all time. And more than that, Bob said, it would be

Not one but two banks. . . . It's getting too risky to go after another train right now. They are waiting for us. So far no one has been hurt, but that won't keep up forever. We all want to get out of this country but we'll be here forever unless we do something. . . . We will ride in, get the banks, ride out and that's all there is to it. Easy, isn't it?[3]

Emmett records that he protested, without success, that some one might be hurt in the raid, and "the people in Coffeyville never did anything to us."[4]

> I tried to prevail on the boys not to come up, for the people here had done us no harm. They said all right, if I didn't want to come that the rest would come and give the town a round-up. I told them if that was the case I might as well come with them.... I knew I would be chased just as hard if I didn't come as I would if I did, and I had no money to get out of the country on.[5]

Bob answered that nobody would be hurt, and asked whether Emmett had a better idea to replenish their dwindling exchequer. Emmett didn't, and so the planning went forward.

Emmett's statement that he tried to talk Bob out of raiding Coffeyville may well have been calculated to soothe the town's angry citizens. When Emmett first talked about how he had objected to the raid, he was badly shot up and in the hands of some mighty upset residents of Coffeyville. Four of their friends and neighbors were dead and others hurt. There had been talk of lynching. Nobody can blame Emmett if he made himself out to be a reluctant robber.

The rest of the chosen raiders fell into line. No doubt they felt as invincible as Bob did, and they were almost broke to boot. Emmett said he had only about twenty dollars in his jeans when he joined the others and the rest of the gang had about nine hundred between them. That was peanuts, comparatively, especially when the gang was thinking about putting the Territory far behind them, and the brothers dreamed of South America.

With bulldogs like the "three guardsmen"—Thomas, Tilghman, and Madsen—hunting them, dozens of other lawmen and rail detectives on the lookout, and nearly everybody else howling for their blood, it seemed prudent to hat up and get out before somebody ran them down. First, however, they needed one last payday.

Whether Emmett's account of planning the raid is accurate or not, it is probable that the operation was indeed Bob Dalton's brainchild. He was, after all, the leader of the gang. He was also, probably, its most intelligent member, although a case can be made for Bill Doolin as his intellectual superior. Bob may well have been mulling over the Coffeyville strike, or something like it, for a long time.

And so the little band of horsemen began to ride north, north for Kansas and a spot in history, five—or maybe six—dusty young men riding north to die. They rose to ill fame suddenly and were snuffed out just as quickly, like a meteor in the night. Their career was, in fact, comparatively short. But while they were at it, they built quite a reputation. They were the "Dalton Gang" and no bunch of outlaws ever attained more notoriety, except the James-Younger gang.

Bob, Emmett, and Grat Dalton were born in Cass County, Missouri. Mother Adeline, by all accounts a rather straight-laced sort, was sixteen years old when she married Lewis Dalton in Independence, Missouri. Dalton (christened James Lewis Dalton) was thirty-six, horse trader, stock raiser, and saloon owner in Westport Landing, now Kansas City.

Adeline was a Younger, aunt to the infamous Younger brothers, a relationship that may have aroused both pride and a sense of competition in her sons. In spite of all kinds of moonshine to the contrary, Adeline was no relation to the James boys. Whatever "bad blood" Adeline may have passed on to her brood, she was twice as tough and resourceful as old man Dalton. She was a whole lot more likeable, too, in spite of being something of a shrew.

Adeline was a God-fearing woman, a dutiful wife, and a good mother. In time, she even got Lewis to give up both drinking and selling the demon rum, "a decision," as one writer put it, that "she lived to regret, since he rarely did anything afterward except bet on slow horses."[6] Nevertheless, the family settled down to farm, after a fashion. Although Adeline did get Lewis to forsake some of his sinful ways, the one thing she could never do was get him to stay in one place very long, especially if that place was home.

They lived for a while in Cass County, Missouri, on land Adeline inherited from her father, at least until Lewis wasted the inheritance on horses that ran second. The family may have spent a little time near Leavenworth, Kansas, as well. The shiftless elder Dalton was regularly someplace else, continuing to indulge in his fondness for racehorses. He traveled the circuit of county fairs and other local celebrations, working as a barker part of the time. Meanwhile, the family got by as best it could. Over the early years, Dalton managed a trip home often enough to keep his long-suffering wife in a state of more or less perpetual pregnancy. Altogether, old man Dalton's occasional visitations resulted in fifteen Dalton kids, thirteen of whom lived to adulthood.

Later the family settled down in Montgomery County, Kansas, not far from Coffeyville. There morose papa Dalton continued his long career as a fiddle-footed professional failure. The family eked out a precarious existence at the Coffeyville place until, in 1882, the father moved his considerable brood south, into Indian Territory. There he leased land south of Vinita, near a place called Locust Hill.

Almost single-handed, Adeline Dalton kept the family going, helped for a while by her brood of boys. Adeline was a good friend. At the Locust Hill place, she rode miles to nurse a sick neighbor, in wild country so infested with snakes and half-wild cattle that it was not safe to travel on foot. A Locust Hill resident recalled Adeline's valiant attempt to build a home for her brood. "She was always gathering carpet rags," the raw material of the crude floor coverings of the day, although somehow no carpets ever appeared on the Dalton floors. In those days Frank Dalton supported the family with his marshal's wages, old man Dalton being, as usual, elsewhere.[7] After son Frank was killed in 1887, Lewis moved his family back north to the Coffeyville area.

The senior Daltons separated after many years. Historians disagree about whether they were actually divorced, as indeed historians do about a lot of other details in the history of the family and the gang. A couple of newspaper reports mention the divorce, however. Most convincingly, so does Coffeyville editor Elliott's daughter, who knew Adeline and said Elliott (also a lawyer) "represented her in her divorce action. . . . Father would not have had her for a client if he had not thought she was all right."[8]

Divorced or not, Lewis did everybody a favor by dying in 1890. In spite of one story that Adeline was "grief-stricken" when the old man died, Lewis's departure from this earth cannot have been anything but a relief to his spouse.

After Lewis passed to his reward, Adeline moved south to Kingfisher, north and west of Oklahoma City. She claimed 160 acres, all good bottom land, and settled in with her daughters, and sons Littleton, Henry, and Ben. The neighbors thought Adeline was "as nice a little old lady as you could find anywhere, well educated and interesting to talk to."[9]

In spite of Adeline's heroic efforts to hold things together, the boys showed signs early on of being as fiddle-footed as their useless father. As the brothers matured, some left home for greener pastures in Texas, California, and Montana, and most of them apparently led honest and productive lives.

One cowboy writer paints the Daltons in downright rosy hues: "These boys, like the average Western man, were big-hearted and generous in every way. They attended the dances in the country and were liked by all the settlers. When the news came that they had held up the Coffeyville bank at Coffeyville, Kansas, many people could hardly believe it."[10] Talk like this is very hard to swallow. By the time of the Coffeyville raid, as we shall see, the criminal exploits of the Dalton gang were well known all over the Indian Territory. No doubt Kingfisher folks liked the boys well enough, at least as long as they did their lawbreaking someplace else. One neighbor said the boys "were all right as far as we could see. . . . They never got into trouble around home. They would go up to Kansas or some place like that to rob banks and trains."[11] And Bob and Bill, the cowboy historian says, were "always perfect gentlemen at the dances," ignoring the fact that Bill lived in California during most of the time Adeline was settled in Kingfisher.

In any case, no matter how popular the Dalton boys may have been, the Coffeyville fiasco could not have surprised anybody at Kingfisher. Nobody who ever read a paper or gossiped with a neighbor could have been startled to hear of what by then was just one more Dalton job, albeit a bungled one.

Whatever their reputation around Kingfisher, we know that Bob, Grat, and Em were tough kids. Both Emmett and Grat had local reputations as fist-fighters, and Grat was assiduously working on a robust case of alcoholism. Bob, as we shall see, was well known as a superb marksman, even in a country in which most men were raised with guns and good shooting was common. Even so, the brothers were well thought of by at least some of their neighbors, in spite of Grat's fondness for hitting people.[12]

In stark contrast to the later careers of his outlaw siblings, elder brother Frank became a deputy United States marshal, riding for "hanging judge" Isaac Parker's federal district court in Fort Smith. Frank had a reputation for both courage and honesty. And he surely was tough—you had to be to ride the wild country for Judge Parker.

In late 1887, Frank was killed in the line of duty. Consistent with the fog that surrounds the rest of the Dalton history, there are at least two versions of how he "passed in his chips," as the cowboys pithily put it. One old-timer said Frank was shot as he tried to arrest a man for the heinous crime of chicken stealing.[13] Another remembered that Frank was transporting a prisoner, left his Winchester leaning against a tree, turned his back a second too long, and got drilled for his pains.

This version goes on to elaborate on the aftermath. Bob, then helping his father on the Coffeyville farm, rode nobly off to obtain a "special" marshal's commission. He then tracked his brother's killer for six months through Kansas, Colorado, and Texas. In Louisiana he caught up with his quarry, pumped him full of bullets, and brought the body back to Fort Smith for the reward.

It's an engaging tale of brotherly love and implacable vengeance but it is almost certainly not true. A similar story has Bob actually present with Frank, and killing both Frank's murderer and the murderer's wife on the spot.[14] A variation on this theme says Bob "saw his brother die," and credits Grat with an attempt to avenge Frank's death, an effort he had to give up because of a "wound in his left arm."[15]

In fact, what happened was this: Frank was killed when he and another officer took on four horsethieves and whiskey runners in a wild gunfight down in the Arkansas River bottoms, out where God wasn't, west of Fort Smith. His body was returned to Coffeyville, where a sorrowing Adeline scraped together the money for a handsome headstone.

The brotherly retribution story is a typical vapor from the miasma of Dalton myth and invention. Take this account from a book called *American Bandits*: "One author writes that Frank Dalton was killed in a gun fight with horse thieves in Texas, in

1885. Yet in ... memoirs are letters from Frank Dalton in 1935 when he was 83 years old and living quietly in Texas writing about his early days with the Quantrill gang."[16] Even if you ignore the hard evidence of Frank's death on the Arkansas in 1887, not 1885, this would have made Frank ten or twelve years old during his "early days with the Quantrill gang."

After Frank's death, Bob became a deputy marshal and so did Grat. Mythology to the contrary, there seems to be no connection between Frank's death and his brothers' service. The officer with Frank Dalton killed three of the outlaws during the fight in which Frank died. The man who actually shot Frank Dalton to death escaped, only to go down for keeps before the Winchester of a deputy marshal called Moody. Nobody else named Dalton was involved in either fight.[17]

Young Emmett, who idolized his brother Bob, rode along with him as a posseman. Had the boys followed the example of their honest, hard-riding, courageous brother Frank, this book would not have been written. Marshal's pay was poor and slow in coming, but the work was surely honorable. It took a brave, tough man to enforce Judge Parker's writ. When the brothers put on badges, fifteen of the court's marshals had been killed in the line of duty in just two years.

And for a while, the brothers did well. They handled some dangerous arrests, in one of which Grat got a bullet through the arm. But the brothers were not made of the same iron as their departed sibling. None of them lasted long at the peace-officer business. Probably, as one writer put it, the brothers "had a taint of outlaw in them all along, but it did not come to the surface until the occasion called it forth."[18]

Precisely what that occasion was depends in part on whose account you read. There is a story that Bob Dalton used the protection of his badge to murder one Charlie Montgomery, who had pinched Bob's Coffeyville girlfriend, his first cousin Minnie. Bob and Minnie (perhaps Adeline's "adopted niece") were indulging in the occasional harmless roll in the hay, according to this tale. Growing suspicious that he was not the only object of Minnie's affection, Bob searched Montgomery's quarters. There Bob found a handkerchief he had given Minnie, raising a reasonable inference that Montgomery had stolen Minnie's heart, and probably the rest of Minnie as well.[19]

Bob, much wroth, reached for his six-shooter and Montgomery and Minnie fled Coffeyville hurriedly, with Bob firing his pistol into the railroad passenger car in which the lovebirds cowered. Later, Montgomery unwisely returned to town to collect some personal chattels and Bob put a bullet in him, explaining afterward that Montgomery was a horsethief.

There are a couple of things wrong with this colorful story. First, there may or may not have been a "cousin Minnie"; if there was, she was certainly not a cousin by blood. Second, Montgomery very likely was a horsethief and general no-good, who probably deserved killing. According to an article in the *Coffeyville Journal* in August of 1888, "[Montgomery] was suspected of . . . running off horses . . . and various petty crimes. . . . Lately he had appropriated two revolvers that did not belong to him, and had secured a horse that was not his own. . . . [H]e . . . started to run in the direction of young Dalton with his pistol presented at an aim."[20] Whereupon, the paper continued, seeing his brother threatened, Bob propelled Montgomery into the next world with a shotgun. Case closed.

Another tale has Bob shooting—by mistake—the son of one Alex Cochran, a resident of Claremore. It seems that Bob was hunting the elder Cochran, who was wanted for shooting a peace officer. The tale goes that Bob spotted young Cochran, on his way to his father with more ammunition. Mistaking young Cochran for his father, Bob challenged the son and fired when Cochran fled.

This incident is supposed to have cast a certain pall over Bob's reputation as a lawman; it "completely discredited the Daltons,"[21] as one writer put it. Well it might have . . . if it were true.

Sadly for the Dalton mythology, this story too is probably a bit overblown. Cochran, said the Vinita *Indian Chieftain*, was one of two hoodlum brothers who had just shot a peace officer. On his way home from town with a resupply of ammunition, he ignored Bob's order to halt and got his leg and his horse both shot as a consequence.

There is also a tale that the Dalton brothers "shot to pieces" an Indian boy accused of being a wanted man.[22] This reference is probably to the Cochran incident, although it may refer to yet another shooting scrape. One pioneer woman may have come closest to the truth about the Daltons, with her observation that, "when the Dalton boys were United States marshals they were cold and cruel."[23] She related a tale about the brothers killing a man and badly wounding his wife during an attempted arrest of the woman's brother. The story sounds very like the fight in which Frank was killed, but perhaps it was another incident altogether. In any case, it reflects at least one contemporary view of the brothers' reputation, even before they turned to the outlaw trail.

Bob had become chief of the Osage police.[24] It seems the tribe, plagued by outlaws, had appealed to the Wichita federal district court for some protection. They got Bob, largely on the reputation of his departed brother Frank. Emmett came with his brother as posseman. Or maybe Bob was no more than a detective for the Osage force, depending on which book you read. What is certain is that he quit the Osage police, perhaps because he would not take a cut in pay, or perhaps because he was caught running booze into the Osage Nation.

About the same time he was accused of selling protection to whiskey runners inside his own marshal's jurisdiction.

Bob shrugged the allegation off, saying the government owed him hundreds of dollars in fees and expenses, and he was "just getting even."

This story may well be accurate. Marshals waited an eternity for their pitiful pay in those days, and the story of Bob turning outlaw because he wasn't paid was current at the time.[25] Some old-timers believed the Daltons got into their first trouble when they collected what the government owed them at gunpoint, a tale that is plainly folklore.

After the Coffeyville raid, brother Ben Dalton talked to the press at every opportunity. According to Ben, his brothers had turned outlaw because they had been "persecuted" in California, framed and hunted for the celebrated Alila train holdup, and because they couldn't get their marshal's fees paid on time.

"The boys couldn't get their money when they needed it," said Ben, "although they had earned it, and they took ways which were wrong to raise it. That was the beginning of their going astray, and that was the cause of all that followed."[26] Whatever the truth of the unpaid wages story, Bob's boss, Marshal R. L. Walker, was unmoved by Bob's lame excuse and Bob was out of a job. So were his brothers.

Young Emmett, who worked as Bob's posseman, also quit the Osage police, probably over a wage dispute. However, one account says there were persistent murmurings that the brothers were not above a little extracurricular money raising with an elementary protection racket. Considering the boys' later history, it does not seem unlikely that they would scruple at squeezing travelers for a few dollars here and there.

The protection scheme was elementary. The boys would plant whiskey in the wagons of pilgrims bound into Indian Territory, where liquor was forbidden by federal law. Later, the Daltons would "discover" the contraband and levy a "fine" on the spot, money that the U.S. Treasury would never see. This dodge had been practiced by other crooked lawmen, who, if the victim were actually arrested and tried, got a share of the confiscated team and wagon.

Still another version of the tale says Emmett and Bob fell afoul of United States Commissioner W. S. Fitzpatrick, whose beat included the Osage agency. Warned that Bob and Emmett were selling whiskey to the Osage, Fitzpatrick investigated, and fired both men when he determined the allegations were true.

Grat managed to get into trouble substantially more serious, although it is not entirely certain what the difficulty was. One tale goes like this. Passing the time of day with other men on a Tulsa street, he accosted a young black boy who was passing by eating an apple. Grat forced the terrified child to balance the apple on his head while Grat shot it off, William Tell-style, with his six-gun. If Grat's cronies were impressed by his prowess, Marshal Jacob Yoes was not, and Grat was out of a job.

Or perhaps it didn't happen that way, because a similar tale is told about Bob Dalton. This story is also laid in Tulsa—on Main Street—and has Bob threatening to kill the unfortunate child if he did not balance the apple on his head.[27] A variation casts a cousin of the clan, John Younger, as the villain who shot a pipe from a half-wit's mouth in Dallas.[28]

Grat may have been fired for a far more prosaic reason—simple brutality—which would surely have been consistent with Grat's temperament. As one newspaper told it, he badly pistol-whipped a man called Delonadale in March of 1890.[29]

Whatever got the boys fired, from this point on the brothers drifted by the most direct route to a life of stealing from other people. One old marshal—"Red" Lucas—said in later years that the brothers all left Guthrie (near Kingfisher) together, "going to the brush" as they put it. Lucas said he wired Adeline, trying to stop

her sons from taking the owlhoot trail. According to him, she sent
her son-in-law to offer the boys five hundred dollars each to "stay
straight," but all to no avail. The boys turned the money down,
allegedly saying, "Take the money back to mother, she needs it
more than we do. We'll get by."[30] And so they would, with other
people's money.

Somehow this tale strains credulity a bit. "I counted the
money," said Lucas, "and cried like a baby." Perhaps he did, but
maybe the whole tale is an invention too. After all, Lucas is the
same man who later said Bill Doolin died of a seizure instead of
buckshot—a "brain spell" produced by a bullet inside his head.
Lucas also hypothesized that Bill Dalton was never really killed
at all.[31]

Bob, though not the eldest, would be the leader, tough,
impetuous, and always ready for a fight. Born in 1868, blond, blue-
eyed Robert Reddick Dalton stood six feet tall. One of his brothers
said he was named for a Methodist chaplain serving with General
Jo Shelby's Confederate troops. If he was, the name did nothing
for his disposition, which was anything but pacific and forgiving.
He was quick to take offense and quite willing to fight anybody.

Bob was a ladies' man, or at least Emmett said he was. Even
while Bob carried on a flaming romance with his storied outlaw
paramour, Flo Quick (we'll meet Flo shortly), he enjoyed "the
favors of Fannie and Edna," who worked out of Fort Smith in one
of the famous mobile bordellos, the "cat wagons."[32]

Like the other brothers, he was an expert horseman, and
was also the best shot of them all. Veteran U.S. Deputy Marshal
Heck Thomas, who could shoot a little himself, called Bob "one
of the most accurate shots I ever saw . . . fired his rifle mostly from
his side or hip, very seldom bringing the gun to his shoulder."[33]
Other frontiersmen agreed, regarding both Bob's accuracy and his
curious propensity for shooting from the hip.[34] "That's one man I
never wanted to aim at me," said one old-time marshal.[35]

Bob practiced his marksmanship every chance he got. A young frontier boy, son of the Osage agency doctor (and also a witness to Bob's whiskey selling) said later that Bob paid him a quarter to throw tin cans into the air while Bob shot at them. The story goes that Bob could put three rounds into a thrown tomato can—from the hip—before his target hit the ground.[36]

Grattan was the eldest Dalton gang member, born in 1865 in Cass County, Missouri, like his outlaw brothers. Grat was also tall and blond, with light blue eyes, and, like Bob, quarrelsome to a fault and ready to fight anybody at the drop of a hat. Old Lewis had named him, legend has it, for an Irish revolutionary. By the age of sixteen Grat was man-sized, truculent, and much given to the demon rum. All in all, he was a good man to stay away from. As veteran western writer Harold Preece neatly put it, "Grat had the heft of a bull calf and the disposition of a baby rattlesnake."[37] There is also every evidence that Grat was downright dense. His chief recreations seem to have been playing cards and drinking all the whiskey he could hold.

Emmett—"Em" to his friends—was the baby of the trio, born in 1871. He too was named for an old-country Irishman, a rebel hung by the British for leading a rebellion against the crown. Em seems to have been a somewhat gentler sort, with a bit of poetry in his rustic soul.

Witness his account of the evening when, he says, he first met Julia Johnson, who would much later be his wife. Riding through the gloaming, Em wrote, he heard organ music from a little church, celestial tones that captivated him. Dismounting, he went inside, to discover Julia, in the blushing prime of girlhood. As we shall see, that meeting may well be pure invention, but it surely is a pretty thought.

Before he became a lawman, Emmett worked as a cowboy on the gigantic Bar X Bar ranch in the so-called Triangle Country, tucked into the vee formed by the meeting of the Cimarron and

Arkansas Rivers. While he earned an honest dollar pushing the Bar X Bar's ten thousand or so cattle, he rode with two other men who will figure largely in this tale.

The first was one William Power, known at various times and places as Tom Evans or Bill Powers. His full name seems to have been William Tod Power, son of a respectable Missouri man. After his mother died, Power's father married one Mary Heard, known to Power siblings as "Mean Mary." Bill and his brother had enough of Mean Mary's strictness, and left home when Bill was about thirteen.[38] Powers—as we'll call him—was a burly man, just under medium height, with black hair and mustache. For a time, he was a hand on Oscar Halsell's big HH spread, down on the Cimarron east of Guthrie. He was known for his fondness for high times and celebration, always ready for a fight or a frolic.

The second man was a farmer's son called Bill Doolin. Doolin was tall and skinny, mustached, and a very dangerous man indeed, as time would tell. He was born in Johnson County, Arkansas in 1858, and seems to have ridden into Indian Territory sometime in 1881.

Doolin was a personable redhead, with something of a reputation as a cow-camp comedian. A cowboy acquaintance called him "just a big-hearted, generous cowboy, and a very likeable fellow."[39] He first got into major trouble, oddly enough, near little Coffeyville, when the 1891 Glorious Fourth celebration degenerated into a gunfight over a keg of beer. Two constables unwisely tried to confiscate the brew, Doolin told them to leave it alone, one thing led to another, and both constables were badly shot up. Doolin was on the run from that day forward.[40]

On the Turkey Track, the big spread across the Cimarron south of the Bar X Bar, worked a rich assortment of hard-cases who would ride at various times with the Daltons and Bill Doolin's successor gang of robbers. Only one of them made the ride to Coffeyville but they are all worth a brief description, if only to dispel some of the artificial romance created around the Dalton-Doolin gangs by authors who should have known better.

Black-faced Charley Bryant was a thoroughgoing hoodlum without, as the judges are fond of saying, redeeming social value. His nickname described an indelible black blotch on the skin of Bryant's face, souvenir of a black powder shot fired at him from point-blank range. He came out of Wise County, Texas, and periodically shook and shuddered with an uncontrollable fever—probably malaria—which did nothing to improve his nasty disposition.

One writer suggests that Bryant may have suffered from a "neglected venereal disease." Another calls his affliction "an advanced case of syphilis." Whatever his problem may have been, Bryant was meaner than a snake, a skinny troublemaker perpetually on the prod, who told Emmett Dalton his ambition was to "get killed in one hell-firin' minute of smoking action."[41]

Bitter Creek George Newcomb won his title by frequently chanting the familiar cowboy boast, "I'm a bad man (or a "wild wolf") from Bitter Creek, and it's my night to howl." Or maybe, as an old-time cowboy told it, Newcomb got his nickname when, as a kid cowpoke, he drank too much "gyp" water out of a creek and made himself deathly ill.[42]

Newcomb was the son of a good family out of Fort Scott, Kansas, where he was remembered as a "pale faced, well mannered boy." Newcomb left Fort Scott at about age twelve, under the wing of Texas cattleman C. C. Slaughter, a relationship that gave Newcomb his other nickname of "Slaughter's Kid." The youngster drifted up into the Indian Territory and rode with both the Dalton and Doolin gangs. Bitter Creek was part of the wild Adair train robbery, of which more later, and was wounded in the Doolin gang's battle at Ingalls in 1893, in which three lawmen died. Newcomb lasted until May of 1895, when he was killed down on the Cimarron for the five-thousand dollar reward on his head.

A saddle-mate of Bitter Creek was gang stalwart and ex–Turkey Track hand, plug-ugly hoodlum Charley Pierce, generally called "Cockeye Charlie." Pierce had been run out of the Blue River country of Missouri by the kinfolk of a girl he had "compromised." From early in life, Pierce was a thief as well as a wastrel, a scowling, shiftless bum who idolized Quantrill, the Youngers, and the Jameses, and dreamed of emulating them.

The last of the Turkey Track crowd was a man who will play a major role in our story, Richard L. Broadwell. Dick Broadwell, also known here and there as John Moore and Texas Jack, came from up Hutchinson, Kansas way, where his father was a substantial rancher in the Medicine River country. Dick was a man deeply wounded by cupid's arrows, deserted by his love (who also departed with his bankroll) one bad day in Houston.

Broadwell was probably the most civilized of the gang, a tall, slender man with fair skin and black hair. He had not started out as a bad hat, just an ordinary farm kid. A man who had watched Broadwell grow up called him "a rather overgrown, awkward, good-natured youth, not naturally a tough, but of that impressionable nature which would be influenced and greatly attracted by a man like Bob Dalton."[43] One source says some people called Broadwell "Jack of Diamonds," from his habit of incessantly singing the song of the same name.[44]

There were some other shadowy frontier characters who may or may not have ridden at times with the Daltons. Besides somebody identified only as "Six-Shooter Jack," there was one Bob Yokum, also sometimes called "Bitter Creek," and at least four other minor-league hard-cases, all of whom were either killed or imprisoned in the next few years.

Not one of the men who would form the Dalton gang was "driven to outlawry," unless you count Broadwell's wounded ego as some sort of societal compulsion. All of them turned to the owlhoot trail because it seemed easier to steal than to work, or it was exciting, or perhaps both. The Dalton boys, especially, had no reason whatever to turn bad. They surely had other options.

They could, for example, have lived on the family home place, near Kingfisher. Adeline held a quarter-section there, all bottom-land along Kingfisher Creek. Kingfisher Creek had an annoying habit of turning into a torrent during heavy rains—it still does—but the soil was good, and Adeline also held a homestead ten miles west, on Cooper Creek. There was plenty to do, but the boys were not interested in the sweat and worry of farming. Significantly, they could also have worked for other lawmen as posse members, but the labor of law enforcement had also lost its interest.

The three Dalton boys last rode on the right side of the law in June, 1890. After that, according to a Fort Smith newspaper, they stole three separate herds of horses down in the Indian Nations and peddled their loot on the hoof in Kansas. In those days the open market for stolen stock was a town called Baxter Springs, over the Kansas line and not far from Coffeyville.

On hand in Baxter Springs to help the thieves lose their loot was the fabled Annie Walker. Annie, sometime lover of the abominable and unmourned bushwhacker William Quantrill, ran a first-class brothel, much frequented by the tough youngsters of the frontier.

The boys barely escaped a Kansas posse after the last theft. They swiftly cashed a horse buyer's check and cleared Baxter Springs no more than fifteen minutes ahead of a deputy U.S. marshal and a couple of possemen. Grat even spent a few weeks in jail over this one, suspected only of furnishing his brothers fresh horses. At last released, he lost no time in riding west.

Safely out of unfriendly Kansas, Bob and Emmett drifted into New Mexico, then as wild and woolly as any place in the brash, brawling West. Riding beside them was the nucleus of what would become the Dalton gang, Bitter Creek Newcomb and Black-faced

Charley Bryant, as well as another rider named Bill McElhanie, who rejoiced in the peculiar handle of the "Narrow Gauge Kid." Exactly what sort of difficulty the boys got into out in New Mexico is lost in the mists of history. Whatever it was, it sure was trouble.

First off, the boys spent some time in the booming mining camp at Silver City, which Harold Preece aptly described as "Babylon-on-a-pithead, a place of florid squalor, with money heaping the varnished keno tables and burro dung littering the bawdy streets."[45]

There, according to popular history, Bob met the fascinating Eugenia Moore, introduced to him by city marshal Ben Canty, an old Missouri neighbor. Eugenia is the stuff of legend. Emmett, with his gift for the sentimental, said she was a schoolteacher, "a beautiful young lady, about twenty-two years old, pure of mind, a fair telegrapher, unusually intelligent and courageous." Eugenia, said Emmett, was a product of northern Missouri who had come out to New Mexico for reasons of health. She was, of course, the child of "a fine old Missouri family." Elsewhere, Emmett calls her a "proficient telegrapher," and says she used that knowledge to make friends with various railroad station agents.[46]

Good Missouri family or not, the story goes that she became spy and scout for the gang and long-term inamorata of Bob Dalton. Emmett says that Eugenia

> was a valuable ally. She was a girl of unusual tact and quick wit and was a loyal member of our band. Riding up and down on the railroad from Parsons, Kansas, to Denison, Texas, she was constantly on the alert for bits of information which might prove of value to us. She being a telegraph operator, she frequently overheard messages in the depots telling of money shipments.[47]

Finally, says Emmett, Eugenia got word of a large money shipment in a Katy express car, and rode two hundred and fifty miles to carry the news to her lover. This tale may require several grains of salt, however, and not only because much of Emmett's "history" is suspect. Consider for a moment the unlikely idea of a single woman spending her days riding hither and yon on the railroad and perpetually hanging about telegraph offices waiting for a hot signal. Even if she did overhear word of a big shipment of money, it is hard to believe she heard of it in time to ride two hundred fifty miles and tell Bob, and he still had time to ride off and rob the train. It's a charming story, but it's about as likely to be true as the equally charming saga of the Three Bears.

Depending on which book you read, Eugenia may have been the notorious and elusive female horsethief Flo Quick, also known as Tom King. Flo's exploits may be nine parts myth, but she was real and she sure makes interesting reading. One prolific writer says Eugenia and Flo Quick were one and the same, a nubile lass who made a profitable sideline out of seducing solid citizens and then blackmailing them.

In any event Eugenia—or Flo, or Tom—has an extensive popular history in connection with the Daltons. She spied, she eavesdropped on telegraph messages, she rode boldly about the countryside "setting up robberies" for the gang. She also appears as Daisy Bryant, in one account either the sometime mistress or the sister of Black-faced Charley Bryant.

Another tale somewhat fancifully credits Eugenia with stealing five horses for the gang's use in the ill-fated Coffeyville raid. In this account also, Eugenia is said to be Florence Quick, the well-known and accomplished horsethief.

Wearing out their welcome in Silver City, the gang planned the holdup of a Mexican gambling hall in Santa Rosa, New Mexico. Eugenia and Bryant were to arrange a hideout for the gang down in Indian Territory, while the others did the robbing.

In Santa Rosa, the boys stuck up a faro game, or maybe, as Emmett had it, a monte game (in another source, it's a Chinese restaurant).[48] Whatever happened, the local citizenry objected to it violently. Worse, they backed up their anger with live ammunition, and the Daltons made tracks forthwith. One account says Emmett was wounded in the arm in the shootout in Santa Rosa. The boys alleged that the faro game was crooked, a predictable sort of excuse, and Emmett took great pains to call the New Mexico affair "OUR FIRST CRIME."[49] Whether any of that apologia was true or not, New Mexico became distinctly unhealthy and the gang split up.

Bob and Emmett made for California at the high lope. There they joined brother Bill, established and well known in rich Tulare County, and newly arrived Grat, who betook himself to Fresno to drink and gamble. Bill, whom we'll meet again, was an ornery sort. He was involved in perpetual disputation with the all-powerful Southern Pacific Railroad over the rights of homesteaders who had settled on the SP right-of-way. Bill had eyes on a seat in the California legislature. Contrary to several accounts, he never got it, but he surely had high ambitions.

Author Richard Patterson says Emmett was still in Oklahoma when his brothers got into hot water out in the Golden State. In *Beyond the Law*, Emmett says the same thing, and Frank Latta agrees. Bob, Patterson says, fled from New Mexico to California with McElhanie, the Narrow-Gauge Kid, not with Emmett.[50] Patterson also says, as do other versions, that the boys went first to Bill's "ranch" near Paso Robles. The details are uncertain and unimportant. What matters is that the brothers got themselves into a heap of trouble, worse by far than anything they had left behind them.

This heap of trouble was the much-disputed episode of the Alila train holdup. Like so much else in the Dalton mythology, there is no general agreement on exactly who did what at Alila. Some things, however, are certain.

Somebody did indeed hold up the Southern Pacific, specifically Train No. 17, at a tiny water stop called Alila, a wide spot in the road in southern Tulare County. It happened on February 6, 1891, at about nine in the evening. What infuriated the citizens and brought lawmen out in swarms was that in the firefight between the express messenger and the bandits, fireman George W. Radcliff was mortally wounded.

It is no longer clear, if it ever was, how the Southern Pacific and the local peace officers connected the Daltons with the crime. Some writers speculate that the giant Southern Pacific needed to convict somebody and simply chose the Dalton boys as victims. Bill Dalton, at least, was something of a burr under the saddle of the Southern Pacific. On the other hand, another writer denies that any of the Dalton boys were in California at all.[51]

Whatever happened, Bob and Emmett were on the run, each with a bounty of fifteen hundred dollars on his head. Grat and Bill Dalton ended up in the Tulare County jail at Visalia, charged as accessories.

Bob and Emmett shook their pursuers, made San Luis Obispo on horseback, and then disappeared again, heading east. On March 8, the brothers left their horses at a station about one hundred miles east of Mojave, boarded a handy eastbound train, and put sunny California far behind them. By the end of April they briefly visited the family in Kingfisher, then disappeared into the tangled and familiar Triangle Country across the Cimarron.

On May 2, Bob and Emmett stole a small bunch of horses near Orlando. Pursued by a band of local ranchers, the brothers turned on the posse at a place called Twin Mounds, killed a man named Starmer and badly wounded another posseman, then escaped with the horses. The epilog is another of those Dalton tales that has been widely told ... but may or may not be true.

The killing—if it happened—sounds like Bob's work because, as the story goes, Starmer had been hit three times, the
holes so close together they could be covered with one hand.[52]
Now the charge would be murder, and Judge Isaac Parker's writ
ran down in the no-man's-land of the Nations. Now deputy marshals would be on their backtrail, and that was a very different
proposition from a band of angry farmers.

After Twin Mounds the brothers lay low for a while. By now
they had several hard-to-find hideouts down in the wild country
of the Indian Nations. One of these was at Hennessey, where Bob
and the omnipresent Flo "had set up an undetected love nest."[53]

One author says Adeline stayed in contact with her outlaw sons. Brother Ben Dalton arranged a rendezvous in Dover, a
predominantly black settlement, where the boys could meet their
mother undisturbed. Adeline brought the boys money, the story
goes.[54] If she did, it must have meant scraping for her last dollar;
the cotton wasn't all that tall for the hardworking woman from
Kingfisher.

Nevertheless, the brothers kept on stealing other people's
money and goods. Black-faced Charley Bryant and Bitter Creek
Newcomb were part of the band by now. The seductive Flo scouted
another job for them, allegedly sleeping with a railroad messenger
to get her information. And so, in May, 1891, the four men held up
a Santa Fe train at Wharton, a two-building stop near what is now
Perry, Oklahoma. It wasn't much of a holdup, the bandits riding
off into the night with only a few hundred dollars per robber. This
raid was, in Emmett's flaming prose, "a blind striking back at all
corporate interests in any way related to their troubles."[55]

Maybe so. Or maybe it just beat working for a living. After the fact, at least, the California encounter with the Southern
Pacific made a convenient excuse for going banditing.

Some accounts say that Bryant wantonly shot down the
railroad agent as the gang galloped away. Such a killing would be

right in character for Black-faced Charley, although there is some question whether the incident is not just another chapter in the Dalton myth. Whatever Bryant actually did at Wharton, he did not live to gloat about it very long.

Bryant got his "minute of hell-firin' action" near Waukomis, Oklahoma not long after the stickup. Black-faced Charley was arrested while in the grip of one of his fever attacks, in bed after an Oklahoma cowman beat him up, or while being treated for his syphilis—take your pick.[56] Back on his feet, Bryant was transported, in handcuffs, in a Rock Island mail car.

Taking advantage of the mail clerk's lack of vigilance, Bryant seized the clerk's .45 and opened up on his escort, Deputy Marshal Ed Short. Short, mortally wounded, nevertheless pumped Bryant full of Winchester slugs and the two died within minutes of each another. Several histories rather sentimentally record that both Black-faced Charley and Ed Short spent some of their last few breaths asking passers-by to take their boots off. Bryant was thus the first of the gang to go. The reward for his capture paid for the shipment of Ed Short's coffin to his eastern home.

Meanwhile, the Dalton gang galloped on about its nefarious business, apparently wasting little time mourning Charlie (who was, in fairness, eminently unmournable). The gang's next escapade was another train robbery, this time on the Missouri, Kansas and Texas near Wagoner, Indian Territory. Black-faced Charley having been erased from the roster by Ed Short's Winchester, Bob recruited more help. This time, Dick Broadwell, Charlie Pierce, Bill Doolin, and happy-go-lucky Bill Powers would ride along.

The gang stopped the Katy train at Leliaetta on September 15, 1891, and the robbery went quietly, without a shot fired except for a couple of rounds designed to encourage the opening of the express car. Some accounts have Doolin galloping, whooping and firing, the length of the halted train, spooking emerging passengers as they climbed down to resist the robbers. Doolin's gallop may never have happened, but it made rousing reading and produced no end of flashy illustrations, then and after.

This time, the Daltons got away with around twenty-five hundred dollars, which made each man's share something less than the per-bandit percentage at Wharton. At this rate, banditry showed a worrisome lack of earning potential. Afterward, the boys again scattered, Bob and Emmett galloping off to a lair near Guthrie, where, of course, the devoted Flo awaited her lover.

Flo is also given credit for the recon before the Leliaetta raid, reporting at the hideout before the raid "resplendent in Spanish chaps and a brand-new sombrero."[57] With or without chaps, she had "dallied joyfully" with a Katy station agent, while posing as a magazine writer researching an article on railroading. She did her scouting, as Harold Preece said, "with an incomparable combination of sex and wit. She was the shrewdest woman outlaw who ever popped up out of the sagebrush. By comparison, Belle Starr was no more than a sly frontier slut."[58]

Well, maybe. The more one reads about Flo—Florence, Tom, or perhaps Eugenia—in her various incarnations, the more she seems too good to be true. Just to confuse the whole story, she also appears as divorcee Daisy Bryant. She is a "full-blown beauty" (of course), who becomes Bob's mistress.[59] The more you read, the more you hope just a few of the tall tales about What's-her-name are the real McCoy. She is just too fine a story to be pure invention.

The Leliaetta raid provides some insight into the unreliability of Emmett's fanciful tales about his outlaw days. Writing years after Leliaetta, Emmett said the take was $9,400, some 1,880 pounds of silver.[60] Now that is literally almost a ton of money. Even so, Emmett has Doolin carrying the loot out of the express car in a sack, and Emmett is supposed to have ridden all night with this monstrous pile slung across his saddle. In *When the Daltons Rode*, Emmett even upped the ante, declaring the gang got

$3,500 per man. It is little wonder that historians are more than a little skeptical of Emmett's "histories."

Meanwhile, on July 7, back in California, Grat Dalton had been convicted of complicity in the Alila holdup, in spite of testimony by a dozen witnesses that he was playing cards and sopping up whiskey in Fresno at the crucial time. The jury was not having any, however, and Grat went back to his cell to await sentencing. Disenchanted with California justice, Grat took it, as the old-timers used to say, "on the heel and toe." Grat's lawyer had won a postponement of sentencing into September, and while the wheels of justice were temporarily idling, Grat and two others slipped out of the Visalia jail, stole a buggy, and vamoosed.

Another version of Grat's escape, entertaining but pure moonshine, was produced by a Dalton biographer known only as "Eyewitness," an inventive sort who dreamed up the following marvelous tale. Sentenced to twenty years, Grat was on his way to prison, traveling the rails with two deputy sheriffs. Grat, in leg irons and handcuffed to a lawman, somehow slipped a cuff, then hurled himself headfirst through the open train window, just as the iron horse puffed across a trestle above a stream. Landing miraculously unhurt, he mounted a horse brought by a waiting accomplice and disappeared.

Anything is possible, but that account sounds a little like something out of *The Prisoner of Zenda*. It further indicates that Grat got himself a horse and headed for home, 107 days cross-country to Kingfisher and his doting mother. It was quite a ride if, as the story tells us, he made it all on horseback. It took Grat across the Mojave Desert—a nasty trip at the best of times—through the wild country of Arizona and New Mexico and then home across the Texas Panhandle.

Some six to eight weeks after the Leliaetta raid, Bill Dalton also disappeared from sunny California. Watched by lawmen, he is supposed to have eluded the detectives by having another man dress in his clothing and drive about in a buggy with Bill's wife. Appearing in Kingfisher, equipped with the gift of gab and a burning hatred of banks and bankers, Bill set up in the land-dealing business and prospered. On the side, Bill became intelligence gatherer and information broker for the gang.

For a while, at least, the Dalton gang could find hospitality at many of the isolated ranches and squatters' cabins scattered across Indian Territory. Food and shelter were readily available, with no questions asked. No lonely farm family was terribly anxious to cross any band of outlaws. Further, many of the people who lived in this wild country were not eager to meet federal lawmen, for good and sufficient reasons of their own. Lastly, the Daltons were liberal with their gold—after all, they hadn't had to work for it—and hard money was difficult to come by.

There is even a tale that one of the gang's suppliers was a deputy United States marshal. In 1890 an Oklahoma City man reportedly paused in his journey at the home of the marshal in question. For reasons unexplained—perhaps protective coloration—the marshal invited the traveler to go with him on a long, difficult ride into the badlands, the "depths of rugged hills and gulches, thickets of timber and underbrush," and in this empty, hostile country the marshal stopped to deliver to Grat and Emmett "two bulging leather saddlepockets" full of food and ammunition.[61] This tale could well be true. Some peace officers worked both sides of the street. Others were not averse to helping an outlaw, in return for the criminal taking his depredations into somebody else's jurisdiction.

While they waited for their brother, or brothers, with or without aid and comfort from the law, Bob and Emmett had suspended operations, even pushing cows a while under assumed names. Now, with Grat back home—deeply bitter, Emmett says— the gang reconvened for business. By the end of May 1892, the brothers sat down to plan with Doolin, Bitter Creek, Charley Pierce, Broadwell, and Powers. This time it would be a major strike, the bonanza they all hoped would set them up for life. It would be another train, this time carrying the Sac and Fox tribal annuity money, 70,000 dollars of it.

Bob planned to stop the train on the first of June at Red Rock station, a one-horse depot about forty miles south of Arkansas City. The train was due at 10:40 in the evening, and arrived right on time. It all seemed innocent enough, but Bob didn't like the look of a darkened smoking car, and let the train stop and pull out again. Emmett painted the picture with his usual flair for the dramatic: "That black smoker, sinister as a vault! Was deadly menace crouching there in rifled readiness?"[62]

Deadly menace sure was, and Bob, wariest of the bunch, smelled a rat. "Look at that smoker," he said. "It's a deadhead, and as dangerous as a rattler."[63]

It was. In fact, it was more dangerous, for the train carried a gaggle of loaded Winchesters, ready and waiting for the gang. Warned that "suspicious characters" had been spotted near Red Rock, Wells Fargo detective Fred Dodge waited alertly in the darkened smoker, ready to pounce. Beside him was Heck Thomas, who had left his new bride to resume his hunting of the Daltons.

Bob's well-honed bandit instincts had served him well, saving the gang from what might well have been a terminal surprise. A few minutes behind this Trojan horse, however, came the regular express, and the gang jumped it as it stood in the station. There was no escort on this train, only the regular crew, and the bandits moved swiftly to crack the locked express car.

In those days, express cars frequently carried a pair of safes. One, the "through" safe, was usually formidable, heavy and hard to move, and often could be unlocked only at the train's major destination; to frustrate bandits, express messengers could not open the through safe at all. The second safe was the "way" safe, containing deliveries consigned to intermediate stops along the train's route. The express messenger had to be able to open this one, but as a rule it contained relatively small change. Any substantial amount was usually locked in the through safe.

After a brief defense by the express messenger and guard—caught playing checkers, according to some accounts[64]—the gang took control of the express car, only to be badly disappointed. The gang's bonanza had gone on through with the first train, well protected by the Winchesters of the guard force. Emmett as usual inflates the size of the Red Rock take, but all they found in the way safe was a paltry prize, less than three thousand dollars, to which they spitefully added the guard's pocket cash and gold watch and the crew's lunchboxes. There was more money in the through safe, which they could not open. One writer says they also looted some "feminine finery meant for Bob's mistress, Flo Quick; Emmett's flame Julia Johnson; and Bitter Creek's little inamorata, Rose Dunn."[65] Elsewhere, the same writer records that they took "three or four boxes of silk stockings."[66] The grass was getting mighty short for the famous Dalton gang.

Rose is none other than the renowned "Rose of Cimarron," who later won fame for shinnying down the side of a building on a rope of bedsheets, bullets whizzing around her, to bring arms and ammunition to her embattled true love, Bitter Creek, during a battle with marshals. Julia married Emmett, much later. At the time of the Red Rock raid, she was indeed between husbands, but her granddaughter said in later years that Julia never laid eyes on Emmett until after he got out of prison in the next century.[67]

One story about the Red Rock holdup illustrates the difficulty of wading through the mythology invented over the years about the Daltons. This tale has Charley Bryant wantonly murdering the station agent as the gang finished its work. The obvious trouble with this horrifying fable is that Black-faced Charley wasn't in condition to shoot anybody: Ed Short had terminated Bryant the better part of a year before.

After Red Rock the gang scattered to confuse pursuit. A number of posses were scouring the country for them, including one led by the formidable Dane, Chris Madsen. One bunch of pursuers found Bob's "love nest in Greer County," but the birds had flown, taking along "Flo's wardrobe, including plenty of silky Montgomery Ward negligees."[68]

In spite of the hot pursuit, the gang members again got away clean. Wells Fargo detective Fred Dodge and a deputy marshal chased Grat across part of the Sac and Fox Reservation without catching him, and that was as close to a bandit as any of the pursuers came.

Even so, the gang must have felt increasingly harried and insecure. The best in the business were after them and hardly likely to quit. As a territorial paper editorialized, "The James boys, with all their deeds of outlawry, surpassed in no way crimes that the devilish Daltons have been known to commit! The time will come when they must give up their liberty or life, but when and how?"[69] The comparison with the James boys may have been a little over-stated, but the paper reflected the anger most citizens felt toward the "devilish Daltons."

Then and now, the gang's exploits were shrouded in a swirling vapor of legend. The tales told about the gang are wonderful without exception, except that lots of them aren't true and lots of others are only partly so. The trick is figuring out which tales offer how much truth.

Along about the time of Red Rock, for example, Flo is supposed to have enticed a yokel into her bedroom and got him arrested as Bob Dalton. Her dupe remained in jail as the law rejoiced, until Chris Madsen took a look at the prisoner and told the officers they had the wrong man.[70] If this story is true—and even if it isn't—Flo was a busy girl. In addition to giving Bob all manner of aid and comfort, she spent some time sharing hearth and home with a Guthrie butcher called Mundy and stole the odd horse or two on the side.

Another tale records Grat being arrested along about this time by a deputy marshal and a small posse. The teller of the tale, a pioneer named Herbert Hicks, was interviewed long years later. He remembered that the arrest took place about a year before the Coffeyville raid, and that it happened this way. Hicks was recruited by a deputy marshal to track down members of the Dalton gang. The lawmen got the drop on two of the outlaws in an isolated barn and captured both. One turned out to be Grat Dalton (Hicks called him "Gratz"). Gratz, said Hicks, laughed and joked with his captors all the way to jail at Claremore, particularly over the fact that he had arrested one of the possemen for a whiskey offense.[71]

There the story ends, leaving to the imagination what happened at Claremore and who the other outlaw might have been. The story is probably the invention of an old man's mind, for there is no independent record of Grat being captured, unless the reference is to some minor arrest made after the Daltons got out of the marshal business, before the gang started raiding trains.

Returning to events we can be reasonably sure of—the gang reunited at a hideout in eastern Oklahoma, a cave in which they could rest up and plan further adventures. There are various claims about exactly where the cave was located, but the only thing certain is that it was close to Tulsa. There they took counsel together and decided on the next strike, a raid on the Katy at Pryor Creek, a station twenty miles north of Leliaetta out in the Cherokee Nation.

While they were camped near Pryor Creek, however, they were seen by an Indian farmer, and Bob changed plans. Sure that the farmer would alert the authorities, Bob changed his objective; "We'll outfox them," he said. "They'll be expecting us at Pryor Creek, but we'll be robbing the train at Adair."[72]

Adair was a substantial town less than thirty miles from Vinita, where the Daltons had lived at one time. One old-timer said that Bob did the recon for this job himself—so much for Flo's famous scouting. Bob "stayed around Fishback's pool hall for a week before getting the lay of the land." In fact, said the old-timer, the whole gang played pool in Adair for "almost a week" prior to the robbery.[73]

Whether the pool-playing episode is true or not (it sounds like pure invention), the gang certainly knew their way around town. They left their horses in a draw at the west side of town (or "behind the pool hall," depending on whose account you read)[74] with Charley Pierce in charge of their vital transportation.

At first everything went smoothly. The outlaws captured the station without trouble, holding a gun on the night telegraph operator and stealing some money as a sort of hors d'oeuvre to the big haul. Katy Train No. 2 was right on time, sliding into Adair station at 9:42 P.M. The train crew was captured without trouble, being invited to shut up and obey "or have their brains blown out." The gang also started blazing away down the town's streets, trying to keep the citizenry under cover.[75]

With the crew accounted for, the gang got into the express car with the help of the usual shots fired into the doors and sides. The fireman was forced to attack the express car door with his pick and the messenger was bullied into opening the safe, which apparently contained little money. What there was, plus some other miscellaneous loot, was loaded into a spring wagon locally stolen to carry the booty.

And about here is where everything began to come unstuck. For suddenly Winchester slugs began to snap around the heads of the bandits, and the night erupted with muzzle flashes. For the train carried eight guards, including veteran Captain Charley LeFlore of the Indian Police. The lawmen forted up in a coal-house next to the right-of-way, and for a few minutes everybody blazed away in the gloom until Pierce showed up with the horses and the gang clattered off whooping into the night, spring wagon and all.

The bandits had gotten the best of this brief skirmish. LeFlore and two others had minor wounds, and the gang had gotten away clean, galloping madly down the streets of Adair. Up to this point, the Adair raid might have been just another holdup, but now the bandits did the unthinkable. According to the local press, as the robbers clattered past the Skinner Store, they fired eighteen or twenty rounds at two inoffensive men on the porch of the store. Both men went down with leg wounds.

And both men were doctors. One of them, Dr. W. L. Goff, was mortally wounded. The other, Dr. T. S. Youngblood, would lose part of his foot. Now there was a rough protocol even among western outlaws, and part of it was that you didn't shoot preachers and you didn't shoot doctors. What the Daltons had done was even worse than talking dirty to a respectable lady, and the countryside was up in arms.

Emmett Dalton calls Doctor Goff's wound "trifling" and, typically, says Goff died of blood poisoning after "unskilled treatment."[76] The allegation is nonsense, for Goff passed away at Vinita before six the next morning, after treatment by two local physicians, and long before blood poisoning could have run its lethal course.

One writer says the doctors were shot in a drugstore, and attributes their wounds to "the high-powered rifles of the cowardly guards."[77] Others, including the egregious "Eyewitness," say the doctors were hit by "wild" shots; one writer even has the doctor a passenger on the train.[78]

In the end, it didn't matter much whose bullet had in fact struck down Doctor Goff. The fat was in the fire. Murder warrants were issued from the Fort Smith district court, and the Katy and the express company ponied up five thousand dollars a head for the capture of the gang. For the first time, virtually every man's hand was against the Daltons. The gang rode west, hoping to shake pursuit and get back into their lair in the Osage Hills. The take at Adair had been about seventeen thousand dollars, hardly enough to finance a quick exit to faraway climes.

It did not take a criminal genius to feel the toils of the law closing about the gang. The robbery of the Katy train at Adair, and especially the death of Doctor Goff, had generated massive public indignation and official energy. The public and the press saw Daltons behind every bush. They were accused of robbing a bank in Southwest City, Missouri, just after the Adair raid. And when robbers took ten thousand dollars from a bank in El Reno, Oklahoma, shortly after the Adair raid, the crime was instantly blamed on the Daltons. Some experienced lawmen doubted the Daltons had had a hand in the El Reno job, but the public leaped to a conclusion and clung to it staunchly.

The reward for the gang was now the biggest bounty yet offered for a single bunch of outlaws. It was plain that even the dugouts down in the Nations were no longer safe havens. The whole countryside was becoming too hot to hold the gang for many days more. It was time to go.

But going took money. The gang's treasury was running low, or at least Emmett Dalton later said it was. If Emmett told the truth, the gang's relative poverty at the beginning of October was another good reason for doubting their involvement in the El Reno bank robbery in July. One more job, then, said Bob, a lucrative raid to restore their fortunes and finance a trip to the high lonesome.

The idea made sense to the others—until the gang found out just what Bob had in mind. This was to be no ordinary robbery. It must have been a little daunting to the bandits to discover that, instead of plundering a train or a small-town bank, Bob intended to ride boldly into a prosperous, bustling county town, in the heart of the business day, and hold up not one but *two* banks.

One has to wonder how much of the raid was the product of rational planning, and how much arose from Bob's vanity. Marshal Evett Nix, for one, thought the raid was the result of "Bob's mad ambition . . . fired with a desire to commit a robbery so daring and so sensational that the entire country would be shocked, and that would establish the Dalton gang as more to be feared than the James boys or the Youngers had ever been."[79]

It may indeed have been Bob's ego, not his brain, that spawned the Coffeyville raid. The plan was obviously more dangerous than it needed to be. Not only would the gang have to split its forces between two objectives, but striking two banks at once doubled the chance of early discovery by the citizens. More dangerous still was the choice of towns. No doubt Coffeyville was a prosperous town, where there was likely to be money in quantity, but it was also the sometime hometown of the Dalton boys, where people were likely to remember them on sight.

Emmett Dalton chalked up the decision to hit Coffeyville at least in part to his brother's vanity. While much of what Emmett later said and wrote can be discounted as self-serving invention, this statement has the ring of truth: "Bob said he could discount the James boys' work and rob both banks of Coffeyville in one day. I said I did not want any of it at all." Emmett made this statement shortly after the bloody end of the raid, while he lay, shot full of holes, in Coffeyville's Farmer's Home hotel.[80] Nobody expected him to survive, and Emmett himself must have known he was likely to die. It seems improbable that in the face of death he would lie about the brother he had loved and ridden back into the fire to save.

Reluctantly or not, Emmett would go on the raid, and in *Beyond the Law* he wrote at length about the planning and preparation. First of all, Bob chose his personnel. He would not take Doolin, Bitter Creek Newcomb, or Pierce. Only his brothers, Dick Broadwell, and Bill Powers would go.

And why not Bill Doolin? By all accounts Doolin was a cool hand in a tight place, a smart, tough gunman who, as the saying went, "would do to take along" on any raid. Later on, Doolin was a successful gang leader in his own right, perhaps a better leader than Bob Dalton had been. Emmett says Doolin was not invited to Coffeyville and that Doolin, Newcomb, and Pierce were dropped from the gang's roster "as they had seemingly gotten so they did not like to ride too long at a time and were too prone to lie around their friends, after they had made a little raise."[81]

Emmett's account to the contrary, however, there is some evidence that Doolin actually *did* ride along to rob the Coffeyville banks. Whether he did is one of the longstanding mysteries of the Coffeyville raid. The whole "sixth bandit" mythology is discussed at length in the last chapter.

Emmett's reasons for Bob's choice of raiders may or may not be the whole truth. We can speculate, as Emmett says, that Bob had decided to take only his most reliable, obedient men. Or he may simply have reduced his personnel to the bare minimum he thought necessary for the job. After all, fewer people meant fewer shares in what he believed would be a major bonanza.

As to Doolin, it is possible that Bob did not want another strong, magnetic leader along—if this was to be the most astonishing robbery of the age, Bob might well have wanted no rival around to share the glory.

Doolin may also have been left behind simply because Bob did not trust him. It seems that before the Leliaetta job, Doolin had ridden coolly into Wagoner and posed for a photograph. Worse, he had ordered a copy sent on to his girlfriend down at Ingalls, Oklahoma, where he had many friends. The photo may have pleased

Doolin's girl, but it also pleased Indian Police Captain Charley LeFlore, who got a copy of it and used it to tie Doolin in with the Dalton gang.

Perhaps Bob considered Doolin so reckless and wild as to be a danger. He had "strutted" up and down the station platform at both Adair and Leliaetta during the shooting there. Daring was one thing; every bandit had sand in his craw. Wild and headstrong were something else altogether.

Pierce and Bitter Creek Newcomb were a constant danger: they talked too much. They were gregarious types, apparently, always ready to pass the time of day with strangers. Who could tell when they would drop a casual boast to the wrong person, an informer, a marshal, a Wells Fargo undercover agent like Fred Dodge? So Newcomb and Pierce were probably left behind because of their propensity to run off at the mouth. One incautious remark in the wrong saloon could get the whole gang hung, legally at Fort Smith or summarily someplace else.

Colonel Bailey Hanes, writing in *Bill Doolin, Outlaw O.T.*, says that Newcomb, Pierce, and Doolin all "quit" the gang before the Coffeyville disaster. Another writer says bluntly that only Broadwell and Powers were willing to "risk their fool necks," taking on two banks at once in a town where lots of people could recognize the Daltons.[82] Prolific author Ramon Adams, in his forward to the Hanes book, concurs: "This seems logical. I do not believe that Doolin, levelheaded as he was, would have joined in such a foolhardy stunt, especially in a town where the Daltons were so well known."[83]

Hanes and Adams have a point. Although others describe Doolin as reckless and foolhardy, even he might have been daunted by the prospect of invading a populous town where three of the gang members were well known. Doolin may or may not have been "levelheaded," but he was far from stupid. And so, when the gang was cut down to five, Doolin may already have decided he wanted no part of Coffeyville.

In any case, the gang split up. The parting was apparently amicable. Bob Dalton told the dispossessed that he "had nothing in mind" just now, but that he would contact them when another job was planned. And so Pierce, Doolin, and Newcomb trotted off toward the outlaw haven at Ingalls, spared to live a while longer. The Daltons, Powers, and Broadwell rode north to die.

Bob knew he might have only days to find the big payday the gang had sought for so long. The gang's days were obviously numbered in Oklahoma. Wells Fargo's ace bloodhound, Fred Dodge, was baying on their track, and riding with him was Deputy U.S. Marshal Heck Thomas.

Deputy Marshal Chris Madsen and dozens of other lawmen were also out on the hunt. Indian trackers headed some of the posses, and the combination of five thousand dollars a head in blood money and the killing of Doctor Goff meant that no place was safe any longer. It was hard to know whom to trust now. Bob's first plan was to hit the railroad again, at Wharton. Here he was frustrated, however, for the pursuers soon got word of the planned raid. Bob and his men turned away from Wharton, but the damage had been done.

Nemesis was even closer behind them now, the worst possible bunch of manhunters to have on your backtrail. Fred Dodge was very close to them, and with him were veteran posseman Burrell Cox, Sac and Fox tracker Talbot White, and that most dangerous of pursuers, the implacable Deputy U.S. Marshal Heck Thomas, whom Fred Dodge called "a man that was known to always get his man—sometimes dead but he got him."[84]

Now and again the hunters lost the Daltons' trail and wasted precious time finding the track again. The bandits had been seen near Blue Springs shortly after the holdup, and on September 21 they had eaten dinner at an isolated ranch. There they bought provisions, "and weren't particular about the price they paid."[85] They were last seen heading in the direction of Vinita, the Daltons' old home country, and then the trail petered out again.

The hunters kept at it, and by the end of September Bob knew it was time to cut and run. Thomas and Dodge were not going to quit hunting, and there was no safe place left to hide. And so, in their hideout near the Mashed-O Ranch, north of Tulsa, Bob unveiled his final plan. This last caper would be an astonishing, history-making raid, two banks in the same town and then a long run to safety—and a thumb-of-the-nose to all their relentless pursuers. One author suggests Bob flatly told his henchmen that anybody who didn't come along was a coward.[86] If Bob said that, it was the kind of talk designed to overcome all objections—no frontier tough could stomach anybody thinking he had shown the white feather.

Bob repeatedly rehearsed his plans for the raid. Bob and Emmett would hold up the First National and the other three would strike the Condon Bank, just across the street. They would hitch their horses, Bob said, at the C. M. Condon building, so that nobody would see them "until we got into the banks."[87] Leaving their horses as near the banks as possible made excellent sense. In the event, however, the gang paid little attention to the location of their critical mounts during the raid.

In short, the gang made no reconnaissance worthy of the name, unless one accepts two highly improbable tales related by "Eyewitness." One says that the boys dropped by Coffeyville from time to time during their "wanted" days. Whether from nostalgia or bravado or both, they called after midnight at the Farmer's Home hotel, demanding and getting dinner from a host either terrified or friendly or both.[88] This might actually have happened. A midnight meal in the old town might be the sort of rash gesture that would appeal to young outlaws feeling their oats.

The second tale is that Bob had been in Coffeyville just before the raid. "Eyewitness" says Bob entered town in the dead of night and rousted out a Slosson's drugstore "manager and partner" called Frank Benson. This visit "Eyewitness" describes—in successive paragraphs—as variously "within the week preceding the famous raid," and "about a week or ten days before the raid."[89] Benson knew Bob, who demanded a gallon of whiskey, not always easy to find in a dry state.

Benson said Slosson's did not have any firewater and told Bob to try elsewhere. Benson, the story goes, told only a close friend or two about Bob's visit. However, "word got back to the marshals through somebody or other, that Bob had been in Coffeyville."[90] "Eyewitness" says Benson's confidants "mocked at Benson as a dreamer of idle things."[91]

It is hard to accept Bob's visit, if it happened at all, as a scouting mission for the raid. Bob would have seen little of the town in the darkness, and presumably was not crazy enough to show himself to a man who knew who he was, not when he planned to surprise the town's banks. If the nocturnal whiskey visit ever happened, or the midnight meals, it must have been before Bob decided on the raid. In any case, Bob would have learned little about the state of the town or the layout of the banks.

One young man named Andy Jones later maintained that Bob Dalton had been in Coffeyville on July 29, possibly the time he is supposed to have visited Benson. Jones said he saw Bob standing at the southwest corner of the Condon Bank, apparently during daylight. Perhaps significantly, the street work had not begun by the end of July, and the hitching racks near the banks were still in place on the twenty-ninth.

A circus was in town that day and Jones told his wife-to-be, Ida Gibbs, that he feared the Daltons might rob the banks that night during the circus performance. After the raid was over, Andy declared to Ida that the trousers Bob wore were the "same he had worn on July 29." There is no record, however, of Jones telling anybody but Ida about seeing Bob, either before or after the raid.[92]

And so, except for these somewhat improbable tales, as far as we know neither Bob nor anybody else in the gang had any current intelligence on Coffeyville. Bob may have been operating on information two years old, impressions and memories of years gone by. He had been in the town as recently as January, 1890, during which visit he ran up a tab of $18.95 at Barndollar Brothers. The bill was for clothing, and it presents an interesting sidelight on what an American dollar was worth in that faraway year. For less than twenty dollars, Bob had bought a flannel shirt, a pair of pants, two suits of underwear, two "half hose" and a pair of Alaskas, whatever those may be.

No doubt Bob's memories were fresh enough for reminiscence's sake, but they were no substitute for up-to-date reconnaissance. Perhaps the relentless pursuit drove Bob Dalton to attack without scouting ahead. Perhaps it was simple arrogance. In any case, he ignored the most basic precautions. He was walking into a hornets' nest with no idea of what the nest looked like or how many hornets lived there.

Better reconnaissance might have told Bob that there were easier pickings than the banks. Periodically, large annuities for the Indian tribes were paid through Coffeyville. In fact, two men from the Condon Bank, one of the Daltons' targets, sometimes carried money to the tribes. The messengers would not have been hard to ambush and rob on some country road, armed or not—certainly a much easier target than two substantial banks in a town center.

Bob intended to strike the banks about half-past nine in the morning, according to Emmett, when "there would not be so many people in town, and we wouldn't have to hurt anyone."[93] This last statement is hard to understand, if you try to take it as true. Neither Bob Dalton nor his men could have been so dense as to think a thriving country town would not be going full blast by nine-thirty on any weekday morning, especially in farm country where people rose early and got about the business of the day.

It seems likely that Emmett simply invented this part of Bob's plan in order to placate the wrathful citizens of Coffeyville. Probably the raid was scheduled for the morning hours in order to strike the banks before anybody made any large withdrawals. In later years, Emmett agreed that insuring the largest possible take was at least one reason for attacking Coffeyville soon after the banks opened in the morning.

The rest of the plan was simple, and based on long experience. After the raid, the gang would make for the familiar thickets and draws of the Osage Hills, a maze in which they could feel confident of losing any posse. From the Osage Hills they would strike west for a rendezvous in the Cherokee Strip. Somewhere along the way, probably after getting clear of all pursuit, the brothers would separate from their henchmen.

Waiting at the Cherokee Strip meeting place would be Amos Burton, a black Texas cowboy who was "noted as a cowpuncher and bronco-buster throughout Oklahoma and north Texas."[94] Burton would drive a team and covered wagon, and bring along a supply of food and ammunition. Emmett says Burton was told nothing of the plan to rob the Coffeyville banks. He probably was also left out of any share of the loot, although Emmett says the gang intended to "pay him liberally."

From the rendezvous, the plan was to drive the wagon on west and northwest. Two of the gang would sit in front, dressed as farmers. The others, with all the guns and saddles, would hide in the wagon. The saddle horses would be led behind the wagon, and the two men in front would "pretend to be farmers." The raiders' ultimate destination was Seattle, from which pleasant city they would drift by ones and twos to South America and safety.

Burton, incidentally, faithfully carried out his part of the scheme, waiting in vain for the brothers to join him.[95]

Another version of the brothers' plan also involved the innocent wagon trip but added Julia and Flo, who would join the boys out in the Indian Nations. The whole menage would then rumble out to New Mexico and thence south to sample the charms of old Mexico, where they would live happily ever after, including, presumably, the doltish Grat.

In preparation for the raid, the gang supposedly indulged in new clothing and treated themselves to fine Mexican saddles, complete with tassels and carvings and silver-plated stirrups. Moreover, Bob "bought ten new Colt forty-fives. . . . Each of the outlaws owned a high-powered Winchester of the very latest model." This story is hard to take seriously, since the same tale has Bob carrying the Bisley Colt that would not be made for the better part of two more years. Harold Preece said Bob and Emmett had two rifles apiece, although what a man could do with two Winchesters at once is hard to imagine. Everybody carried "100 rounds," although the tale does not say whether these were pistol or rifle rounds.

As to the obligatory business of fond farewells, Emmett, positively wallowing in sentimentality, tells of his sad goodbye to Julia. He sat in the Johnson home, he says, listening to his beloved play the "big organ . . . melodies suffused with sadness, carrying some indefinable lament or reproach as if to remind one constantly of life's swift passing."[96]

Not long afterward, Emmett says, Bob was plunged into black depression. Eugenia had been ill, it seems: "Autumn leaves were already falling in her dark eyes while yet summer tossed green and vital outside."[97] Soon Bob received a letter from Ben Canty up in New Mexico, telling him that the light of his life was dead. "Boys," said the stricken gang leader, "Boys, I don't care what happens to me now."[98]

And then the boys went off to say good-bye to Mom; at least, in *Beyond the Law* Emmett talks about riding "near to Kingfisher" where Adeline Dalton lived, and implies that it was on this final foray. He goes on, with somewhat contrived sentimentality, "I know that for one I wanted to take a chance and see her again. But discretion overcame the calls of affection for me as well as for Grat and Bob, and we rode on by in the night without even a friendly 'Hello.' Mother was never to see two of her boys alive again."[99]

Emmett also talks about the visit to Kingfisher in *When the Daltons Rode*. "For a moment we saw her in a distant window," but Adeline's sons were too afraid—or too ashamed—to go to the house. They decided, according to Emmett, that it was "better she should not know how close we were, her three outlawed sons."[100] In old age, brother Littleton Dalton said that the gang visited Kingfisher on the way to Coffeyville, staying the night.[101] Littleton probably has this visit mixed up with another one, since even Emmett says the boys did not go into the house.

The notion that the gang rode anywhere near Adeline's homestead on the way to Coffeyville is hard to buy. Emmett's tear-jerking statements in his books—and Littleton's faded memory—simply cannot be accurate. Kingfisher lies north and west of Oklahoma City, and the gang started out from a point north of Tulsa, far to the east. To pass Kingfisher on the way to Coffeyville, the gang would have had to traverse most of the wild, roadless territory twice, a manifest impossibility in the time they took to travel from the Tulsa hideout to their target.

Whatever sentimental farewells there may have been, on the second of October the raiders saddled up and rode through the Osage Nation, pushing their ponies north. Emmett's horse went lame about this time, and so he and Bob stopped at the sprawling Mashed-O Ranch, northeast of Tulsa, to find another mount. The Mashed-O foreman was still friendly, and might well trade horses with Emmett.

Emmett got a horse at the Mashed-O, all right, but it turned out to belong to Ed Chapman, a deputy U.S. marshal. Just how this came about is most unclear. Emmett boasts that Chapman had been bragging about catching the Daltons, but dissolved into a froth of fear when Emmett and Bob showed up at the Mashed-O.[102] Emmett says Chapman volunteered not only his horse but his services and all his Winchester cartridges.

According to Emmett, he paid one hundred dollars for the horse, although after the raid Chapman alleged that Daltons had stolen the animal. The truth of this curious business has never been sorted out. Emmett's version sounds like another of his inventions. All we know is that the brothers did acquire Chapman's horse, by fair means or foul.

One old-time marshal says the gang began the ride north on September 25, stopping a while north of Skiatook to pick up two dapple gray horses. From there, the gang drifted on to a ranch on Candy Creek, where they stayed three or four days making final plans for the strike at Coffeyville.[103] There they posed for a final picture, dapple gray horses and all, a photo which, if it ever existed, is lost to history.

The gang may have stopped also—or instead—on a homestead at a place called Pegg's Prairie. There, according to the memory of Claude Timmons, a pioneer who was then a boy, Bob and Grat, Broadwell and Powers (the pioneer called Powers "Tim") slept and ate. The pioneer lad did not mention Emmett but recalled that Bob gave Timmons's mother a twenty-dollar gold piece even though she said she would take no pay for feeding passersby. When the mother said she had no change, Bob answered, "Keep the change, it didn't cost me anything."[104]

This one has the ring of truth. Bob's answer to the lady of the house is exactly the reply one would expect from a long-rider. It has the right touch of Bob's braggadoccio, and it reflects the habitual openhandedness of the outlaw. Courtesy and generosity went a long way to create good feeling; if it did not make allies, it surely helped ensure silence.

However Emmett got Chapman's horse, wherever the raiders may have stopped along the way, the gang kept on to the north without being intercepted, reaching California Creek, about twenty miles from Coffeyville, on the third of October.

The Dodge-Thomas posse was only a day behind. As Dodge told the story, they had learned from an informant that the Dalton gang was off on a job. They did not know where, only that "Bill Doolin was opposed to doing as Bob Dalton wanted to do whatever it was.... The only thing we had was that Bill Doolin had told Bob Dalton that it was a Death Trap." Dodge's informant also told the posse that Doolin had "Dengue fever."[105]

On the other hand, Heck Thomas never mentioned Doolin as part of the raiding party. His story of the pursuit included these words: "We located their hide-out on October 3, got full information that five men still composed the gang, and were ready to take them, when they suddenly pulled out for the north."[106] They found the gang's lair near the Mashed-O not long after the outlaws had left it. Thomas thought he and Dodge were only about twenty-four hours behind the gang at California Creek. At that point rain washed out their quarry's tracks.

Dodge then left the rest of the posse searching for the lost trail, and rode to the Sac and Fox agency. The gang's tracks had led toward the line of the Santa Fe, and Dodge wanted to warn the railroad it might be in for trouble. No sooner had Dodge reached the agency, however, than he learned the Daltons had already struck at Coffeyville. He rode back to his posse's camp, picked up Heck Thomas, and rode for Guthrie. There Dodge conferred with the marshal's office and with the local sheriff—nobody knew then whether there were still more bandits on the loose, and Dodge was a careful man.

There is every likelihood that Dodge and Thomas's remorseless pursuit was a significant factor in the Daltons' debacle at Coffeyville. Emmett called Thomas "Nemesis," and acknowledged the marshal's dogged pursuit. It is reasonable to suppose that Thomas's constant pressure on his backtrail may have moved Bob to attack Coffeyville hastily, without full information. In any case, Wells Fargo later concluded that Heck Thomas had contributed substantially to the gang's demise, and said so in concrete fashion: "[W]hile it has not been marked by capture, we feel that your work, more than anything, brought about the extermination of this gang ... and are happy to hand you, from our railway and express pool, a check herewith in the amount of $1500."[107]

Whatever route the gang took, they halted on California Creek and, as Emmett said, "talked it over." Emmett later maintained that he was still trying to talk the others out of hitting the Coffeyville banks. When the rest of the gang would not change their minds, Emmett says, he resolved to go with them. Leaving California Creek behind them in the twilight of the third, they rode on north.

Thanks to the rain, the Daltons had gained a little time, and by the night of the fourth they were about twelve miles south of their target. They halted for a while in the trees along Hickory Creek. And then, after dark, they rode on down to the bottoms of Onion Creek, where they made a dry camp on the land of some people named Davis. There was a snap of frost in the air, and the "Indian hunting moon was a sharp sickle in the sky."[108]

They fed their horses on corn stolen from a nearby field belonging to a farmer called Savage, and ate a sparse dinner of biscuits and hard-boiled eggs. About two in the morning on the fifth, according to Emmett, the bandits burned all incriminating paper over a small fire. Emmett pulled from his watch his treasured picture of Julia; Bob parted with Canty's letter announcing the end of Eugenia. Emmett says they flipped a coin to see which party would attack which bank.

Here, for the last time, Emmett says he asked his confederates if they "were still coming up here." They were, they said, and that was that. Emmett wanted to ride into town and take a personal look at what they would face the next day, but Bob vetoed the idea. "No," he said. "No. You might be recognized."[109] The gang would go into battle without fresh information about their objective, and they would pay for their ignorance in blood.

And so, on the morning of October fifth, the bandits got up early, fed their precious mounts, and swung into the saddle. They rode north, moving up out of the Onion Creek bottoms. Surely journeymen at their trade, they would have checked their weapons and ammunition carefully one last time, and seen to their horses' hooves and shoes. They knew what they had to do. They were armed to the teeth. There was nothing more to talk about, and each man would have to deal with his private devils alone.

Many years after, a retired Coffeyville cigar maker named Blakely added one more interesting detail to the gang's preparations. He had visited Emmett in prison, he said, and Emmett had told him that he and Bob had downed a pint of whiskey apiece before mounting up to ride into town. If it hadn't been for that Dutch courage, Emmett said, they would never had tried their daring raid on a town that knew them well.[110]

Maybe so, maybe not. None of the Daltons lacked for courage at any time, and there was certainly nothing inhibiting Bob's marksmanship when the shooting started. Still, a bellyful of white lightning might have affected the Daltons' judgment, and might have led them to leave their horses where they did, rather than tether them somewhere more sheltered and easier to reach.

According to Emmett, Bob was in high spirits, laughing as he said, "On to Coffeyville! This is the last trick!"[111] Bob had tied his coat collar up with a handkerchief against the morning chill, and Emmett joked with him, "Just wait till we get to Coffeyville.

You won't need any coat, brother. It's going to be hotter than hell up there."[112] How very right he was.

4

A SCENE OF PEACE AND SPLENDOR

THEY RODE IN FROM THE SOUTH early on a Wednesday. It was a lovely day, a marvelous autumn morning. An old-time marshal described the scene precisely, if a little floridly: "Those who have experienced October in southern Kansas can imagine the clear sky, the balmy bracing atmosphere, and the general beauty of the day in which all nature seemed to rejoice at existence. No firmament was ever quite so blue, and the slight tendency to frost had left the air spicy and keen ... and as the sun ascended it shone upon a scene of peace and splendor."[1]

A Coffeyville citizen who survived the raid waxed equally poetic: "Indian Summer was here, with its mild sunshine and purple haze. The bandits, like young Lochinvars, came out of the West."[2] The comparison to Sir Walter Scott's bold hero is stretching things a little, because the gang seems to have attracted no particular attention. They were just a little clutch of nondescript, dusty men, and nobody paid them much heed. Strangers were not uncommon here. Still, to anyone who took the trouble to look closely at these riders, there were things about them that might have been food for thought.

For one thing, they were armed to the teeth, all of them. A man carrying a gun was not an unusual sight in Coffeyville, of course. Everybody in Kansas knew how to shoot; self-defense and hunting were part of life. Even so, most men in settled towns usually went unarmed in these last years of the nineteenth century, unless they were hunting or there was trouble in the wind.

These roadstained men were different. All of them carried Winchesters in saddle boots. More than that, all of them wore sidearms as well, a small arsenal of handguns, two or more to each man—although some of their handguns were concealed, like the Colt in Bob's boot and the .38 caliber British Bulldog tucked away in his vest. Even in frontier country where any man might wear a gun without arousing comment, five—or six—heavily weaponed men riding together should have caused some interest. If anyone wondered about them, as far as we know, nobody was disturbed enough to try to find a lawman. Perhaps it was the day: bright and bracing, a clear, wonderful morning, the kind that makes people eager to work and achieve.

Still, there was even more to notice about these silent visitors, if you were paying close attention. They had come a long way; they and their mounts were travel-worn. And they came from the south, from the direction of the Indian Territory and the Nations. Many an ordinary, honest man came out of the Nations, sure enough. But so did bad men, killers, robbers, rustlers, booze runners, fugitives. The wild land to the south remained the haunt of a hundred hunted, dangerous men and more, including that famous and desperate band called the Daltons. Somebody should have wondered.

Because their family had lived near Coffeyville for a while, the Dalton boys had tried to disguise themselves. Emmett, thinking ahead, had let his beard grow out. Grat had stuck on an unconvincing set of black false side-whiskers and a mustache, and Bob hid his face behind both mustache and goatee. Bob apparently added a mask before he entered the First National Bank and

Powers also had his face at least partially covered during the actual holdup.[3]

Elliott, the best authority on the raid, wrote that three of the raiders tried to disguise themselves with false whiskers. Bob, he says, was still wearing a false mustache and goatee when the fighting stopped, and Grat still had his stuck-on mustache and side-whiskers. The disguises were torn from their faces as they lay lifeless in Death Alley.[4]

"Eyewitness" adds, somewhat confusingly, that the bandits were "apparently disguised" as they rode into town, but also says that Bob, Grat, and Broadwell put on beards when they dismounted in the town itself. This notion is a most unlikely proposition, considering that the bandits would have had to stick on their phony whiskers in broad daylight, with dozens of citizens watching. As with other details on the Daltons, however, reports conflict. In conversation with author Harry Drago back in 1928, Emmett Dalton derided the notion of false whiskers. "That's hogwash," he told Drago. "We wore no disguises when we rode into Coffeyville. If we could have put our hands on false whiskers, we would have been ashamed to wear them."[5]

With or without false hair, the raiders rode in from their dry camp in the timber patch, crossed a plowed field, and headed across Onion Creek. A young girl saw them there, as they came out from under the bridge and put their horses up the sloping north bank of the creek. She was a daughter of James Brown, on her way to town, and she apparently thought little of the strange riders.

The girl lost sight of the gang not long after that. She turned east, down what was then the main road into Coffeyville, and rode out of our history. The bandits walked their horses on north, over a road somewhat less traveled. There was nothing furtive about their progress: William Gilbert, whose home they passed, thought they looked like a marshal's posse; small groups of lawmen were not an unusual sight in this part of the world.

In any case they seemed pretty ordinary, and they were talking and laughing together as they trotted along the dusty road that would later be called Buckeye Street. Passing some sheep and goats, the bandits "baa'd" at the animals. Gilbert went on about his business and thought no more about the weatherworn riders passing by in the clear morning light.

A little farther north the gang struck another east-west road, a dusty, rutted strip that led on east to become Coffeyville's Eighth Street. Here, near a dairy farm and cheese factory, they turned their mounts toward the town and their deadly business. They did not move fast. After all, they would need their horses badly later in the day. Those horses were deliverance, and must be conserved at all costs.

A number of citizens passed the raiders in the dust of the dry road, for this was farm country, where men and women rose early to attack the problems of the day. R. H. Hollingsworth and his wife, driving their rig west, passed the raiders less than a mile west of the town. According to Elliott, the Hollingsworths not only noticed that the riders were heavily armed but thought they appeared "peculiar."

And if Marshal Evett Dumas Nix is correct, the riders must have looked a little stiff as well. The bandits, he says, had their Winchesters concealed under their coats. That would be a considerable feat, considering that the men were straddling saddles, which would hike up their coats, and their Winchesters were long-barreled weapons.

Another writer alleges that the gang carried their Winchesters "rolled in slickers behind their saddles."[6] I suspect this account is also invented, for such a slicker would look as if it were wrapped around a broomstick, making an unusual and ungainly roll sure to attract unwanted attention. Why go to such trouble anyway? People often carried rifles in saddle scabbards; such a sight would alarm nobody.

Marshal Nix also makes mention of the fancy Mexican saddles, replete with carving, spangles, and similar ornamentation. And on top of all this, says Nix, the bandits had large "hair-covered pockets" on the sides of their saddles, "each carrying several six-shooters."[7] All of which is a little hard to believe, since the post-raid inventory established that each man—Bob possibly excepted—carried no more than two revolvers.

Moreover, the citizens who saw the raiders on their way into town noticed that the riders were heavily armed. There could have been little attempt to conceal either Winchesters or sidearms. Sticking a rifle under a long coat, or duster, or trying to wrap it up in a blanket roll or poncho, would achieve nothing besides exciting enhanced curiosity and alarm in anybody who saw the riders. My guess is that the gang simply rode into town as if they belonged there, most of their sidearms in ordinary holsters, their Winchesters carried in saddle boots the way honest people carried theirs.

However the bandits were dressed and equipped, a lot of people saw them without taking fright. A hundred yards or so after the Daltons passed the Hollingsworth rig, John M. and J. L. Seldomridge passed by the little group of riders on the dusty road. The Seldomridges also remarked that the horsemen were heavily armed. Moreover, they noticed that the gang was "apparently disguised," and concluded that they were "on some peculiar mission."

Indeed they were, but neither pair of citizens was worried enough to turn back into town and raise the alarm. However, both the Hollingsworths and Seldomridges thought there were six men riding together, six men and six horses. Except for a bank employee, who many years later talked of a sixth bandit, nobody else remembered seeing more than five raiders.

Since all four peaceful citizens noticed that the newcomers were heavily armed, and two noticed their disguises, they certainly paid some attention to these dusty riders. It may well be that they observed more closely than anybody else did—or could—later that bloody day. It is just possible, therefore, that at that point in the raiders' ride into town, there *was* a sixth rider in the bandit party. If so, there may be a good deal of truth to the stories about the bandit who got away.

The Daltons moved on through the calm of the morning, until the dusty track they rode turned into Eighth Street and the quiet countryside became a busy community. A good many Eighth Street residents watched the bandits trot past them, trailing a little cloud of dust. Nobody who saw them on Eighth Street, or later, noticed more than five riders and five horses. The bandits stuck close together, riding in two groups: the three Dalton brothers were side by side in front; behind them rode Dick Broadwell and Bill Powers. In the bright clear morning, grim death rode matter-of-factly closer to the bustling heart of Coffeyville. And nobody paid much attention.

Now the riders reached the corner of Eighth and Maple, next to the Episcopal church, a comfortable white wooden temple with a graceful spire. There they turned south into the center of Coffeyville's business district, past the Long-Bell Lumber Company office and its substantial warehouse, just west of Coffeyville's two thriving banks.

In 1892, the heart of Coffeyville lay generally between Eighth and Ninth streets, which ran east and west. The town's major north-south business streets were Walnut and Union. They converged between Eighth and Ninth, where Union ran in at an angle from the northeast to meet Walnut, just as it does today.

At that point there was an open area, a sort of plaza, which lay at the bottom of the V formed where Walnut and Union Streets ran together. In the center of the V was a pie-slice block of buildings, its sharp end pointed south. The southernmost of the buildings in the pie-slice, facing the plaza, was the Condon Bank. The Condon was a solid, reassuring building, built to last. It was two stories tall, constructed of conservative red brick and ornamented with metal facings, one of which bore the bank's name in large, proud letters.

There were offices above the bank, and at least some of these were occupied at the time of the attack. The bank lobby itself was nicely furnished after the elaborate fashion of the day, complete with a carved walnut counter and an ornate cashier's cage protected by a metal grating.

Directly east of the Condon, facing it across Union, was the First National. At the time of the raid it was a frame building of one story. Some time after the raid, the First National was pulled down, and a 1938 photo shows a two-story brick grocery store on the site. The bank then moved its operation across the street, just behind the Condon, into a handsome building with metal bay windows and very Victorian ball finials along the line of the roof.

The Condon, beautifully restored, still faces south across the plaza. The old First National facade has also been restored, so that from the outside, at least, it looks as it did that memorable autumn of 1892. The First National's second location is also restored, so that the whole Condon Block is today a graceful reminder of that day of lightning from a cloudless sky.

On the east side of Union, facing the pie-slice block, were many of Coffeyville's leading businesses. Besides the First National, there were two hardware stores—A. P. Boswell's and the emporium called Isham Brothers and Mansur's. In the same line of storefronts were Cubine's Boot and Shoe, Rammel Brothers' drugstore, Smith's barber shop, and Barndollar Brothers' dry goods. Behind this line of businesses, running northeast-southwest, parallel with Union, lay an alley.

Running east and west between Walnut and Maple, parallel with Eighth, was another alley, much used for deliveries to the stores in the block. You could see straight down it from the front of the First National and Isham's, across the plaza from the alley's mouth. Onto this alley opened the back of John Kloehr's livery stable, the city jail, Davis's Blacksmith Shop, the massive warehouse of Long-Bell Lumber Company, a lot owned by Police Judge Charles Munn, and still another stable.

Coffeyville was a busy town and a prosperous one. Many of its buildings were of red brick, like the Condon Bank, solid and comfortable and permanent. Structures of more than one story were common, and contemporary pictures show the plaza area jammed with horses, buggies, wagons, and busy people.

On the northwest corner of the intersection of Walnut and Eighth stood McCoy's Hardware and Ullom's Restaurant. As the gang came in view of this corner, they discovered their first setback. It probably seemed a small thing at the time, but in fact it was a disastrous failure in the gang's planning and reconnaissance. In the end, it meant death for four outlaws, and agony and prison for Emmett Dalton.

"I'll be damned!" said Bob. "Look, the hitch rack's gone!"[8]

The gang had intended to tether their horses on the north side of Eighth Street, in front of McCoy's, or in front of the Opera House, which stood diagonally across the street directly behind the Condon Bank. They discovered, however, that the Coffeyville city fathers were upgrading Eighth at that point, giving it curbs and gutters. As a result, the street was pretty well torn up, stone had been piled up ready to use—and the hitching posts in front of McCoy's had been temporarily removed.

And so the gang rode on, south a little farther on Maple, until they struck the alley running east-west between Maple and Walnut. Down this narrow gut they rode, until they found room to tie their horses by a wood fence in the alley. There were a number of other horses tied in the alley as well, most of them grouped behind Davis's Blacksmith Shop, which backed up onto the north side of the alley and fronted on Eighth Street. At least one account of the raid has Grat, Broadwell, and Powers tying their horses right in front of the Condon Bank, but this is surely an error.[9] All the horses were left together, tethered in that deadly alley.

The constricted little passage in which the raiders found space for their mounts had no name in 1892. Today it is appropriately called Death Alley. That lurid label may seem melodramatic if you read it in a book. But if you walk down that commonplace alley even now and you have any imagination at all, the name seems far less fanciful. For there are crude outlines of human forms painted on the pavement, and they are painted at the places where real living men fell gasping down to die, with their own blood splashed and splattered on the walls and street around them. Even in broad daylight there are ghosts in Death Alley.

Today there are still a few bullet holes in the wall of the alley. Or at least there are pock marks there that might have been made by slugs one grim morning in 1892. Perhaps the marks were really made by Winchester bullets, although the shape of them makes you wonder. Or maybe they aren't bullet holes at all and somebody after the fight just said they were, out of orneriness or civic pride or hunger for the tourist dollar.

The Dalton gang tied their horses to a pipe, or rail, at the back of a lot owned by, of all people, Charles Munn, Coffeyville's police judge in those days. Their choice of tethering places is astonishing. For the fence by which their horses were tied was a long 350 feet away from Walnut Street to the east, and across Walnut lay the gang's targets, the Condon and First National banks. The banks and the horses were a very long way apart, a long way for an armed stranger to walk to his target. It was an even longer way for a desperate, hard-pressed man to run, especially with a whole town shooting at him.

Surely there must have been empty spaces at other hitching posts closer to the banks. Walnut and Union joined near where the two banks faced each another, and two ranks of business houses faced onto the little plaza. Just south of the two banks the plaza opened onto Ninth Street. They might have left their animals there or in the alley which ran northeast-southwest behind the buildings on the east face of Union.

It is hard to imagine that no empty hitching post or fence existed within a hundred feet or less of the Daltons' targets. As our map clearly reveals, there were all sorts of nearby streets and alleys in which a horse might be tethered. Even if the flourishing little town were so busy that Bob Dalton and his men could find no place to leave the horses, there were other expedients.

The raiders could have ridden another block or two, killing time until spaces opened up at some rack close to their targets. As far as anybody knows there was no timetable they had to meet. Or they might have done what cavalry troopers would have done: leave one man to hold the horses at some convenient spot close by, while the other four robbed the banks. For instance, there is no reason why the horses could not have been left in the care of Powers or Broadwell in the alley behind the First National.

After the event, at least, Emmett Dalton recognized the terrible risk the gang had run in tethering their horses down the alley, so far away from the objective. In *Beyond the Law*, Emmett agreed that the raiders had originally intended to leave their mounts at the corner of Eighth and Walnut, a short walk from the Condon Bank. Because those hitching rails were down, Emmett wrote, the gang looked for another place to park their essential means of escape. It does not appear that they looked around the town for a convenient spot. Instead, they headed directly for the deadly alley.

It was a lethal error.

The raiders committed a couple of other major blunders in planning. First of all, they did no reconnaissance worthy of the name, in spite of the Daltons' familiarity with Coffeyville, or maybe because of it. They obviously did not know that their chosen hitching rail was down; they did not know the layout of the banks, as we shall see; and they had plainly given no thought to how to save their skins and liberty if the raid went sour. There was no emergency plan in case of failure or resistance, and that is the most surprising thing about the whole bungled attempt. These men were all old campaigners, far too experienced to stage a raid without adequate reconnaissance. Yet that is exactly what they did.

And they failed entirely to give any thought to a line of retreat. For example, there was a door at the side of the Condon Bank. It opened out of the cashier's office at the northwest corner of the bank, onto Walnut Street and to a stairway that led to upstairs offices. Using this exit would have put the whole building between them and the deadly nest of rifles in the hardware stores east of the plaza. In the event, the robbers at the Condon did not even know about this safe back exit, which might have saved their lives.

And, as any military veteran could have told them, the gang needed what modern soldiers call a "base of fire." This would have given them a haven on which to fall back in case something went haywire, as the farmers said, one or two men who could cover a retreat to the horses with powerful and accurate rifle fire. Instead, all the gang members were fully committed in robbing and intimidating inside their targets. When they emerged from the banks and ran head-on into the Winchesters of the townsmen, there was nobody to cover them.

Perhaps this sloppy preparation was a function of haste. The gang knew they were being hunted everywhere. They may even have known that the implacable Heck Thomas was close on their backtrail. Or their lack of planning may have been the product of simple negligence. Or arrogance. After all, these men were successful robbers, victors in holdup after holdup. Their names were legend, and no doubt they counted on fear multiplying both their numbers and their prowess. Maybe they simply held ordinary people in contempt. This was, they might have said, a hick town of sodbusters—farmers and plough jockeys and shopkeepers, surely no threat to long-riders like themselves. Whatever they thought, they didn't know as much as they should have about Coffeyville—or its people.

And so the dusty men dismounted in the little alley. They secured their horses to the rail, pulled their Winchesters from the saddle boots, and walked together east down the narrow alley. They kept on down its long expanse, past the city jail and the rear of John Kloehr's livery service. And at last they moved out into Walnut Street and the pleasant open space of the town plaza.

As they left the mouth of the alley, they walked between Slosson's drugstore on their right—south of them—and the rear of McKenna and Adamson's dry goods store on their left. Still nobody paid much attention to them, even a stonecutter who closely followed them east down the alley. He noticed the guns the strangers carried, but he attached no significance to them—or so he said afterward. The head bookkeeper for Adams Grain Company saw them too, but thought they were a hunting party.

As the raiders strolled across Walnut, the stonecutter turned north, away from them. Behind them a Consolidated Oil Company team pulled a tank wagon into the alley, westbound. The driver, young J. P. "Pat" Moran, apparently noticed nothing about the little group of armed, hard-faced men. He went on his way, stopping about one hundred feet up the alley to make a delivery to Slosson's. When the first shots roared out minutes later, Moran was still inside Slosson's, jawing with the clerks.

If Moran paid no attention to the purposeful little group of dusty men, neither did anybody else. Coffeyville was busy as usual that Wednesday morning. The streets were full of parked rigs and horses, and the stores were full of people. The town had been that way since eight o'clock and ordinarily the Daltons might have disappeared in the crowd. But not today.

For it happened on that morning that Aleck McKenna was sweeping the sidewalk in front of his business, McKenna and Adamson's Dry Goods. He clearly saw the Daltons leave the alley and walk into the plaza, and now the gang had lost the immense advantage of complete surprise.

McKenna knew the Daltons. He instantly recognized at least one of them, even through the forest of hairy disguises they affected. He knew this Dalton by his walk and the shape of his head, and he watched three of the bandits split off from the other two and enter the Condon Bank, dead in the middle of the plaza. He must also have realized that most of the facial forestry he was seeing was false, and become more suspicious still.

Alarmed, Aleck McKenna kept his eyes on the three raiders inside the bank. When he saw a Winchester leveled at the Condon's startled employees, McKenna instantly began to spread the alarm. There were *Daltons* inside the Condon, and more inside the First National, and rifles brandished, and big-time trouble on the way![10]

Charley Smith, son of the owner of Smith's Barber Shop, helped spread the news down to Boswell's and Isham's. Long after the raid, J. P. Moran, the driver of the oil tank parked in the fatal alley, declared that he had given the first alarm. Two clerks in Slosson's drugstore would not believe his excited words, he said, and they laughed at him. They would not laugh long.

In both *Beyond the Law* and *When the Daltons Rode*, Emmett wrote that still another citizen, a drayman called Charles Gump, recognized the raiders and shouted, "There go the Daltons!" Emmett also made the astonishing assertion that Bob fired at Gump to keep him from arousing the town. Immediately a dozen dogs began to bark, said Emmett, but the citizens, "held numb with shock," failed to react to Gump's warning and Bob's shot.

Either Emmett's memory failed him or he took significant literary liberties with the facts, for this part of his story is manifest nonsense. Bob Dalton was not stupid enough to fire at Gump, thereby alerting the whole town. There is no contemporary mention of a single shot early in the robbery, especially not by Captain Elliott. Illogical as the whole episode is, other writers have perpetuated it.[11]

Gump was standing by the city fire pump, a heavy-duty rig with a four-man handle, chatting with Billy Hughston, a city constable. Gump had teams hired out to haul for the street work and was supervising the use of his teams when he saw the bandits moving toward the banks "at a dog trot and heavily armed."[12] Though Gump did not know the Dalton boys, he instantly concluded that was who the strangers were and began to yell the alarm.

The chances are that McKenna gave the first alarm, and that Gump and others passed it on. Whoever first gave it, the bad news got around in a hurry. Citizens ran from all directions to fight off the invaders. Nobody seems to have been armed initially. The bad old days of rampaging cowboys and liquored-up hoodlums were long enough gone for few men to be carrying a weapon on an ordinary, peaceful business day. Nearly everybody owned a gun, or more than one, but a sidearm got in the way when you pulled out a bolt of cloth or measured coffee or hefted a sack of feed. So most men left their guns at home, pegged over the fireplace or hung from the hall tree.

Only one man in the whole plaza area had a weapon: George Cubine, whose uncle's thriving boot and shoe shop was just three doors north of the First National. Cubine had brought his Winchester to the shop just a day before the raid, to keep it away from his children.[13] Now Cubine grabbed the weapon and ran out to defend his town. Like Charley Gump, other citizens hurried to Boswell's and Isham Brothers' hardware stores, where clerks began to hand out Winchesters and revolvers and shotguns to anybody who wanted a weapon. There were lots of volunteers.

Ammunition was broken out—some of the citizens simply reached behind the counter and helped themselves—and the men of Coffeyville loaded their weapons and took up positions to meet the threat to the peace of their city. John Kloehr came down from his livery stable on Ninth Street to pick up a 73 Winchester and join his friends at Boswell's. Outside the store citizens pushed wagons together to give themselves some cover.

Harness maker Parker Williams left his shop above Boswell's and went downstairs to get a weapon. He chose a Colt .44 rather than a rifle, however, and, thus lightly equipped, made his way to Barndollar Brothers' store next door. He wriggled out onto the awning that covered the street in front of Barndollar's and cocked his weapon. He would be terribly vulnerable in the fight to come, sheltered only by a wooden sign, but he would have a marvelous field of fire.

Over at Isham's, more citizens armed themselves. Gump, the teamster, left his team in Union Street when he heard the alarm, and rushed to choose a double-barreled shotgun. Loading it, he found shelter behind a heavy iron post holding up the awning in front of the store. Instead of facing Condon's, as most of the other citizens seem to have done, he concentrated on the entrance to the First National, just point-blank range north of him on the same side of the street. Any bandit that left the front door of the First National was a dead man, or should have been.

The owner of Isham's, Henry H. Isham, thoughtfully shut his safe before he picked up a rifle and took position behind a heavy iron stove in the front of the store (a vantage point that makes a lot more sense than the store roof, where one account puts him). One of Henry's clerks, Lewis Dietz (sometimes "Diets") armed himself with a revolver and moved up beside his boss. The other clerk, Arthur Reynolds, chose a Winchester and prepared to back up the other two.

They were joined by Lucius Baldwin, twenty-three years old and a clerk at Read Brothers on the corner of the alley and Walnut. As he left Read's, his boss, Haz Read, warned him not to go outside, but the young man would not listen. Instead, he walked across to Isham's and picked up a short-barreled revolver.

Meanwhile, inside Condon's Bank, Grat Dalton, Bill Powers, and Dick Broadwell were still unaware of the army forming across the street to destroy them. They had troubles enough inside the bank, for they were getting no cooperation at all from the spunky staff.

At first, things went smoothly for the outlaws. Bank man Charles T. Carpenter looked up from his work at the sound of clanking spurs and found himself staring into a Winchester. The first man in, probably Powers, leveled his Winchester at the unarmed Carpenter and demanded cash, by God, and the sooner the better.

Grat, Powers, and Broadwell had entered the bank by a door on the southwest corner of the building, one of two front entrances, the other being a few feet away on the southeast corner. Broadwell took a position by the southeast door, and Grat, yelling profanely at Charley Carpenter, ordered Carpenter to raise his hands.

About this time John Levan, an elderly customer, chose the wrong moment to walk into the bank through the southwest door. He immediately found himself lying on the floor under the muzzles of the bandits' Winchesters. Carpenter and Levan were quickly joined by cashier Charles M. Ball, who heard the tumult out in front and walked out of his office to find himself in a staring contest with the baleful, unwinking eye of a leveled Winchester.

A third bank employee, bookkeeper Thomas C. Babb, quietly moved from his seat at the rear of the office into the vault, and made himself small. Soon after the bandits' entrance, D. E. James, another customer, walked innocently into the bank. He, too, became an unwilling close-up spectator of one of the West's most ferocious fights.

Grat was in a hurry. He moved quickly behind the bank counter, Winchester in hand, and tossed a two-bushel grain sack to Ball, the cashier. Hold that open, Grat said, and you—turning to Carpenter—you fill it with all the money from the cash drawer and the counter. Helpless, Ball and Carpenter did as they were told.

At about this time, according to Carpenter, and as reported by Elliott, there was an interruption. Luther Perkins, a substantial citizen who had an office on the second floor of the bank building, suddenly opened the northwest door to the bank and stuck his head in. Perkins, who owned the building, had been upstairs with J. H. Wilcox and Joe Uncapher, who were watching the citizens milling about in front of the hardware stores.

Perkins had seen Emmett and Bob Dalton go bursting into the First National, and was eager to warn the staff of Condon's. Seeing three dusty hard cases and three cocked Winchesters already infesting Condon's, Perkins instantly repented of his errand. "Oh, Charlie," he said to Carpenter, slammed the door, and departed in some haste.

If this story is true, and Perkins really interrupted the robbery, his sudden appearance and disappearance do not seem to have rattled or hurried Grat Dalton, a further demonstration of Grat's glacially slow wit. Far from leaving the bank, he now turned his attention to the vault, and ordered both Ball and Carpenter into it. He also discovered Babb quietly hiding there, and treated the young man to his usual display of profanity.

The vault doors were open, an inviting sight to the long riders. Inside, more doors stood open, the outer and inner doors to a Hall "burglar-proof" safe. Here Grat discovered three bags of silver dollars. He ordered these dumped into the grain sack along with the currency, and this was duly done. This addition increased the bandits' loot by some three thousand dollars—but it also increased the weight of the sack by around two hundred pounds, making the bag of booty virtually unmanageable.

Now the robbers faced still another set of doors, the way into a large chest or strong box, and these were firmly closed. They also bore a stout combination lock. And here Grat ran out of luck. Open the inner doors, he ordered, but Ball just shook his head. I can't, Ball said. I can't because they're on a time lock set for 9:45, and it's not 9:45 yet.

At least that was how Captain Elliott told the story in his newspaper two days after the raid. In Elliott's little book, published later, Ball tells Grat that the lock is set for 9:30, and it's only 9:20.[14]

Banker Carpenter, who ought to have known, said afterward that the bank clock had read 9:40, and that the conversation between Grat and Ball went something like this:

Ball: "The safe is on a time lock. It won't open until 9:30."
Grat: "What time is it now?"
Ball (solemnly consulting his watch): "9:20."[15]

It doesn't really matter exactly what Ball said about the time, or how long he told Grat the lock would take to open. The important thing was that Grat Dalton gave another demonstration of the lack of planning and care the gang showed throughout the raid. At the same time, he conclusively proved that he was not, as modern kids say, a rocket scientist.

For when the gutty Ball looked at his watch and innocently said it was only 9:20, Grat believed him. All Dalton had to do was look at the bank's own wall clock to know that Ball was blandly lying to him. Moreover, the iron safe doors that looked so formidable were ready to open to anybody's slightest touch. There was indeed a time lock but it had long since gone off. It had been set for 8:00—apparently bankers' hours were a trifle different in those hardworking days. Grat could have reached into the safe and taken what he wanted.

Charley Ball was an immensely courageous man, or an immensely foolish one, depending on your point of view. He blandly laid his life on the line for his employer's property, in spite of all the threats and curses and the leveled Winchesters and the tell-tale clock on the wall. There were something like forty thousand good American dollars in the vault, and no FDIC to cover his friends and neighbors—or his bosses.

And so it is probable, for these reasons and because of the spirit of the times, that Ball took his long chance entirely out of concern for his town and his friends and the men whose salt he ate. Emmett, in a typically whiny passage, later called Ball's bluff a "shifty falsehood," and complained that Ball's stratagem, not the bandits' greed, was "to cause the death of eight men."[16]

Whatever his reasons, Ball successfully ran his most extraordinary bluff. For Grat bought Ball's story, hook, line and sinker. Carpenter helped out by turning the door handle to demonstrate that it would not open—apparently he turned but did not pull, and Grat accepted Carpenter's demonstration as he fell for Ball's honeyed words.

"We can wait," said Grat, and prepared to do so. "We can wait."

But he couldn't. Grat Dalton did not have ten minutes to wait. In fact, he had less than ten minutes to live.

Perhaps Grat sensed that he was running out of time, for he soon began to fidget. He turned again to the bank employees: "God damn you! I believe you are lying to me. I've a mind to put a bullet through you. Open it up or I will shoot you; you have been blowing too much about what you can do. Where is your gold?"[17]

There isn't any, said Ball, not even in that safe you're waiting for. And with colossal cold courage he glibly explained that the bank's books the night before showed a thousand dollars in paper money and another three thousand in silver, all of which Dalton already had taken. Some more currency had been ordered, Ball said, but that had not yet been delivered from the express office.

Throughout all of this palaver, none of the three bandits at Condon's seems to have noticed that the alarm had been given and the town's defenders were gathering outside at almost point-blank range. Dick Broadwell, in particular, standing by the southeast door, must have been absolutely entranced by the exchange of threats and explanations between Grat and the bank men. He managed to miss completely the excitement of a swarm of citizens milling about, giving the alarm, arming themselves, and pushing wagons together. He could not have looked out of the bank's windows or through the glass panes in the door, or he would surely have seen the angel of death flexing his wings just a few feet away across the street.

Over in the First National, Bob and Emmett, both masked, barged in with cocked Winchesters and immediately had their hands full. There were only two of them and they had walked in on three unsuspecting customers, plus three bank employees. The customers included J. H. Brewster, a prominent local building contractor who had built the county court house, A. W. Knotts, and C. L. Hollingsworth. Nobody was armed, and nobody was stupid enough to rush those Winchesters empty-handed.

Bob and Emmett were equally unaware of the terrible danger gathering all around them. Their failure to see their peril is easier to understand than the blindness of the bandits in the Condon Bank. For one thing, Bob and Emmett did not have as good a view of Coffeyville's streets as that from Condon's. The First National's windows gave directly out on Union Street, so their only direct view was of the northern side of the Condon's building. Also, they were a little busier than were their comrades in Condon's, and quickly got even busier.

Two more citizens, Jim Boothby and Jack Long, strolling into the business district, met Jess Morgan "shaking his umbrella and yelling 'they're robbing the banks!' "[18] Apparently not alarmed by this startling announcement, Boothby and Long walked on past the First National and Boothby looked in the bank door. Emmett saw him and snarled, "Get in here, you sob!" Boothby, suitably impressed by leveled Winchesters, complied without delay.

Captain Elliott says Boothby walked unsuspectingly into the bank just behind Bob and Emmett, and was trapped before he realized a robbery was under way. He tried to back away, but had his mind changed by an invitation waved by a rifle barrel. Being a man of good sense, Boothby did not argue.

Long, apparently still a youngster, was treated differently. In a moment, Emmett Dalton punched his gun against the window and said, "Get away from here, son, before you get hurt."[19] Young Long hesitated long enough to hunker down and look beneath the curtain on the bank window. Inside four citizens stood with their hands raised, and that was enough for Long. He did indeed get away from there, moving over in front of Rammel Brothers' drugstore where shoemaker George Cubine stood, holding a Winchester.

Emmett and Bob had entered the foyer of the bank and moved around a screen that stood between the heavy doors and the cashier's area. Cashier Tom Ayres was behind his window and teller W. H. Shepard was sitting at a desk behind the counter, near the vault. Bert Ayres, the bookkeeper, was at his own desk in a private office to the rear of the bank. Cashier Ayers and teller Shepard were surprised and unarmed. They could offer no resistance but they were not about to cooperate.

Emmett stayed in the front of the bank to cover the customers, cashier, and teller. Bob strode down a hall into the back of the bank and ordered Bert Ayres up to the vault. One writer has Emmett rousting Ayres out of the back of the bank, but this appears to be an error.[20]

Once the robbers had everybody together in the front of the bank, Bob called cashier Ayres by name and told him to open the vault and pass out the money. The Daltons were impatient—when Ayres did not react fast enough to suit them, he was bombarded with curses and a threat to shoot him. Ayres brought gold and silver out to the counter all right, but he did it as slowly as he could, making, as Elliott put it, "as many trips as possible."

Ayres scraped together what money there was on the counter and in the cash drawer. This went into the grain sack the Daltons produced. Now it was time for the safe, a solid, square affair bearing the bank's name neatly engraved across its front.

Open it, ordered Bob Dalton, but courageous Bert Ayres shook his head. I can't, he answered. I don't know the combination.

At this point Bob Dalton turned to cashier Tom Ayres, young Ayres's father: "Tom, you go and get it."

The elder Ayres, willing to bide his time and probably concerned for his bold son's safety, stepped in and got some money from the safe. This he dumped into the sack with the money from the counter and drawer.

Is this all the money? asked Bob.

No, said the cashier. No. There is still some gold in the vault. Do you want that too?

"Every damned cent," said Bob, so Tom Ayres entered the vault again and returned with some gold coin. And here the cashier showed a flash of the same steel that was showing in both his son and in young Ball over at Condon's. That's all there is, he said. But Bob Dalton was not nearly as credulous as his brother Grat. He went to see for himself. He returned furious, carrying two more packages of currency, each containing five thousand dollars. These also went into the sack. He picked up a box full of gold watches, as well, but put it down again when the bank men assured him it contained only papers.

By now the bandits had accumulated a substantial pile of loot. Emmett's grain sack was stuffed with more than twenty thousand dollars of tax-free First National money, a reasonable grubstake for flight to Seattle. And apparently Bob was now convinced that he had all he was going to get.

Either that or he was becoming edgy, although there is no indication that he had any notion that the devil was loose in the street outside the bank. He and Emmett obviously intended to leave the bank the way they had come in, no doubt planning to collect their three comrades and fall back to their horses in a group. The Daltons herded the three bank employees and the four captive citizens out through the bank's front door onto the Union Street sidewalk, and started to follow.

Bob and Emmett had every reason to congratulate themselves. They had made a good haul. There had been no shots fired, no trouble beyond a little cursing and threatening, no inquisitive sheriffs, no alarms. All that remained was to cover a little over a hundred yards to the horses and safety.

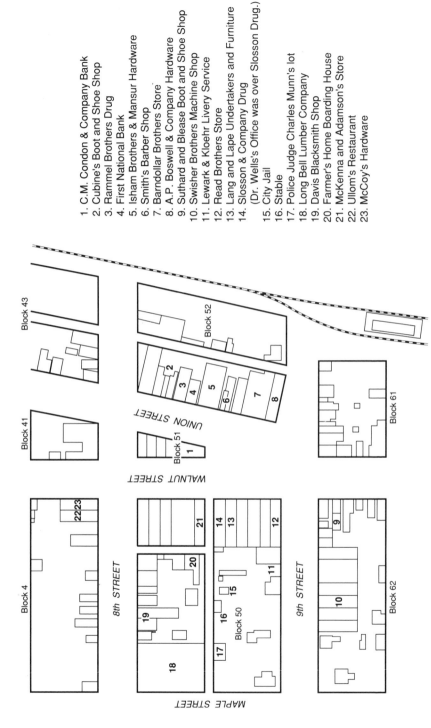

1. C.M. Condon & Company Bank
2. Cubine's Boot and Shoe Shop
3. Rammel Brothers Drug
4. First National Bank
5. Isham Brothers & Mansur Hardware
6. Smith's Barber Shop
7. Barndollar Brothers Store
8. A.P. Boswell & Company Hardware
9. Suthard and Blease Boot and Shoe Shop
10. Swisher Brothers Machine Shop
11. Lewark & Kloehr Livery Service
12. Read Brothers Store
13. Lang and Lape Undertakers and Furniture
14. Slosson & Company Drug
    (Dr. Wells's Office was over Slosson Drug.)
15. City Jail
16. Stable
17. Police Judge Charles Munn's lot
18. Long Bell Lumber Company
19. Davis Blacksmith Shop
20. Farmer's Home Boarding House
21. McKenna and Adamson's Store
22. Ullom's Restaurant
23. McCoy's Hardware

Downtown Coffeyville in the autumn of 1892. Based on a map courtesy of Coffeyville Historical Society.

Coffeyville, Kansas, about 1880. Courtesy of *Coffeyville Journal.*

Walnut Street about 1892. Courtesy of *Coffeyville Journal*.

The west side of Walnut Street about 1895. Courtesy of *Coffeyville Journal*.

Frank Dalton, shortly before his death in 1887. Courtesy of Western History Collections, University of Oklahoma Library.

Bob Dalton with unidentified woman, Vinita, Oklahoma, about 1889. Courtesy of Western History Collections, University of Oklahoma Library.

Grat Dalton. Courtesy of Wells Fargo Bank.

William Todd ("Bill") Power, or Powers. Courtesy of Patrick Waddle, Vinita, Oklahoma.

The Condon Bank at Coffeyville, Kansas, 1892. Courtesy of Western History Collections, University of Oklahoma Library.

Bullet holes in the Condon windows. Courtesy of Coffeyville Historical Society.

Death Alley after the raid. Courtesy of Coffeyville Historical Society.

First National Bank Lobby, 1892. Courtesy of *Coffeyville Journal.*

The Dalton Gang after the raid. Left to right: Bill Powers, Bob Dalton, Grat Dalton, Dick Broadwell. Courtesy of Western History Collections, University of Oklahoma Library.

Lucius Baldwin. Courtesy of *Coffeyville Journal.*

Marshal Charles T. Connelly. Courtesy of *Coffeyville Journal.*

George B. Cubine. Courtesy of *Coffeyville Journal.*

Charles Brown. Courtesy of *Coffeyville Journal.*

John J. Kloehr. Courtesy of *Coffeyville Journal*.

William M. Dalton, ca. 1884. Courtesy of Western History Collections, University of Oklahoma Library.

5

A FLASH OF LIGHTNING
FROM A CLEAR SKY

PAINTER J. R. HAMES was perched on a ladder leaned against the side of the Condon Bank. On another ladder stood his boss, and between the two men stretched a chalk-line, with which they were laying out a big sign to be painted on the wall. And as they carefully measured and snapped their line, all hell broke loose. There was a shot and then two or three more, and then a roar of gunfire, and it was all around them.

Hames, "a crack painter but too fond of hard liquor," was nicked in the leg by one of the opening shots. However eventful Hames's night before might have been, he skinned down the ladder with wonderful agility and disappeared at a dead run, his boss with him, leaving painting, chalk-line, and ladders abandoned in their wake.

The battle of Coffeyville was on.

The first shot may have been fired by a seventeen-year-old, William Harry Lang, or at least he said so afterward. Lang clerked at Slosson's drugstore in those days, in spite of the fact that he was the heir to the Lang & Lape Furniture and Undertaking emporium. After getting off his single round, Lang apparently had second thoughts. He ran into the lot behind Slosson's, watched the rest of the fight from behind a wooden fence, and lived to tell the tale.

As Bob and Emmett cleared the doorway of the First National, herding the bank employees before them, Emmett suddenly called to Bob, "Look out there at the left!" Just a step or two later, gunfire roared from the doorway of Rammel Brothers' drugstore just next door, and bullets cut the air past the Daltons. George Cubine, with his Winchester, and express agent C. S. Cox, wielding a .44 revolver, had cut loose at the bandits at what amounted to point-blank range. Sadly, Cubine and Cox were not good shots; they missed both bandits entirely.

Bob and Emmett jumped back inside the bank, as did Bert Ayres and W. H. Shepard, to get out of the line of fire. Tom Ayres and the customers kept running out at the front, and the elder Ayres turned hard left for Isham's, where he snatched a Winchester and ran back to cover the front of the bank from Isham's north door.

The shots fired by Cubine and Cox broke the quiet of the morning, and a full-scale war broke out on the peaceful streets of Coffeyville. This chapter follows what I think are the most reliable accounts of the fight, but the precise sequence of events is lost forever in the mists of time.

Emmett insists that the firing began after "Gump, injured, had given the alarm."[1] This statement is surely at odds with Emmett's own preposterous statement that Bob had earlier fired at Gump and hit him to prevent his alerting the town. Neither does it fit with Jack Long's account of the raid, or anybody else's, for that matter.

All over town noncombatants sought cover. Unarmed people crowded into cellars and doorways, mothers snatched children from their play and hustled them indoors. Little Minnie Falk was playing with her brothers and sisters in the yard while her mother churned butter on the porch. When the roar of firing rumbled up from downtown and a passerby shouted the alarm, Mrs. Falk hastily shooed her children into the house, thoughtfully rolling the churn in behind them. She may later have reflected on the

time her husband had refused to prosecute Grat Dalton for stealing a saddle from him, noting that it had been a first offense, and
young Grat was "a likeable lad."[2]

About a half-block south of the Condon, young Ida Gibbs
stood on the sidewalk watching the battle. Behind her was the
frame building in which she worked as Adams Grain Company's
assistant bookkeeper. With her stood the rest of the Adams staff,
plus some dressmakers who shared the building. Ida was philosoph-
ical about the danger: she knew "that old building would never
stop a bullet if it came this way," so she stood in the open and
watched the whole show.

Many years after, Charley Gump told a Kansas City newspaper that "everybody who wasn't pumping a gun was hiding out."
Gump told a story of a panicked deputy sheriff who ran into a
store and hid beneath some plows. As bandit bullets smashed
into the store, the deputy reportedly howled in terror, "pile on
more plows!"[3] Well, maybe, although there is no indication besides Gump's of another lawman in the midst of the fight, let alone
of anybody sheltering under iron implements; some memories get
fresher with the years.

As some of Coffeyville's defenders concentrated their fire
on the facade of First National, and other citizens began to pour
lead into the lobby of Condon's, at last it dawned on Grat and his
men that they were in very deep trouble.

Up on the awning of Barndollar Brothers, Parker Williams
was sheltered behind his wooden sign, banging away at the plate
glass of Condon's with his pistol. Broadwell returned the fire with
his Winchester, and one of his rounds whistled clean through an
open window on the second floor of Barndollars' and smashed into
some crockery stored on shelves there. Whatever damage he did
to Barndollar stock, Broadwell missed Williams completely.

Broadwell's terrible marksmanship, at very short range, was
only part of an amazing amount of bad shooting done by the

Condon contingent of raiders that bright morning. The citizens were no great shakes at shooting either, at least not in the first part of the battle, but somebody—perhaps the redoubtable Williams— got a round into Broadwell and Dick dropped his Winchester and clutched his left arm. "I'm hit!" he yelled. "I can't use my arm!"

As the firing rose to a steady roar, a Coffeyville girl watched Grat and his men "running back and forth in the Condon bank, and I thought of rats in a trap seeking a way out. . . . The firing was continuous like bunches of firecrackers exploding, both shotguns and rifles."[4]

Now Bob Dalton got into the fight. Moving back to the front of the First National, he opened up with his Winchester and immediately drew blood. At this time, not before, he put Charley Gump out of action with a single bullet. The round tore through Gump's hand and went on to knock his shotgun stock into fragments.[5] Another account has Gump shot by Bill Powers, but this version gives Gump a pistol instead of a scattergun, calls him a laborer, and sounds contrived.[6]

Other citizens helped Gump back into Isham's and the fight went on. Meanwhile, Emmett had tied up the mouth of the sack of loot and was ready to move. Indeed, for the two Daltons it was high time to go.

"You hold the bag," said Bob to Emmett. "I'll do the fighting."[7]

About this time, Isham's employee Arthur Reynolds ran out of the store and began to fire his Winchester at Broadwell over at Condon's Bank. Broadwell, not yet hit, returned the fire, and a ricochet tore through Reynolds's right foot from little toe to instep. Another account says Reynolds was shot by Bill Powers, but only after Reynolds "slapped a bullet into Bill Powers that half-turned him around."[8] It was "a center shot" that mortally wounded Powers.[9] Whoever shot Reynolds, other men ran to help him back into Isham's, in great pain and out of the fight.

Isham's clerk Lou Dietz was also hit about this time, by a Winchester round that knocked him down and out but did him no serious harm. Dietz was carrying an iron spanner in his pocket, and the bullet that would have punctured his vitals banged into the spanner instead, floored Dietz, and glanced off to tear completely through a massive roll of wrapping paper.[10]

Inside Condon's, rifle bullets and buckshot were tearing through the windows and smacking into the walls. Altogether, the citizens of Coffeyville would pepper the bank with something like eighty rounds of rifle and shotgun fire. The raiders were shooting back, but their return fire did nothing to suppress the steady bombardment from the citizens. Grat asked the bank employees whether there was a back door to the bank—they told him, with their customary gall, that there wasn't.

And he believed them. It did not occur to any of the three bandits in Condon's to go and see whether there might be a door leading out on the west side of the bank. If in fact Perkins did appear in the Condon's office and then flee when he saw the bandits, it should have occurred to one of the outlaws that Perkins came from somewhere. Assuming he did not fall from heaven, there had to be a door opening from the outside into the back of the bank.

But none of them even looked.

Grat now ordered Ball and Carpenter to carry the grain sack full of loot to the southwest door. They got as far as the foyer outside the counter, but the citizens' fire was so heavy that they retreated behind the counter again. About this time one of the bandits was hit, crying out that he could fight no longer: "I am shot. I can't use my arm. It is no use, I can't shoot any more."[11]

Elliott describes the wounded bandit as "one at the southwest door," which would probably mean Powers, since that had been his vantage point from the start of the holdup. The arm wound, however, sounds like Broadwell's, since that seems to have been where he was first struck. It is possible that both men were hit while they were still inside the bank—certainly arm wounds would go a long way toward explaining the extraordinarily poor shooting by the bandits in the Condon Bank.

Over at First National, Bob Dalton quickly realized that there was nothing but death waiting for him and Emmett out in front of the bank. Union Street was a trap. He remembered the back door, which he had probably seen when he first entered the bank and rousted young Bert Ayres out of his back office. Bob and Emmett herded Shepard in front of them to that back door and ordered him to open it. The three men stepped out into an empty lot, bordering the alley behind the line of buildings fronting on Union Street.

They ran into trouble immediately.

To their right, coming out of the back door of next-door Isham's, was young Lucius Baldwin, the clerk from Read Brothers who had ignored his boss's sage advice to stay indoors. Nobody knows where Baldwin was bound. He apparently said nothing to anybody when he left Isham's, but he walked directly toward the two bandits and the helpless Shepard. Surely Baldwin recognized Shepard, and he may have assumed the two Daltons were simply more armed citizens he did not know.

In any case, he strode innocently down the alley. Emmett says Baldwin's short-barreled revolver was "leveled at us,"[12] but other accounts say Baldwin held his weapon down by his side. Both Daltons covered him with their rifles and told him to stop. Apparently, Baldwin did not understand what they said—he did not react at all. He simply kept on coming, his weapon swinging uselessly beside him.

As the young man lay dying moments later, he said he had mistaken the outlaw brothers for citizens defending the town, particularly because First National teller Shepard was with the bandits. In any case, Baldwin strode directly to his death. At about fifty-foot range Bob Dalton said, "I have got to get that man," and shot him down. The round struck Baldwin on the left side of the chest and went clear through him.

A rather more dramatic account tells us that Bob and Emmett went out the back door, only to meet "instant fire from men who had been posted to cut off just such a retreat by Charles T. Connelly, the city marshal."[13] The same source has poor Baldwin running after the two Daltons "firing wildly," and can safely be discounted as a reliable source. In fact, Baldwin's little Colt was never fired at all.

Young Jack Long, perpetually curious, had walked through Rammel's to the alley after Bob and Grat had dodged back inside the First National. Now he watched the brothers emerge into the alley and confront Baldwin. Long afterward, Long confirmed that Bob tried to face Baldwin down without killing him. As Long remembered, "I heard Bob Dalton tell him two or three times, 'Boy, throw that gun down—I don't want to hurt you.' But Baldwin stood there like he was froze, and Bob shot him."[14]

As Baldwin crumpled, his young life finished, Emmett and Bob turned their backs on Shepard, ignored young Long, and sprinted north toward Eighth Street. Behind them, Baldwin was carried into Isham's, which was rapidly starting to look like a hospital ward, with blood splattered everywhere. Apparently nobody pursued Bob and Emmett—maybe nobody but Shepard and Long saw them go. The outlaws ran out of the alley and turned left into Eighth Street, out of sight of the defenders and safe for the moment. About this time Bob and Emmett met a boy called John Sibert, who had run downtown to see what the excitement was about. Young John started to question the outlaws, but got only a shove in reply. "Keep away from here, bud, or you'll get hurt," said Bob and "placidly strolled along with Emmett, snapping his fingers and whistling through his teeth."[15]

As Bob and Emmett came to the corner of Union and Eighth, they had a clear view down past the First National, the

Condon Bank, Isham's, and Boswell's, and could hear the roar of firing as the citizens steadily poured bullets into the Condon's windows.

Now Bob Dalton, without question the best marksman among the raiders, found more targets for his deadly Winchester. Down in front of Rammel Brothers' drugs, immediately north of the First National, stood bootmaker George Cubine, facing south toward the First National. Jack Long was near Cubine, and had just told the cobbler that "they're coming this way." About that time Bob pulled down on Cubine.

Bob could hardly miss his unsuspecting target, a man El-liott says had been Bob's friend in years gone by. Friend or not, Bob drove three bullets into Cubine from behind. Cubine was dead when he hit the ground, a bullet through his heart. He was also hit in the thigh and ankle, probably after he was down. A fourth bullet from Bob's rifle holed the plate glass window of the drugstore. Em-mett says Cubine "swung down on us," and Bob shot him "before he could fire," but this statement seems to be pure invention.

In spite of the hail of bullets from point-blank range, an-other citizen ran to Cubine as he lay on the sidewalk. Shoemaker Charles Brown, an older man and Cubine's workmate, saw that Cubine was beyond help and tried to avenge him, seizing the fallen man's Winchester. Brown was a Civil War veteran but he had no chance against the Daltons, already poised and ready to shoot. Four more shots roared out from the outlaw brothers, and Brown went down beside Cubine, dying.

Some unreliable accounts of the fight overdramatize the parts played by Cubine and the other fallen citizens. One book says Baldwin and Cubine "dashed to Connelly's aid," even though there is no question that both men were dead or dying well before the gallant marshal was shot down.[16]

No doubt the murderous barrage from Bob's Winchester created something of a diversion, but it was not nearly enough to help Grat, Broadwell, and Powers. Back in the Condon Bank, bullets smashed through the windows and slammed into the wall, while the captive customers and bank employees huddled on the floor for safety.

Long said much later that Broadwell came out of the bank in the midst of the shower of bullets from Isham's, walking "back and forth in front of the bank for a while, looking in all directions. Broadwell was sure a wild looking human, and I heard he was just as wild as he looked."[17] There is no obvious reason to doubt Long's statement, although it is difficult to imagine anybody surviving unhurt in the open, within point-blank range of the rifles at Isham's, and perhaps Broadwell did not. This may have been the moment Reynolds got a slug into Broadwell.

It is also a little hard to see why an experienced outlaw would wander into the open to make a target of himself. If Broadwell did, it is reasonable to think that he was already hit, perhaps hurt badly enough that he had ceased to think rationally, or had decided to spend his last minutes on earth showing off all the sand in his craw. Half a century after the fight, Emmett said that Broadwell was "drilled through the body by a bullet in the first volley,"[18] so it is just possible that pain robbed Broadwell of all caution.

At last dim-witted Grat reluctantly decided the time had come to run for it, loot or no loot. "Let's get out of here!" he yelled. And it finally dawned on him that a hasty retreat carrying two hundred pounds of silver was not an encouraging prospect. One story of the raid says the bank employees were forced to carry "two bushels" of coins "toward the waiting outlaw horses," but "lost their nerve" in the process.[19] Well they might, with the torrent of fire smashing into the bank from Isham's, but this wrinkle in the story has no foundation in fact; the Condon employees never left the building at all.

In any case, Grat ordered Ball to open the bulging grain sack and pass him the currency, which he stuffed inside his vest. The bandits in the Condon were ready to run. Grat led. Firing as he ran, he dashed out of the bank's southwest door into the sunlight, sprinting for the alley and the all-important horses, suddenly so very far away. Broadwell and Powers ran behind him, their eyes no doubt fixed on the alley mouth as on the gates to the promised land. They ran, one account said, "with heads down, like facing a strong wind."

They ran the gantlet of a murderous swarm of bullets, an interlocking cross fire from Boswell's and Isham's, tearing at them as they ran diagonally across the coverless expanse of Walnut. They turned to fire at their tormentors, snapping bullets back at the phalanx of flaming rifles concentrated in front of Isham's. Behind his iron range, Henry Isham "was throwing bullets up that alley as fast as he could pull the trigger"[20] and everybody else was banging away furiously at the men running for their lives down Death Alley.

Jack Long, still on the sidewalk, had at last decided that his position "seemed like a hot spot." Acting on that massive understatement, he drew back into the drugstore as a bullet from Bob's Winchester bored into the door behind him. For Bob and Emmett were giving Grat, Powers and Broadwell what covering fire they could. As Bob and Emmett crossed Union and ran up the steps to the raised sidewalk on the west side of the street, they spotted banker Tom Ayres and his rifle in the north entrance to Isham's.

About this time Long poked his head out of cover again, just in time to see Tom Ayres's head, framed in a horse collar that hung as a sign in front of Isham's. Then Bob pulled down on Ayres from about seventy-five yards and put a Winchester bullet through Ayres's face. The slug went in below Ayres's left eye and exited at the base of the skull. It should have killed him, as a couple of writers say it did.[21]

But it did not. Other citizens ran to pull Ayres to shelter, and a fellow townsman called George Picker shoved his thumb down hard over the wound to shut off the blood. Picker, forty-two, was English-born, a mason and contractor. Without medical training, he instinctively did precisely what was wanted to save Ayres's life. Beyond hope, the gallant Ayres would live, thanks mostly to Picker's crude but effective first aid.

And the wound to Ayres did nothing to stop the bullets reaching out for Grat Dalton, Bill Powers, and Dick Broadwell as they raced for safety in the alley. Grat and Powers were hit almost immediately—dust puffed from their clothing as the Winchester slugs tore into their bodies. Both men stayed on their feet, however, staggering on into the alley and making doggedly for their horses tethered behind the sheriff's block. The town echoed with the ceaseless hammer of rifle fire, and above the roar rose the screams of wounded horses, thrashing wildly, dying in that deadly alley.

One source says a lawyer named Biddison was blazing away with a pistol from his office above the Condon Bank. A second writer says Broadwell was downed by Joe Uncapper (he means Uncapher) with a shot in the back that "crippled him badly."[22] Uncapher was on the second floor of the Condon building, and still another writer says Broadwell was wounded by "a shot fired from the second floor of the . . . Bank."[23]

Powers tried to find shelter in a building partway down the alley, but the door was locked. And so he was left exposed in that pitiless, barren passage, no hiding place left, until a rifle slug took him in the back and he fell, dying, into the dirt of the alley beside his horse. He never had a chance to mount.

Grat temporarily found cover. Dodging behind the oil tank wagon parked in the alley, he managed to reach a stairway leading to the back door of Slosson's. The covered stairwell pushed out into the alley a little, and it gave him temporary shelter from the murderous fire from across the plaza. Grat fired several times at his tormentors without coming close to hitting anybody, then tried again to reach his horse, stumbling, bleeding and gasping, down that lethal alley.

Down toward the west end of the alley was Herman Duemcke's cigar factory, a thriving little business Duemcke ran behind his home. Hearing citizens crying out for somebody to cut loose the bandits' horses, Duemcke, unarmed, hurried toward the alley, groping under his apron for his knife. Realizing he had left his knife in the factory, Duemcke dashed back to recover it. His lapse of memory may well have saved his life, for while he ran to get his knife, all hell broke loose in the alley.

Meanwhile, another group of citizens was closing in on the tormented outlaws. As Grat and his companions made a run for their horses, liveryman John Kloehr, barber Carey Seaman, and town Marshal Charles T. Connelly were together by Read's store at the southwest corner of the plaza. Kloehr, an excellent shot, had borrowed a .44 Winchester at Boswell's. Seaman, just back from a hunting trip, reached into his wagon and grabbed his own shotgun, still loaded with buckshot. Now all three men ran west on Ninth Street, hoping to get between the bandits and their horses.

Lawman Connelly was unarmed—that was how peaceful little Coffeyville usually was—and so he ducked into Swisher Brothers Machine Shop, on Ninth, and found a rifle. From Swisher's, Connelly ran across a vacant lot and through a gap in the fence on the south side of the alley. Tragically, the marshal had miscalculated. Wheeling left out of the opening in the fence, he turned to face the outlaws' horses, where he must have expected the gang already to be. But the marshal had his back to the stairwell behind which Grat Dalton was taking refuge from the steady fusillade from the plaza.

Grat Dalton cut the marshal down with his 1886 Winchester. It took just one .38-56 bullet from behind, fired from about twenty feet away, and Charley Connelly was down and dying in

the alley. A couple of accounts of the fight have Grat and Connelly shooting it out dramatically: "both men's pistols roared as
they approached each other and both fell dead."[24] According to
these stories, the marshal went down "gun blazing."[25] Sadly, this
heroic picture is almost surely not so. The best evidence is that
Grat simply shot the marshal in the back and Connelly had no
chance at all.

   With the marshal down, Grat, bleeding badly, tried again to
get to his horse, staggering west past Connelly's body. But Kloehr
and Seamen were in the alley by now, and as Grat turned back
toward Isham's, John Kloehr trained his rifle on Grat and drove
a .44-40 bullet through the outlaw's throat. The Winchester slug
broke Grat's neck, and he went down in a heap, not far from
Connelly.

   Dick Broadwell came closer to winning clear than any of his
friends did. Badly hurt, he still managed to find some cover in the
Long-Bell Lumber Company yard. Because their frantic rearing
interfered with his aim, he killed the horses hitched to the oil
tank. Then, snatching his chance during a pause in the firing, he
mounted his horse and turned to run.

   He wasn't quick enough. Before Broadwell could clear the
alley, both Seamen and Kloehr opened up on him. Kloehr hit
Broadwell with a rifle bullet, and Seamen smashed a load of buckshot into the outlaw's body. Blood soaking his clothing, Broadwell
grabbed the saddle horn and managed to stay mounted. Reeling
in the saddle, he made for the edge of town, anyplace away from
that terrible fire. He would not get far.

   At this point, "Eyewitness" produced a new hero, a diminu-
tive rabbit from a hat. Enter "the young son of Mr. Russell," who
appears with a "heavy Colt revolver" and blazes away at Broadwell as the bandit gallops past. Broadwell "uttered a yell as if
touched in a vital spot," but rode madly on, firing his Winchester

blindly behind him. "The young fellow's aim had been true," says "Eyewitness," judging from the size of the wound in Broadwell's abdomen.[26] The boy hero does not appear in Elliott's narrative.

Bob and Emmett were also trying to get to their horses. According to Emmett, Bob was still confident and spoiling for a fight. "Go slow!" he told his brother, "Go slow, I can whip the whole damn town! I hit two of them. Now let's get to the horses. The rest ought to be through by this time."[27] Emmett says he and Bob got to the alley ahead of Grat and his party, and turned back to help their comrades escape the Condon. As they did so, there was a "sudden crash" of firing in the plaza, and Grat and the others began to run for their lives.

Bob and Emmett had run south from Eighth Street, past the Farmers' Home down a narrow passage that would bring them out into the alley about even with the rear of Slosson's drug. Along the way, Bob snapped a fruitless shot at a citizen, F. D. Benson, who was climbing through a rear window at Slosson's.

Editor Elliott wrote that as they turned into the alley, Bob and Emmett surprised young Bob Wells, a teenager, who was hunkered down behind a platform with a .22 pistol. Wells was apparently lying in wait for the two Daltons, but the youngster's ambush misfired. He turned his head to look straight into the barrels of the outlaws' Winchesters, and forgot all about heroics. Bob paddled young Wells with his Winchester stock, and the boy ran for cover.

Bob and Emmett might well have spared Wells because of his youth. Emmett says they did. Editor Elliott says that's the way it happened, and Elliott is surely the most reliable historian of the Coffeyville fight. There is also the evidence that Bob and Emmett would have spared young Baldwin if they could have.

Still, it is not easy to imagine that kind of mercy from these two hard-case bandits. They had, after all, just killed three men and horribly wounded a fourth. It is hard to believe that Bob and Emmett would spare an armed male of any age while they were running for their lives in the heat of battle.

As soon as Emmett and Bob ran into the alley, they were in full view of the citizens over at Isham's. Bob was looking up, apparently fearing he would be fired on from a rooftop or second-story window. Instead, a round from somebody at Isham's slammed into him, and he tottered over to a pile of cobblestones stacked behind the jail and sat down hard. He was still game, still working the Winchester, but he was dying as he fired, and he hit nobody.

Elliott says Bob got off four rounds as he sat, bleeding, with his back against a building. One of his bullets holed a big Isham's window, another struck a churn near Henry Isham, and the third slammed into a window frame inches from a fifty-pound box of dynamite. Now dynamite normally requires more than the shock of a bullet to explode it—a hundred movies to the contrary notwithstanding. However, if it is a little old, and has begun to "sweat" little drops of TNT, it becomes unstable. In that condition it gets nasty and treacherous, and takes very little shock to explode. We don't know the condition of Isham's dynamite, or how carefully it had been stored, but if it had been around a while . . .

Although Bob Dalton's life was running out into the dirt of the alley, he kept trying. Seeing John Kloehr inside the fence behind his livery stable, Bob tried to shoot. He could not even raise the rifle to his shoulder, and his shot went wild. Pulling his bleeding body erect, he fired and missed twice more. Now Kloehr answered, a single round that tore into the outlaw's chest and knocked him down.

Another account says Henry Isham nailed Bob from across the plaza. That Isham dropped Bob is certainly possible, for Isham was a fine marksman and had a clear shot. Whoever fired that last round, Bob Dalton was finished.

Emmett remained miraculously unhurt until late in the fight, and he was still carrying the grain sack full of the First National's money. In the alley, he says, one round struck him in the body and another broke his arm. Somewhere along the way another slug smashed into his belt, crushing a cartridge into mashed brass and lead (you can still see the belt and cartridge in the Coffeyville museum).

Emmett stayed on his feet, however, and his horse was still standing, although both Bob's and Powers's mounts had been killed in the cross fire. Emmett swung into the saddle, still clutching the grain sack, and was immediately hit several times, including wounds in the left hip and left groin.

Whatever his other failings might have been, Emmett Dalton was long on courage. As he started his run for safety, he looked back to see his brother "leaning up against a rock. All thought of money—of my own life or of escape vanished. I only knew that I had to reach Bob."[28] Clinging grimly to the saddle, Emmett turned his horse back toward Seaman's shotgun and Kloehr's rifle, into the teeth of the rifle fire from Isham's, reaching down to try to pull Bob up across the saddle with him. Dying, Bob Dalton looked up at his brother and whispered, "It's no use." Or perhaps, as Emmett wrote in *Beyond the Law*, Bob muttered, "Good-bye, Emmett. Don't surrender, die game."[29] Nobody can know for certain whether Bob said anything at all to his brother—he was very near death, if not already gone, and we have only Emmett's word for what passed between them.

It really doesn't matter much either way. Whatever Bob may or may not have said, nothing was any use for either of the brothers, for about this time Carey Seaman fired both barrels of his shotgun into Emmett's back and the last of the brothers toppled into the dust of the alley. What Emmett wrote about that moment has the ring of truth:

I felt myself falling. I had been shot again with buck-shot. I fought back the feeling. I was there to save Bob. Maybe I was just getting sleepy.... The strange fancy that maybe I had not slept enough the night before darted across my mind, and I began to curse myself for my folly. But the numbness was growing.[30]

Still conscious, Emmett could see Powers, lying still now, "his hands thrown out in the form of a cross."[31] Bob, says Emmett, was still alive, blood seeping from his nose, and fired one more wild shot down the alley. Then the bandit leader's rifle slipped from his hands. Smiling at his brother, Bob Dalton died.

Now somebody shouted, "They are all down!" and citizen defenders flocked into the alley from Isham's and Boswell's and all around the plaza. Emmett raised his remaining uninjured hand in token of surrender, and the Coffeyville fight was over.

Even the last moments of the gang have been drenched in purple prose. One book describes how "a thick group formed around Bob Dalton in his carmine puddle on the clay. The body heaved in its blood but he kept yelling 'Ride!'"[32] The same writer created an exciting—and highly unlikely—picture of Emmett's last seconds in the fight. It has him

struggling among the horses. He was wounded four times when he got into his saddle and sat huddled with his gloves clasped on his groin. Men lowered their rifles, expecting him to fall, as men shot in the groin do, generally. But all the brothers were valiant. He spurred his horse down the alley and swung from the stirrups to seize Bob's arm. Politeness ended. Carey Seaman blew in his side with a fast shot.[33]

Even without the inventions of irresponsible writers, Death Alley was a charnel house. Bob and Emmett and the grain sack full of money lay close together in that blood-spattered passage, just a little way from the quiet form of dying Marshal Connelly. Grat lay a little distance farther on, still grotesquely decorated by his false whiskers, his vest stuffed with eleven hundred dollars in Condon Bank money. Powers was dead also, his rifle empty. Winchesters and hats were scattered on the ground between puddles of blood, and dead horses sprawled in the alley.

Broadwell had gotten clear of the deadly alley, but a posse of townsmen soon discovered him about half a mile west on Eighth Street, or maybe, as author Drago says, by the creamery on the Independence road, north of town. He was crumpled dead in the dirt in a puddle of his own blood, his horse standing quietly beside him.

Miraculously, nobody in the crowded little town had been hurt by a stray round. Emmett suggested later that Marshal Connelly might have been hit by a slug fired from Isham's, but that seems an unlikely possibility based on Captain Elliott's contemporary narrative. Nobody is sure how many shots were fired. It is probable that the bandits emptied their weapons at least once. Emmett Dalton wrote later that "each of the boys loaded and reloaded their Winchesters."[34] Certainly the townspeople poured lead at the invaders as fast as they could load and shoot.

With few exceptions, the Coffeyville battle had been fought with rifles and shotguns. No matter what you see in the movies, the six-gun was and is a point-blank weapon, reliable and deadly, but designed for close-range killing. The bandits, professionals in their way, had stuck to their shoulder guns. When the citizens cleaned up the battlefield after the shooting died away, they found that none of the bandits' numerous revolvers had been fired. And it had been rifles and scatterguns that had done for the Daltons.

Altogether, something approximating fifteen weapons—mostly rifles—had fired fairly steadily for ten or twelve minutes. The townspeople counted some eighty bullet marks at the Condon, plus evidence of the strike of shotgun pellets. Add to that the rounds that peppered the alley, those that took effect in human flesh, those that struck the storefronts east of the Condon, and those that flew off into thin air, and the total of shots fired is conservatively a couple of hundred.

The shooting finished, Coffeyville began the grim business of dealing with the bloody debris of the raid. There was a great deal of it. Long and two others went into the alley, along with a crowd of other citizens. One of the three kicked a bulging feed sack on the ground, commenting that "they even brought their horse feed with them." Read, the First National president, knew better, and scooped up the sack, crammed with the bank's money.

Babb, the bank employee, began to gather up the weapons strewn up and down the alley. He thoughtfully checked inside Bob Dalton's coat, and carefully removed the British Bulldog, unfired, from Bob's vest pocket. Somehow the stubby Webley never made it to the auction of Bob's possessions. Perhaps it stuck to Babb's fingers for a time; today it rests in the Coffeyville Defenders Museum.

Mostly, the townspeople began to talk excitedly, and to curse, and to cry, all trying to come to grips with the awful fact that some of their fellow citizens had been torn from them for good, men they had seen and spoken to most of the days of their lives. And so, while they picked up the debris of battle, the citizens started mourning the defenders of their peace, mourning their neighbors, relatives, and friends.

6

MEN WHO DID THEIR DUTY WELL

The world likes a man who does his duty well.

—John Kloehr

So FAR, the focus here has been mainly on the Daltons and the gunslingers who rode with them, and only incidentally on the citizens of Coffeyville. Beyond some of their names and a few details, such as how some of them earned their daily bread, we have looked little at those who fought off the Dalton gang—the people who really mattered in Coffeyville that bright October morning. This chapter is dedicated to the major figures in the Coffeyville fight, the citizens of the town, the living and the dead.

To know a town, a place, a country, you have to know something of the folks who live there, especially the people who are willing to fight for what they are and what they have. The defenders of Coffeyville sure didn't fight for money. Marshal Connelly had thirty-one dollars in the Condon on the day of the raid; Lucius Baldwin's deposit amounted to a paltry twenty-eight dollars. None of the other men killed or wounded—except for banker Ayres—had any stake at all in either bank.

We have already met one of the leading citizens of the city, David Stewart Elliott, editor and owner of the *Coffeyville*

Journal. He is the historian of the raid, a real eyewitness, and the sole reliable source on what actually happened on that October morning. Elliott was in the plaza area when the fighting erupted and walked through the clotted blood and tattered corpses in the alley just after the powdersmoke had blown away. You cannot get much closer to your subject than that. Elliott saw and heard everything with the eyes and ears of an experienced journalist.

Elliott came from elsewhere, like most of the rest of Coffeyville's citizens; this was still frontier country, attracting the adventurous and the self-reliant. Elliott was surely both. He was a Pennsylvanian by birth, a lawyer, admitted to the bar in 1869. He had been a newspaper editor in Bedford County, Pennsylvania, until he went out to Kansas in 1885.

During the Civil War, Elliott served with two Pennsylvania regiments, a brief three-month hitch followed by three years in E Company, 76th Pennsylvania Volunteer Infantry.

Elliott was admitted to practice in Montgomery County in 1885, shortly after his arrival in Coffeyville. He already had roots in the town, being related by marriage to the Barndollar merchant family. His family joined him, coming into town through a flood, riding on a railroad handcar. In the summer of 1885 Elliott became editor of the *Journal*, and in the next year he founded the *Coffeyville Weekly Journal*, which he ran until 1897.

Elliott seems to have been the sort of man who is never happy unless he is endlessly busy. In addition to editing both *Journals*, he also practiced law. As his daughter said, one of his clients had been Adeline Dalton, whom he successfully represented in the action that severed her forever from grumpy Lewis Dalton. David Elliott knew the brothers in life, and recognized them in death in that terrible alley after the fight.

Not content with his three jobs, Elliott was also a great joiner. The Montgomery County *History* summed him up: "His tastes led to the formation of his fellow men into associations, political parties and other organizations and the promulgation and advocacy of their principles."[1] At his death, the county historian tells us, Elliott was a member of no less than sixteen lodges.[2]

No doubt Elliott was an eminent, respected man in his thriving little town. As he walked through Death Alley, the desperately wounded Emmett Dalton called to him, "Colonel, take my guns," and Elliott did so. Apparently Emmett thought well of Elliott. In later years he wrote that he did not ask to be paroled while Elliott was alive, because he "did not want to embarrass him." One may be permitted to doubt the purity of that statement, but at least it indicates that Emmett harbored good feelings for the editor long years after the fight.

When the Spanish-American War broke out, Elliott again answered his country's call. He sold the *Journal*, then organized and commanded Company G of the 20th Kansas Volunteer Regiment. G Company, 115 men strong, got what training they could in a store on South Walnut in Coffeyville. The unit departed with "a great outflow of patriotic spirit," headed for the docks of San Francisco. From there, Elliott and his men were shipped to the Philippines and into a shooting war.

Elliott survived a ferocious firefight at Caloocan, near Manila, but his luck ran out the next day. On the twenty-seventh of February, 1899, Elliott was killed by a sniper. A month and a half later, brought home by his two soldier sons, he was buried in Coffeyville's Elmwood Cemetery with full military honors.

Newspapers in the last century, like Elliott's *Journal*, had a distinctive style. They were, after all, the chief source of information in any town. They carried all sorts of features, including serialized novels: in early 1893, for example, the *Coffeyville Journal* ran Bret Harte's *Sally Dows, An After-War Romance of the South*. A paper like the *Journal* spent much space on local happenings, the essential stuff of everyday life in any American small town. In late 1892, for example, the paper dealt with such varied items as these:

"The poor fund committee of last year had a balance of $13.40 after making numerous distributions in the way of charity. This amount was this morning turned over to the present committee for this year's work by Mrs. Duckworth."

Subscription to the *Journal* for a year cost a dollar and a half (in advance, please). It was full of advertisements for local business, rendered, after the custom of the day, in seven or eight different typefaces to attract attention. Also advertised were items from corsets to canned goods and exotic elixirs to cure every ailment under the sun: "Are you billious, constipated or troubled with jaundice, indigestion, sick headache, foul breath? ... [Y]our liver is out of order and your blood is slowly being poisoned.... Herbine will cure any disorder of the liver, stomach or bowels."

The paper featured not a little gossip, some delivered tongue-in-cheek: "A man committed suicide in Independence Saturday. There is nothing strange about this, as it requires a good deal of patience to live in that town. His name was Polk Dye; what it now is we do not know." Readers could also learn about puzzling and bizarre events elsewhere in the world, like this somewhat ominous news: "A Chinese sailor en route to New York died from a disease 'common to Chinamen'"—whatever that might mean.

Finally, the *Journal* delivered itself of dozens of wry comments on the foibles of the world, significant and otherwise, mostly otherwise. For example, "The Los Angeles school board is run by a woman. The board consists of four Republicans and four Democrats and one lady. The party men vote solid, and the lady runs the business as she desires." Or "Walter Gardner ... working at a cotton gin near Galveston, was discovered mashed flat between a pressed bale of cotton."

On the whole, newspapers of the last century were considerably more flowery and fussy than the bland, uninteresting, sometimes illiterate prose of today's papers. Elliott's *Journal* was no exception. Like other papers in the 1890s, it was much given to multiple headlines and subheadlines. The *Journal* of Friday, October 7, 1892, carried Elliott's long story of the raid, under a headline that surely grabbed people's attention.

"DALTONS!" it shouted in huge letters, and then, "The Robber Gang Meet Their Waterloo in Coffeyville." There followed no less than twelve more subheads before the story itself began, and one of these subheads was sure to sober its readers: "Four Good Citizens Dead," it said, and good citizens they certainly were.

Today, when so many people live in huge cities and daily watch television broadcasts replete with murders and violent robberies, we have grown hardened to tragedy and death. Most of it scarcely touches us. How can we respond to all the evil in the human race? A century ago in a small community like Coffeyville, on the other hand, people lived closer together. What happened to their neighbors affected them deeply. Nobody in town was "an island, entire of itself," to borrow from John Donne.

Nobody could ignore the empty pew in church, or the crepe on the door of a favorite store. Everybody missed a friend, an acquaintance, or a treasured relative. Nobody could forget that a man they all knew was suddenly gone, snatched away untimely by a bullet from one of society's professional parasites.

The men who had died had run businesses, after all, performed services, and tipped their hats to say good morning on the street. They fixed your shoes and boots, and they taught your kids, and they sold you dry goods. They were lodge members and creditors and debtors and hunting chums and political opponents, and they sang in the church choir and brought fried chicken to the Fourth of July picnic. They were neighbors. The departed men had been part of a placid, comfortable, and honorable life, in which people mostly did what they said they would and neighbors didn't lock their doors, and hardworking men and women died in their beds in the fullness of time.

And so, when the last echoes of the Winchesters died away and the citizens had congratulated themselves on whipping a famous band of outlaws, sadness began to set in. Editor Elliott put it pretty well, as he usually did, and I think he reported the town's reaction quite literally: "[T]he city went into mourning over the death of Marshal Connelly, George Cubine, Charley Brown and Lucius Baldwin. Stalwart men wept great tears of grief, whilst the women and children cried and wrung their hands in agony."[3]

Elliott's description of the town's reaction may sound a little dramatic to us now, but the chances are that it is entirely, depressingly accurate. Everybody knew the men who had died so suddenly. Everybody knew their families, and their friends, and now remembered the last time they had talked to these brave men. The city grieved and remembered its dead.

The ancient and honorable trade of shoemaking bred upright, conscientious, and courageous men. Saint Crispin was a shoemaker, and England's great warrior-king Henry V did not hesitate to invoke the name of that humble man when he led his bowmen to smash the French at Agincourt in 1415. Coffeyville had valiant shoemakers, too. More than willing to take up arms, two of them died defending their town. King Hal would have liked them, for they fought his kind of fight.

Charley Brown was fifty-nine on the day of the raid. Brown was a New Yorker, who left Rochester at fifteen to try his luck in the California gold fields. He returned to New York in 1861 and served for a while in the Union army. Still restless, he moved to Michigan after the war, married there, and moved to a Coffeyville farm in the autumn of 1883.

He had made and repaired shoes and boots in Coffeyville since 1888. Although he is sometimes referred to as Cubine's partner and had worked at Cubine's, Brown apparently ran his own shop, one door north of Rammel's. The Methodist Episcopal

Church buried Brown with appropriate solemnity, the Saturday after the raid. He left, as the *Journal* sympathetically put it, "an aged widow in dependent circumstances." Brown's obituary summed him up as "an honorable, upright, industrious citizen [who] enjoyed the confidence and respect of his fellow men."[4]

He was an ordinary, hardworking citizen, who loved his town and his friends enough to lay his life on the line and lose it. It probably never occurred to Charley Brown that he "should not get involved." That pusillanimous, selfish notion is more a product of our own century, in which many people seem to have convinced themselves that they owe their neighbors nothing.

Saint Crispin's trade was also followed faithfully by George B. Cubine, forty-six years old, a journeyman bootmaker who worked at his uncle's shop two doors north of the First National Bank. Out in front hung a sign shaped like a giant boot.

Cubine came from Walker's Creek, Virginia, a tiny place near Mechanicsburg. He had come to Coffeyville in 1875 to live with his uncle, Confederate veteran J. W. Cubine, one of the men who made Coffeyville boots famous throughout the West. J. W. sold 372 pair of his fine boots in 1891, a pretty fair output for custom-made footwear.

Cowpunchers were particular about what they wore on their feet, and many treasured the well-made Coffeyville boot. It was a high boot with an extension up toward the front of the knee and a modified heel that fit stirrups well. And it was comfortable; Cubine and his peers made the left and right boots to different lasts, a great luxury compared to the old stretch-it-to-fit-yourself footwear other people made.[5]

In 1881 George had married a local girl, Alice Keyton. Of their three children, only young Charlie survived to lose his father to Dalton bullets. It was not only Alice and Charlie who would mourn their husband and father. For as Cubine's obituary sadly put it, "The blow falls with crushing force on an aged mother, a helpless invalid brother, a married sister and brother. In the family of his uncle, where he made his home for many years, there is a bitter mourning as over a dear son and brother."

The somewhat stilted words of the newspaper expressed the feelings of the whole town. Relatives were touched, to be sure, and friends. But so to some degree was everybody else who called Coffeyville home. Cubine was a well-known and highly respected citizen. He was buried in the bosom of the Methodist Episcopal Church that Thursday, while stores closed in his honor and people hung out crepe mourning garlands all over town. Cubine's lodge brothers, the Modern Woodmen of America, participated in the funeral, after the custom of the day. "The funeral," said the *Journal*, "was very large." In contrast, the dead bandits were buried without fanfare that same day.

Lucius Baldwin was the youngest of the citizens killed, and the only one born and bred in Kansas. Just twenty-three, he had been born in Burlington, up in Coffey County on the Neosho River, some sixty or seventy miles from Coffeyville. Baldwin was the son of a preacher, an "itinerant minister," as the *Journal* said, of the omnipresent Methodist Episcopal Church.

The Baldwins had seen a lot of raw, rugged new Kansas. Lucius's father had served his flocks in the little towns of Centroppolis, Pomona, Malvern, Neodesha, Blue Mound, Ottawa, Fredonia, Americus, and Grenola, and at one time in Coffeyville itself. Most of the elder Baldwin's churches had been small ones; several of the towns in which he served are not even on the map today and others remain tiny hamlets. Reverend Baldwin could not have made much money, but he was strong in the Lord. He raised a stalwart son and even managed to get Lucius to Baker University for a year, when the boy was sixteen.

Baldwin's father had retired in Burlington and died there, and young Lucius had gone to work for the Read family, who had known the elder Baldwin while he was pastor in Coffeyville. Lucius was true to his faith, active in the Methodist Episcopal Sunday school and choir, and in the Methodist youth association called the Epworth League. Baldwin was buried in Burlington, and the *Journal* mourned with the rest of the town. The newspaper was even moved to quote a little appropriate scripture in Baldwin's obituary, reminding its readers that, in the pretty biblical phrase, Lucius was "not dead, but sleepeth."

Sleeping too was Charles T. Connelly, the town marshal, a slender man with a neat beard. Connelly was forty-seven that autumn. A native of Indiana and a Civil War veteran who had enlisted at seventeen in the Ninth Indiana Volunteer Artillery, Connelly had come to Kansas in 1885.

He was a teacher by profession, a veteran of many years in the classroom. He had taken the marshal's job only temporarily, as the man most likely to run out of business the last disreputable dives in Coffeyville. Tragically, he was due to turn in his badge and begin work as principal of the West Side School that very fall. He had taught school in Coffeyville and had, as his obituary said, "enjoyed the confidence and the esteem of his pupils." Connelly left behind his second wife, Sarah, and one child.

The marshal was buried in Mount Hope Cemetery, Independence, Kansas, on the Friday after the raid, the Methodist Episcopal Church again officiating. The *Journal* noted with approval that the Missouri Pacific Railroad "kindly furnished two coaches, free of charge, and placed them at the disposal of the family and friends of the dead Marshal Connelly, for the purpose of conveying them to Independence."[6] Before the marshal's body was shipped to Independence, however, Connelly's town said goodbye to him. Coffeyville held its own funeral on October 7, at the Methodist Episcopal Church. Connelly's lodge brothers, the Modern Woodmen, turned out in a body, along with a host of citizens.

The town did not forget those its fallen citizens left behind. Just two days after the fight, Coffeyville held a citizens' meeting at which people began to collect money for the families of the fallen. The town formed a relief committee and sent a circular out to banks, railroads, and express companies, asking for donations. Bankers all over the United States sent money in response. And the townspeople, in traditional Middle American style, began to dig into their own pockets.

The response to the committee's appeal was so great that by early December, more than $13,000 had been paid out to the defenders' survivors. Cubine's, Brown's, and Connelly's widows each got $1,650, and the same amount went to Baldwin's mother. Among other payments, the town put $1,140 in trust each for Connelly's daughter and Cubine's son. Reynolds and Gump both received some compensation for their injuries but Ayres the banker did not, perhaps because he would not diminish the shares of people less well-off than he was. On top of all this largesse, the Katy dipped into its coffers, paying $1,000 each to Baldwin's mother and to the widows of Cubine, Brown, and Connelly.

For the fighting citizens who survived, there was much honor and praise. And the center of attention, deservedly, was the quiet liveryman, John Joseph Kloehr (the family pronounced their name "Clair," and still do). Kloehr was Bavarian by birth, born thirty-four years before the fight in a hamlet called Aschachbad, near Kissingen. Kloehr's parents, Joseph and Margarete, were millers, of a family that had followed that honorable trade "for generations." They emigrated to America in 1858, in the great immigration days when the young United States built its muscle of hardy stock from all across the world.

The Kloehrs moved to Kansas in 1870, settling in Coffeyville two years later. John Kloehr grew up with Coffeyville, where his father ran the Southern Hotel. The elder Kloehr built a handsome brick residence for his growing family on a 220-acre tract near town.

John worked as a butcher at first, after running cattle on the Canadian for a year and spending another season prospecting in Colorado. In time he began to trade in horses, and from there it was only a short step to the livery business. He had been ten years a liveryman when the Daltons rode up Eighth Street out of a clear fall morning. Kloehr did business on Ninth Street, but his premises backed up on the deadly alley where the Dalton gang went down.

Ultimately, the Kloehr stable became a solid brick building, fifty by one hundred and eleven feet, with stalls for sixty-eight animals and undivided space for many more. John Kloehr kept about thirty horses for hire. In later years the business was turned into an automobile garage, where Coffeyville's citizens could keep their precious cars between their once- or twice-weekly outings.

Kloehr was snatching a nap on a cot at his stable when the shooting started on October 5. A citizen called Harris Reed ran in to announce breathlessly that the Daltons were in town, and John hurried out to find a Winchester.

Kloehr was a practiced rifleman, a hunter and trapshooter, good enough to travel to out-of-town shooting tournaments. He also belonged to the local gun club, where, as Elliott put it, "he has acquired some skill and considerable practice as a marksman." Indeed he had.

John Kloehr was and remained a pillar of the Coffeyville community. In 1884 he had márried Katie Huff, an Indiana girl, and the couple raised four children. Kloehr served his town as alderman, school director, and deputy sheriff, and his descendants still live in Coffeyville. Kloehr was a modest man, who did not like to talk about himself. Even within his own family, the subject of the Dalton raid was not mentioned. As his grandson said, "It wasn't discussed in our family. He wasn't particularly proud of his part in the raid. It's a terrible thing to kill somebody … I don't remember him ever saying anything about it."[7]

Henry Isham (say "Eye-sham"), no mean shot himself, was part owner of Isham Brothers and Mansur's hardware emporium. He was born a New Yorker but he had lived in Coffeyville almost a decade by the time of the raid. Having been both banker and merchant back in his home state, he now devoted his time to his large hardware business, working with his brother and son-in-law. Like other hardware stores of the day, Isham's carried firearms and ammunition, and when the Daltons struck, Henry did not hesitate to arm himself and his neighbors.

After the raid, Isham stayed on in Coffeyville, running his thriving business just as he always had. And in the autumn of 1906 he quite literally died in harness, collapsing while waiting on a customer. He was dead by the time doctors got to his store.

Tough Tom Ayres, the valiant banker, came very close to death. Without Picker's crude first aid, he would surely have bled to death. Ayres was an Illinois man, a lawyer like Elliott, admitted to the bar in 1871. He settled in Coffeyville about 1880, where he opened a banking business under the name Ayres and Steele. That modest business grew, and in time became the First National.

After the Coffeyville fight and a long recovery, Ayres left town in 1893. He moved to Sioux City, Iowa for a while, but returned to Coffeyville in 1895. Ayres practiced law and served a term as mayor of Coffeyville. He also speculated in other ventures—including a well that produced a small quantity of crude oil, a harbinger of things to come.

One of Isham's clerks, T. Arthur Reynolds, who ran to back up his boss and his neighbors, needlessly got a bullet for his pains. Reynolds was only twenty-three, and showed a good deal more courage than sense—he was the man who moved out onto the sidewalk under fire to engage Broadwell, then at the southeast corner of the Condon. He was terribly exposed as he worked his Winchester, and he very quickly stopped an outlaw slug.

The bullet that struck Reynolds probably came from Broadwell's rifle. It tore through the clerk's foot, entering at the base of the little toe and exiting the instep. It was a ricochet, too, which means that the slug was probably distorted when it hit Reynolds. It would have made an ugly and very painful wound, and it immediately put the gallant clerk out of the fight to stay.

Lou Dietz, the other Isham's clerk, was also wounded. It is curious that Elliott does not mention the wound, because he commented on the various hurts suffered by other citizens. Still, it seems fairly clear that Dietz was knocked out, or at least knocked down, by the bullet that slammed into the iron spanner in his pocket. Until then, and maybe afterward, Dietz staunchly traded shots with the Daltons, firing down the alley from behind one of the cast-iron stoves at the front of Isham's store. In the years after, Dietz traded in real estate and ran the Brown Palace Hotel for a time. He later moved to California, disappearing from our history.

The town barber, Carey Seaman, cut his neighbors' hair at Smith's barber shop, next door to Isham's and just south of it. It was his shotgun—both barrels, apparently—that finished Emmett Dalton as he reached down to his dying brother. Seaman was a family man and a respected citizen.

Cool-hand Charley Ball, who so blandly bamboozled dull Grat Dalton, was a transplanted Indianian. He had worked in the Condon Bank at Oswego before he came to Coffeyville in 1886. Fittingly, Ball rose to become president of Condon's in 1916. He died in 1922.

Charley Gump lived on in Coffeyville, in time working in his son's auto shop on Central Street. He was an expert in what was then called "toggery," building canvas or cloth tops for cars.

Gump was apparently willing to forgive and forget the slug from
Bob Dalton's Winchester. He was the only citizen actually to visit
Emmett Dalton in later years, as we'll see in the last chapter.

At terrible cost, the citizens of Coffeyville had defended
their town and won a measure of glory in the process. The
Washington Post spoke for the whole country:

> What this country needs is a multiplication of Coffeyvilles. Towns
> of that caliber should be distributed freely all over this glorious and
> happy land. Wherever robbers, murderers, incendiaries and bandits
> congregate, some new Coffeyville should spring up in the night,
> populated by Browns, Connellys, Kloehrs, Baldwins and Cubines,
> and filled with a spirit of emulation in marksmanship. No county
> in any State should be without its Coffeyville.[8]

7

WHEN THE SMOKE CLEARED

We left Coffeyville's citizens gathering in Death Alley, surrounded by drying puddles of blood and the other ugly debris of battle. Elliott picked up Emmett Dalton's guns, Read retrieved the sack full of his bank's money, and Walter H. Wells, one of the town doctors, ran to do what he could for dying Marshal Connelly. Other citizens flocked to the alley from all directions, those who had fought and those who had not. A few people made off with snippets of the bandits' clothing and tufts of hair from their horses, by way of souvenirs. As one paper reported, "Bits of cloth and pieces of belt, pass now as relics of the departed Daltons, and are in current demand."[1]

One pilgrim took the train all the way from Kingfisher to visit Coffeyville and prowl the scene of slaughter. This ghoul returned triumphant, bearing a "small piece of plank with a splash of Bob's blood on it . . . and a little piece of his pants," which, he told his neighbors, had been methodically snipped into small chunks suitable for souvenirs.

Willing hands carried Marshal Connelly over to Slosson's drugstore, and Emmett Dalton was also taken there. Connelly was dead by the time Doctor Wells could examine him, but Emmett was still breathing. Doctor Wells ordered him taken upstairs to the doctor's office, where Wells went to work to salvage what he could.

As the cleanup in the alley began, somebody ran from the Farmer's Home boarding house—it stood where Death Alley and the alley south from Eighth Street meet. He was carrying a rope, whoever he was, and some of the citizens began to get ideas about lynching Emmett Dalton. One famous story has a mob invading Doctor Wells's office, where the doctor struggled to keep Emmett alive.

Wells was a longtime resident, a transplanted Marylander who had fixed cuts and croup and broken bones and worse in Coffeyville for a decade. He knew his fellow citizens. The doctor had his hands full coping with Emmett, who had, in Homer Croy's words, "as many holes in him as a collander."[2] Wells didn't need the extra bother of a gaggle of furious citizens intent on summarily fixing anything that ailed his patient. Emmett had a total of twenty-three chunks of lead in him, and that was trouble enough for one day. Nevertheless, the doctor dealt with the emergency without turning a hair.

The angry townspeople apparently intended to tie one end of a rope to a pole outside the window and the other end to Emmett's neck. Thereafter, their plan called for propelling Emmett out of the doctor's window, thereby saving the taxpayers a good deal of money and trouble. The doctor rose to the occasion:

"No use, boys," said Doctor Wells. "He will die anyway."

"Doc," said a voice from the crowd, "Doc, are you certain?"

"Hell, yes," quoth the doctor. "Hell, yes, he'll die. Did you ever hear of a patient of mine getting well?"[3]

That broke the tension a little. Somebody laughed, and the mob took its leave. Apparently Elliott helped Doctor Wells talk the mob out of extinguishing Emmett, and no doubt other cooler heads assisted too. Even so, there was a lot of understandable anger amongst the solid citizens of Coffeyville, and feeling against Emmett would continue to run high for days to come.

A little of the town's sorrow and anger was vented by a bizarre sort of ceremony in the alley. Somebody set up a hayrack on the south side of the alley, and boards from the Long-Bell lumber yard were leaned up against the rack. Then the citizens dragged the corpses of Broadwell and Powers and Bob and Grat Dalton over to this makeshift easel and propped them up in a row. They laid the outlaws out on their backs and folded each man's hands across his chest. Somebody took a photograph—complete with a Winchester resting on the bodies of Bob and Grat—before the bodies were unceremoniously dumped in the city jail.

Somebody discovered, presumably during the movement of the bodies, that if you pumped Grat's right arm up and down, jets of blood spurted out of the hole in his throat. A good many folks amused themselves by trying out this somewhat macabre experiment in hydraulics, both in the alley and later on, after Grat's mortal remains became part of the heap in the jail.

Naturally enough, business in Coffeyville ground to a halt. People stood in the streets and talked to their neighbors about the grim crew that had so suddenly descended upon their quiet town that terrible day. As Elliott told it, "Knots of excited men gathered at every convenient point, and the dreadful occurrences of the day were discussed. The afternoon and evening trains brought hundreds of visitors from adjoining towns. Telegrams inquiring for particulars, offering help and extending congratulations to the living and condolence to the friends of the dead, came pouring in."[4] Apparently the whole nation was interested in the drama played out in little Coffeyville. Among the telegrams that streamed into town—seventeen of them within two hours—was one from James Gordon Bennett, famed editor of the *New York Herald*.

The press had a field day. All over the country, reporters ground out reams of copy, savoring every juicy detail of the raid over and over again, inventing what they could not learn. The raid became a ninety-day wonder, threatening to crowd out the saga of Peary's new assault on the North Pole. It even rivaled progress reports on the case against ax-wielding Lizzie Borden, the scandalous maiden of sedate Fall River, Massachusetts.

Up in Stillwater, Minnesota, an enterprising reporter sought out Cole Younger, still serving time after the botched, bloody, Northfield, Minnesota, raid of 1876. Cole denied any connection with the Daltons, no doubt disappointing his interviewer. Meanwhile, in Louisville, Kentucky, somebody got hold of Frank James, who delivered himself of this pious observation: "No, I did not know any of them, but have often heard of their raids in the Territory. I was satisfied that they would be wiped out sooner or later, as it is the general end of desperadoes."[5] The *Kansas City Star* chimed in, on a somewhat frivolous note: "The fact that the Daltons owned a lot in the cemetery at Coffeyville emphasizes the propriety of their course in going to that place to get killed."[6]

John Kloehr's marksmanship won him all manner of fulsome praise in America's newspapers. Charley Ball's astonishing bluff got good notices, too, as reported by the *St. Louis Globe Democrat*: "[E]ight minutes was the time consumed by Cashier Ball in his one-act skit of 'The Bogus Time Lock.' That eight minutes saved the bank treasure and cost the Dalton gang its existence."[7]

The *Minneapolis Tribune* announced the result of the battle in true western style: "The deadly epidemic of lead colic in Coffeyville, Kan., has rid the country of the worst gang of outlaws since the days of the James boys." Not to be outdone, the *Louisville Post* pronounced solemnly, "The destruction of the Dalton gang in Kansas marks a new departure in the administration of justice, and the outcome will have a most beneficial effect on border ruffianism." A somewhat supercilious *Philadelphia Ledger* sneered genteelly at the lawlessness of the backward West: "Only a western town could relate such a tale of blood." And the *Pittsburgh Dispatch* combined encomiums for Coffeyville with a snide little stab at its own local lawmen: "There are plenty of citizens who are not scared at the crack of a rifle or pistol.... It is only in Pittsburg that the posse hunts for holes on the call of the sheriff."

An incautious Kansas politician named Jeremiah "Sockless Jerry" Simpson was heard to defend the Daltons, provoking most justly the wrath and indignation of the *Journal.* Simpson is quoted as saying: "The Dalton boys were no worse than the national bankers and thousands of others in Kansas who are engaged in pretended lawful pursuits, while really they are robbing the people. They are to be no more condemned for their acts than the bankers they robbed."[8] Or words to that effect.

It was not a wise thing to say, especially for a congressman, even if he was a spokesman for the "people's party," and therefore the avowed foe of banks and bankers. Simpson's speech provoked a sulphurous letter to the *Journal,* reporting this insult to Coffeyville: "I had often heard it said that Mr. Simpson was a foul mouthed fellow but I had never believed that a member of Congress from the great state of Kansas could be so lost to manhood and common decency as to utter such a statement."[9]

Elliott, both a devout Republican and a passionate Coffeyvillian, jumped ferociously on Simpson's stupid comment, rising to sublime heights of rhetoric with this flaming broadside: "Business men of Kansas, whether republicans or democrats, what do you think of a party that will put forward a man so devoid of principle as a leader and mouthpiece? ... Brave men of Coffeyville, rise in your might and resent insult."[10]

But for a little time, Coffeyville had more pressing problems than rising and resenting the polemics of Sockless Jerry. Since nobody was sure that there were not more bandits lurking outside the town, there was some unease about a retaliatory raid by whatever survivors and sympathizers might be about. As it turned out, the town would have plenty of help. At 9:42 A.M. on the day of the raid, up in Parsons, Kansas, the telegraph key began to clatter, bringing news of the beginning of the big fight: "The Daltons are holding up the Condon Bank. Shooting has started."[11]

Without delay, Superintendent J. J. Frey of the Katy piled fifty armed men on a special train and highballed south to help guard the town. The Parsons men were too late for the fight, of course, but they arrived in plenty of time to reassure everybody that there would be no retaliatory raid. "They made the run," said Elliott rather proudly, "in thirty-two minutes."

So help was near at hand. Still, the town remained uneasy for weeks. Nobody knew how many bandits there had been—some newspapers talked about six, at least. And nobody knew how big the gang really was. In fact, early on, nobody even knew for sure who all of the dead bandits were; early reports mentioned "Tom Heddy, desperado," and "an unidentified desperado."

But as the smoke blew away and the peace began to seem more assured, the town turned to mourning its losses and savoring its victory, and to many other tasks, some of them quite mundane. Among the more routine tasks was the balancing of the banks' books. Ironically, the First National was astonished to find a surplus when the money was counted the next evening.

The surplus was only $1.98, to be sure, but it was a surplus nevertheless. Considering that Bob and Emmett had carried more than twenty thousand dollars out of the bank, around several corners and down Death Alley, a couple of dollars' profit was not a bad result. And when its staff counted the pennies, the Condon Bank was also unhurt—it had lost no more than twenty dollars.

Nobody had much hope for Emmett, gasping for life up in Doctor Wells's office, his battered body punctured by more than twenty holes of assorted sizes. Doctor Wells set to work, however, and Emmett continued to breathe. He was in great pain, but would not agree to amputation of his arm as the doctor suggested. Apparently he was something of a public spectacle, for all his suffering, as "hundreds" of the curious gaped at him as he lay in bed. Bouquets of flowers appeared in Emmett's room, sent, said the press, by "foolish women," not further identified. Whether it was the flowers or the skill of Doctor Wells, Emmett slowly began to mend, to the point where the sheriff began to give thought to moving him to a safer place.

The other wounded citizens were seen to, as well. Cashier Ayers was the worst hurt, and "for days hung between life and death." He was in great pain but he hung gamely on, and by Friday was making excellent progress. He would recover entirely, except for a scar and partial facial paralysis, to remind him forever of his courage on the day the bandits tried to push his town around.

The other wounded would also recover, to the town's obvious delight. And as time passed, a little of the citizens' anger abated also. Even so, on Friday County Sheriff John Callahan postponed plans to move Emmett to Independence from the room at the Farmer's Home where he was being nursed.

Callahan feared, perhaps with reason, that the men of Coffeyville might be tempted to shuffle Emmett off this mortal coil without worrying overmuch about due process. This "desperate gang," as Elliott put it in the Friday *Journal*, "cost Coffeyville some of its best blood," and no doubt the town agreed. The sheriff was probably wise to keep Emmett indoors, where he could more easily be protected.

On Friday, poor old Adeline Dalton arrived in town, up from Kingfisher accompanied by her sons, the peaceful Ben and the bellicose Bill, and by her daughter Eva Whipple, who also lived near Kingfisher. Adeline found one son clinging to life by an eyelash and two more of her boys already in the ground. There is a story that Julia Johnson showed up too, rushing to the side of the stricken Emmett, but this tale seems to be part of the "childhood lovers" myth Emmett carefully fostered in later years.[12]

Adeline was courteous and quiet, and apparently was treated politely and sympathetically by the people of Coffeyville. On October 14, after the fashion of the time, she placed a note of thanks in the *Journal:* "We desire to return our sincere thanks to the citizens of Coffeyville for their uniform kindness to us during our stay.... We have no enmity against any one what ever on account of the late terrible tragedy."[13]

In sharp contrast to his dignified mother, Bill Dalton was loud and belligerent, shooting his mouth off in public at every opportunity. He began to fulminate about revenge, and made no friends with intemperate remarks like this: "The boys were wrong in trying to rob the banks, but they were right when they shot the men who were trying to kill them!" When Adeline pleaded with him to pull in his horns, Bill thundered, "They can't bluff me. I say what I please!"[14] And he did, long and loud and over and over. He made noises about suing the city, alleging that money and personal effects had been stolen from the corpses of his brothers. "I know that one of the citizens robbed the bodies of $900 which Emmett claimed they had before coming to Coffeyville."

"Nonsense!" said the *Journal,* no doubt speaking for the whole town. "Will's actions and words and his bank account are all interesting straws to watch when considering the question of his being a silent partner in the late firm of 'Dalton Brothers, bandits and outlaws,' whose business cards should have borne the inscription 'Train and bank robbery a speciality.'"[15]

The *Journal's* comments were hardly conciliatory, but then nobody in town felt very conciliatory. Four brave Coffeyville citizens were barely cold, and here was another Dalton carrying on as if his murderous brothers were the victims, instead of the killers. Bill was furious about the *Journal* article, and raged to Deputy Marshal Heck Thomas, "I came near going over just now and shooting me a newspaperman. By God, the next one that braces me *will* be shot!"[16]

One source says that "when a careful accounting was made of the money afterward, it was found to be $900 in excess of the sum lost. . . . If the $900 was ever turned over to the Dalton family, no evidence of it appears in town records."[17] It's a tantalizing reference, but as far as I can find, there is no evidence that any extra money was mixed in with the cash taken from the banks. All accounts of the raid indicate that the banks' money was stashed either in Emmett's bag or in the front of Grat's vest. Bob carried none of it; his own nine hundred dollars, if he had it, would not have become mixed with the bank's.

On the other hand, nine hundred dollars in cash turned up in the inventory of Bob's meagre possessions a little later on, along with his horse furniture, weapons, and gold watch. So it turns out that big-mouthed brother Bill was right after all.[18]

Even so, when Bill Dalton carried on about Bob's money, he managed to do it in such an abrasive, arrogant way, that nearly everybody was instantly antagonized. And, as if the business of the money were not enough, Bill then sued to recover the horse his brother Bob had ridden. A man from the Indian Territory had claimed the animal after the raid, alleging it had been stolen from him. Bill managed to get a writ of replevin—helped by Heck Thomas, always fair and evenhanded.

Unfortunately, some of the public got the idea that the replevin writ was a deputy marshal's commission, and the resulting complaints gave rise to a congressional inquiry and indignant denials by various United States marshals. By the time this brouhaha had simmered down, Bill Dalton was long gone, off on the owlhoot trail.

The Thursday burial of the robbers had not, understandably, been accompanied by any great ceremony. The bandits were

treated to black-lacquered coffins at public expense, and were put
away in Elmwood Cemetery the afternoon after the raid. Providing coffins was as far as public decency went, for the outlaws' only
marker was the pipe, or rail, to which they had tethered their
horses in that deadly alley.

In addition to Adeline and Bill Dalton, Dick Broadwell's
brother, George, arrived on the Friday, coming to claim his
brother's body. With him was one H. A. Wilcox, Dick's brother-in-
law, described as "a prominent and leading citizen of Hutchinson,
Kansas."[19] They would take Broadwell's body home with them,
they said, and apparently did so quietly, ruffling no feathers among
the townsfolk. Both men were solid citizens, George a salesman for
the Boston Tea Company, Wilcox a grocer. Wilcox spoke for them
both. "We are as greatly shocked by this occurrence as you, and entirely ignorant of Dick's being with this gang. We had not heard of
him since May. He never was wild or a drinker or gambler, and . . .
we always thought him to be straight and law abiding."[20] Wilcox
and George Broadwell got Dick's remains dug up, dressed in a new
suit, and encased in a finer coffin. Then they shipped Dick back
to Hutchinson and planted him again, presumably with suitable
ceremony and appropriate sentiments.

For some reason, Powers had also been exhumed when
Broadwell's relatives reclaimed Dick's body. Nobody appearing to
retrieve what remained of Powers, he was reinterred next to the
Dalton brothers. No one in Coffeyville knew anything about Powers or his family and probably no one cared very much. He would
stay put forever beside Grat and Bob up in Elmwood Cemetery.

The next notable arrivals in Coffeyville were Heck Thomas
and Fred Dodge, in town to confirm the details of the raid and
establish who was entitled to the rewards. Thomas and Dodge
had heard about the fight on the Sixth, over at the Sac and
Fox agency. They rode about one hundred miles into Guthrie
to catch the train, and made Coffeyville on the Eighth. It was

fitting that they should visit the town, for they had been among the most dogged pursuers of the gang. Years later, Emmett would tell Heck Thomas that he was "the one lawman the gang really feared."[21]

Dodge set about trying to sort out who had shot whom, setting out stakes where the bodies had lain in the alley and trying to establish the events of the fight in some sort of logical way. He finally settled for a kind of town meeting, at which the citizens were told to decide among themselves who had done what. Wells Fargo and the railroad would abide the town's decision, Dodge said, and added that "we did not want to have any Voice in this adjustment what Ever."[22]

It was a wise idea. Dodge had solved the vexing problem of disappointed claimants rather neatly, and found it "surely a load off my Shoulders—No Complaints to Come to us, No Damage Suits, No Comebacks at all."[23] Dodge records that the townspeople liked the idea, and "agreed that this was a Fair and just proposition" (he was much given to capitalizing words, pretty much at random as the mood struck him).

Along the way Dodge talked to modest John Kloehr—Dodge called him Klauer—the reluctant hero. Kloehr told Dodge he was bothered by all the notoriety, afraid that "his neighbors would think he was trying to Hog it all."[24] Dodge found that the papers had lionized Kloehr, whom some of them called Jim Spears, to the extent that their news stories reported Kloehr had "[K]illed about all of them. They did not get his name right or much Else about him, and he was pretty sore."[25] Kloehr walked over the scene of the fight with Dodge, and told the detective he had killed only one man, Grat Dalton. Dodge notes: "He said that he sighted for his Head, but Undershot a little for he hit him in the Neck right on his Adam's Apple and it Broke his Neck."[26]

Kloehr's modest recital to Dodge ties in well with the quiet liveryman's reputation as a solid, self-effacing citizen. It also lends

some weight to the claim that it was lead from Isham's Winchester that downed Bob Dalton, rather than a bullet from Kloehr's
weapon.

Kloehr was the chief hero of the fight in the eyes of the press,
if not in his own retiring estimation. His fame spread far from little
Coffeyvile. A group of Chicago bankers presented Kloehr with a
gold badge, an ornate, beautifully crafted star with a diamond in its
center. On a gold ribbon at the top appeared an inscription with
which the town would surely have agreed: "The Emergency Arose,
The Man Appeared." The badge rests in the Coffeyville Defenders'
Museum today. On the back, the donors had inscribed another
suitable sentiment—"Presented by friends in Chicago, who admire
nerve and courage when displayed in defense of social order."

The *Kansas City Star* even suggested that Kloehr should
run for governor of Kansas, which pretty well summed up how
everybody felt, if you don't count what remained of the Dalton
family and what was left of the gang. Kloehr's letter of thanks to
the bankers who gave the badge clearly demonstrated the caliber
of the quiet liveryman. He accepted the badge, he said, for

> defending the best I could the interest of the city and my friends,
> and upholding the law, as I think every citizen should. . . .
>
> [W]hatever may have been the result of my work, it was not due
> to my having any more courage than many of my neighbors whose
> names have not been heralded over this great nation of ours as has
> mine.
>
> I value this magnificent emblem . . . and I shall treasure it as
> emblematic of the fact that the world likes a man who does his
> duty well.[27]

Kloehr was offered other gifts and mementos of that awful
October day. One of them, at least, came unexpectedly. Approached by a stranger, as he often was, and asked his name, Kloehr

modestly answered, "Jim Spears." Kloehr may have given that false name to other well-wishers, because both the *Kansas City Star* and the *Kansas City Times* also called him Spears in their stories of the raid (and the *Times* called him Kloche in still another story).

The stranger, as it turned out, did not ask out of idle curiosity—he was a representative of Winchester, and he knew more than he let on. Before long, the modest Kloehr received a presentation rifle from Winchester, an octagon-barrel Model 73 with beautifully finished woodwork. The weapon was engraved, perhaps tongue-in-cheek, "Jim Spears, Coffeyville, Kansas, compliments of the Winchester Repeating Arms Company."[28]

The notoriety Kloehr hated pursued him for years. In March of 1906, for example, the *Topeka Globe-Democrat* ran a preposterous article purporting to be by "John J. Kloehr," full of glaring inaccuracies, such as having Death Alley run north and south intead of east and west. Worse still, the column dripped with the sort of high-falutin' language Kloehr would never have used: "The Daltons ... in them the lust of slaughter was inborn." It was full of patently invented quotations, like this one attributed to Bob Dalton, working his Winchester in Death Alley: "Hell! There's Kloehr; I hate to do it, but he's got to fall!" The whole column was an obvious invention, cobbled together from other people's more or less accurate accounts of the raid.[29]

On October 10 Thomas and Dodge left Coffeyville to rejoin their possemen, whom they met on the twelfth. There was still much work to do—plenty of bandits remained out there in the badlands. In fact, the town still worried about reprisals by the rest of the gang, wherever they might be, and perhaps by friends and sympathizers of the Daltons. The citizens' concern was heightened on the twelfth of October, when an anonymous note arrived in town, addressed to John Kloehr. It was an alarming message, quite enough to make the townsmen reach for their Winchesters all over again.

I take the time to tell ... the citizens of Coffeyville that all of the
gang ain't dead yet by a damn sight ... and we shall come and see
you. I would have given all I ever made to have been there the 5th.
You people had no cause to take arms against the gang. The bankers
will not help the widows of the men that got killed there and you
thought you were playing hell fire when you killed three of us but
your time will soon come when you will go into the grave and pass
in your checks.... So take warning.

Yours truly,
DALTON GANG[30]

To this day, nobody knows who wrote this ugly little missive,
which was mailed in Arkansas City. Heck Thomas believed it was
sent by Bill Dalton, who by that time, as we have seen, had become
a monumental pain in the saddle for all of Coffeyville. By this
time Bill had accompanied Adeline to Independence, following
Emmett, but then had disappeared.

The writer could have been Dalton, of course, but it also
could have been almost anybody else, anybody literate, that is,
which narrows the field considerably. The letter is not, at least, the
work of an uneducated person. The writer correctly used "shall"
in the third line, instead of the colloquial "will," and took the
trouble to spell "ain't" properly, hardly what you'd expect from a
semiliterate dolt. If Bill Dalton actually sent the letter, as Heck
Thomas suspected, it might even have been written for him by
somebody who had the training and ability to write reasonable
English.

Whoever wrote the letter, it put the whole town on alert,
and all the old fears returned. The tension rose still further next
day, when the railroad agent at Wharton telegraphed Fred Dodge
to warn that a group of hoodlums had passed his station. The
agent theorized, on no evidence we know of, that the criminals

were "presumably en route to Coffeyville to wipe out the place."[31] According to Glenn Shirley's excellent *West of Hell's Fringe*, Dodge received an equally improbable tip that "forty whites and half-breeds under the command of one of the survivors of the Dalton gang" were on their way to exterminate the town, and "no mercy would be given."[32] While Dodge does not mention this tip in his own book about his Wells Fargo days, the wild story of a small army advancing on Coffeyville is just the sort of tale one would expect to appear in the wake of the bloodbath in Death Alley.

Dodge passed all this encouraging news on to the Coffeyville mayor, and the town prepared for the worst. Wires were sent up the railroad to both Kansas City and Parsons requesting more weapons, and a Katy railroad car at the depot was turned into a fort. The town was blacked out, and armed citizens mounted guard at bridges and other strategic spots. The citizens also built an enormous bonfire in the plaza, to be touched off to provide shooting light if raiders threatened the town after dark. Then people loaded their weapons and waited, tense and alert.

But nothing happened.

At least, nothing happened at Coffeyville. Instead, on October 13, a small band of bandits held up a train at Caney, Kansas, only eighteen miles west of Coffeyville on the Missouri Pacific. Nobody knows exactly how many outlaws participated, but the chances are that there were four. Three of the raiders were Bill Doolin, Bitter Creek Newcomb, and a sometimes farmer called Ol' Yantis. Yantis was still an apprentice at armed robbery. He had probably been brought into the new gang by Bitter Creek, who, it is said, had a thing for Yantis's sister. The last man was Bill Dalton.

It was the old familiar pattern—the train crew was jumped in the darkness at a small station and shots were fired into the express car until the messenger surrendered. It was apparently Bill Doolin's first raid as a gang leader and it was a financial flop. The gang got something around a hundred dollars, hardly pin money for enterprising criminals. Coffeyville again reacted in anger and anxiety. Caney was too close for comfort, and the townsmen reached for their Winchesters once more.

And again nothing happened—until, on the cold afternoon of November 1, three bandits hit the bank at Spearville, Kansas, made off with almost seventeen hundred dollars, and vanished to the south, hightailing it for the border. The leader was Bill Doolin, and Glenn Shirley suggests that the "revenge" letter sent to Coffeyville may have been sent by Doolin to draw the attention of the law in that direction. It is an eminently reasonable theory. Doolin was nobody's fool, and must have guessed at the reaction a threat to Coffeyville might produce.

At Spearville, Doolin was backed by omnipresent Bitter Creek Newcomb and the unattractive Yantis, who hailed from near Orlando, Oklahoma, north of Guthrie. The three bandits escaped a party of hunters, who poured bullets after them as they fled Spearville, but the hunt was up.

Sheriff Chalk Beeson of Dodge City, Kansas, weighed in with a posse, and the three outlaws split up. Yantis killed a farmer for his horse, and made it home to his sister's farm near Orlando. The posse found him there, led by Beeson and Tom Hueston, city marshal of Stillwater, Oklahoma. Summoned to surrender by Chalk Beeson, Yantis snatched a revolver from a shoulder holster and blazed away at the lawmen. Three of the posse fired together, bringing Yantis down mortally wounded.

It would take longer to run down Doolin.

He raised quite a gang this time, keeping on Bitter Creek and adding a memorable collection of hoodlums including, not surprisingly, the bitter and surly Bill Dalton. Also joining Doolin were excowboy Little Bill Raidler and hard-case hoodlum Red Buck Waightman (sometimes Weightman). Waightman had been released from prison in the fall of 1892; he promptly stole seven horses, and signed on with Doolin. Another recruit was Texas horsethief and cattle rustler Dan Clifton, also called "Dynamite Dick," whom one old-time marshal called "one of the meanest men I ever knew; he would steal anything from anybody."[33] Dynamite Dick fit right in.

Then there were veteran outlaw Charley Pierce, expert rifleman Roy Daugherty—known to one and all as "Arkansas Tom"—and Tulsa Jack Blake, a Kansas cowboy wanted for a couple of murders. Doolin added "Little Dick" West, a scrawny, peculiar youngster who made a fetish of sleeping in the open, rain or shine, and idolized Bill Doolin.

Altogether, the Doolin gang was a pack of very dangerous men, more dangerous, people said, than the Daltons had ever been. More good men would die before the Doolin gang was accounted for, too. Among them were three deputy marshals killed in a single fight at the outlaw town of Ingalls, Oklahoma, on the first of September, 1893. There were more robberies, much pursuit, and a great deal of shooting. And before they were exterminated, Doolin and his followers provoked a famous and extraordinary order from federal District Judge Frank Dale in Stillwater. It came after the three marshals had died at Ingalls, and the judge had had a bellyful of Doolin and his men.

"Quit trying to bring this gang in alive," said Judge Dale. "Bring them in dead!" The order seeming a mite extrajudicial, deputy marshals Madsen and Thomas made certain they had heard right—"Do you really mean that?" asked Madsen.

"I do," said His Honor, and so it was to be.[34]

Before the Doolin gang went down for keeps, there were further alarums and excursions around Coffeyville. After the Ingalls fight, there were all sorts of reports that the gang had been sighted here, there, and everywhere. As if that were not enough trouble, the town had a typhoid epidemic that fall, and the doctors made their night rounds walking down the middle of the street, lantern in one hand and cocked revolver in the other.

In early January of 1894 the *Journal* reported that the Doolin gang was skulking about the Coffeyville area, waiting for a chance to massacre the citizenry in revenge for the deaths of the Dalton boys. A similar alarm occurred toward the end of January. On both occasions the citizens turned out to defend their town—and nothing happened.

In time, the law did indeed catch up with Doolin's hoodlums. Arkansas Tom had been captured at Ingalls, trapped in the upstairs hotel room from which he had shot three lawmen. He was a long time in prison after that, which helped him become, willynilly, the longest-lived of the gang. In spite of repeated chances to go straight, Arkansas Tom finished up the way he started, killed in a 1924 shoot-out with lawmen in Joplin, Missouri.

Little Dick West, who later joined the inept Al Jennings "gang," was run down by a Heck Thomas–Bill Tilghman posse in 1898. The lawmen caught West in the early morning, on his way to groom a horse, his hands under the straps of a brush and currycomb. West tried to run and fight at the same time but failed dismally in both endeavors. While he was trying to get rid of comb and brush and draw his pistols, the possemen blew enough holes in him for Little Dick to depart this life by the shortest route.

Charley Pierce and Bitter Creek were killed in 1895— some say murdered for the bounty on their heads—by the Dunn brothers down in Oklahoma. Tulsa Jack also passed to his reward in '95, when a peace officer's slug exploded a bullet in the outlaw's cartridge belt during a fight out on the Cimarron. Red Buck Waightman, probably the most vicious killer of the bunch, died under a hail of lawmen's bullets the next year. Dynamite Dick Clifton lasted until 1897, when he took on two deputy marshals in a firefight in Oklahoma and came in last.

Little Bill Raidler was the only one of the bunch who did not die with his boots on. Already shy two fingers from a Heck Thomas rifle bullet, Raidler ran into a posse headed by Bill Tilghman in 1895, at Elgin, Kansas. At the point-blank range of ten feet, Raidler shot at Tilghman and missed—Tilghman and other officers did not. Shot six times, Raidler went first to the doctor and then to prison. After a spell behind the cold gray walls, Raidler was paroled—Tilghman helped him—but died in 1905, crippled by his wounds.

Which leaves Doolin, the leader of the pack, and bitter, vengeful Bill Dalton.

Doolin lasted until 1896. In that year, he had hidden out for a while in New Mexico, sheltered at the ranch of western writer Eugene Manlove Rhodes. In August, Doolin returned to Oklahoma to collect his long-suffering wife and their son. It was a mistake.

For on a bright moonlight night, as Doolin led his horse down a lane near his father-in-law's farm, he was challenged to surrender. The deep voice in the night belonged to the tireless Heck Thomas, out in the shadows with a posse, tipped off, ready, and waiting. Thomas, as always, gave his man a chance to surrender. Doolin, true to form, opened fire with his Winchester and then reached for his revolver. Heck's eight-gauge shotgun bellowed in the gloom, and Doolin went down for keeps. There were twenty-one buckshot holes in his scrawny body, and the Doolin gang was finished forever.

Doolin's corpse was taken into Guthrie to be embalmed and buried. The embalmer, who ran a furniture store on the side, very nearly lost his investment, as crowds of curious people trampled through his store to see the body, climbing all over his polished furniture to see over the heads of other citizens. "I could have made plenty of money," the embalmer said later, "if I had charged 25 cents admission to view the body of Bill Doolin."[35]

Even dead, Bill Doolin remained a fount of folklore. There was, for example, the widely held belief that Doolin died of tuberculosis. After his death, the story goes, a band of lawmen propped up the corpse and filled it with lead, the better to claim the reward. In view of the famous integrity of Heck Thomas, the tale is nonsense. Nevertheless, it persisted, and many years later any number of old-timers were prepared to swear it was the truth.[36]

Mason Frakes (also called William Marion) Dalton was and remains an enigma. Maybe, with his brothers, he actually was part of the celebrated California train robbery at Alila. Or perhaps not. What is sure is that after the Coffeyville raid, after he took his mother to Independence, he left the straight and narrow for good, if he had ever been on it.

He is described as a "fine-looking man," and pictures of him seem to support this description. However, one writer calls Bill "supposedly . . . the smartest of the second batch [of Adeline's children], a con artist. He was the worst of the five."[37] Judging from his belligerent speeches after the Coffeyville fight, he saw very little wrong in robbing people and nothing whatever objectionable about shooting them if they resisted.

He rode with the Doolin gang in a number of robberies, had a horse shot out from under him in the wild Ingalls battle, and gunned down an elderly storekeeper in Sacred Heart, Oklahoma, when the tough old man resisted an attempt to rob him. On his last raid, Dalton led three other men into Longview, Texas, in May of 1894. There, in a wild shoot-out, Dalton's band got away with a little over two thousand dollars in crisp bills, leaving one lawman and one bandit dead behind them.

No doubt the nice new bills gladdened Bill Dalton's heart. They would also get him killed. For when crisp currency showed up in Duncan and Ardmore up in Indian Territory, local authorities checked with Texas and found that the new money was loot from the Longview holdup. According to the Ardmore store owner who received some of the bills, they were passed by a woman and child. The woman would not talk to local lawmen, but the child said they had gotten the money from the woman's husband, and told where the man was hiding out.

And so Bill Dalton cashed in his chips, as the frontier saying went, in June of 1894, when lawmen surrounded his wife's house near Elk, Oklahoma. Dalton tried to escape, scrambling through a window and sprinting for cover, revolver clutched in his hand. He ran fast, but not fast enough to outrun the Winchester bullets that pursued him.

Summoned to halt, Dalton turned and raised his revolver, but a .44 Winchester bullet tore into his body before he could get off a shot. One writer says Bill Tilghman killed Bill Dalton.[38] In fact, the famous marshal was not in on the death this time. Deputy Marshal Loss Hart drove a slug through the outlaw's heart, and Adeline had another son to mourn. One variation on the tale, which has the cruel lawmen shooting poor old Bill in the back as he played with his daughter, is pure moonshine, a creation of the ever-inventive Emmett Dalton.

There is a strange tale that Bill Dalton appeared in the Medora country of the Dakota Badlands the following year. He came north with a trail herd, the story goes, and stayed "to rest up a bit." In time, he conspired with two other men to rob the Northern Pacific, but backed out at the last minute. Instead, he rode to a deserted line camp and killed himself.

Curiously, the story does not read like an invented tall tale. The writer, an old-time cowboy, seems convinced the man he knew was Bill Dalton, "quick as a rattlesnake and a dead shot." He describes the criminal he knew as "a small man."[39] Bill is described by contemporary newspapers as five feet, nine inches and about 170 pounds, which was certainly not "small" for the time. It's probable, then, that the Dakota cowboy knew an imposter, a would-be badman who called himself Dalton and ate his own bullet when he found he did not have the sand to hold up a real, live train.

As the chilly last days of 1892 ran out, echoes of the raid still rang faintly in Coffeyville. In December, editor Elliott reluctantly gave up Emmett's revolvers. He had been served with a writ of replevin sued out by Bill Dalton, whom the *Journal*, in obvious pique, had taken to calling "Billious," and "that exemplary candidate for heaven." The *Journal* was also involved in a nasty little feud with the *Independence Tribune*, apparently arising from the *Tribune's* allegations that Elliott had "stolen" Emmett's revolvers.

In the course of the quarrel, the *Independence Reporter*, which Elliott called the "*Tribune's* baby," editorialized that Elliott and another Coffeyville newspaperman should "have their wind shut off." That intemperate comment provoked a ferocious reply from the *Journal*, which said, among other things, "The scoundrel who undertakes the 'shutting off' job is informed that the very same Winchester that spoke so effectually on the 5th of October is within easy reach."[40] Strong words. But the feud apparently petered out with time, even though the *Journal* took the occasional potshot at Bill Dalton into the spring of the next year.

In January Bob's and Grat's personal possessions were auctioned off by John Callahan, the county sheriff. There was little to put on the block besides Grat's horse, just the gear the bandits rode and carried when they rode into town, horse furniture, weapons, a couple of gold watches, and Grat's diamond ring. Curiously, the sale inventory shows only two Colt revolvers belonging to Bob. The Bulldog is omitted from the list.

One of Bob's handguns went for thirty-one dollars, and his Winchester brought sixty more. Grat's rifle was worth only twenty-eight dollars to Doctor Hall. John Kloehr bid for and got a couple of useful souvenirs of the fight. Kloehr bought Grat's horse for ninety dollars, and got Bob's saddle for $23.50. That doesn't sound much like the "fancy Mexican saddle" of folklore, and for good reason. The saddle is a fairly ordinary western rig, without silver plates or tassels or carving. It sits quietly in the Coffeyville museum today.

The leather of Bob's saddle is tooled a little and it carries a couple of hearts made out in silver-colored studs, but nothing more. Kloehr may have bought both horse and saddle for his livery business; if so, it may be that both relics of wild outlawry appropriately finished their days in mundane service to mankind.

Altogether, the Dalton boys' possessions netted $294.25, which was at least enough to pay off some longstanding debts. Barndollar Brothers finally got its 1890 bill paid off, and the few other creditors were satisfied out of what remained.

Emmett gave away what possessions he had. According to a story in the *Star and Kansan* of Independence, Kansas, his pistols, recovered from Captain Elliott, went to F. J. Fritch, Emmett's lawyer. His Winchester he gave to Sheriff Callahan, who had done his duty in preserving Emmett's life in the angry days following the raid. Emmett directed that his horse be sold, in at least partial payment of his medical bill. His "scarf pin" he sent to Adeline, languishing in Kingfisher.

Emmett Dalton recovered from his wounds, surprising nearly everybody. After a preliminary hearing in November, he appeared before the judge again just before Christmas. Two men carried him into court in a chair fixed to a pair of poles. Since he pronounced himself unready to plead and was without a lawyer, *State v. Dalton*, number 7287, was continued. The *Journal* clucked worriedly, "It is rumored that he will plead not guilty and will use every quibble of law to prevent conviction."[41]

On January 16, a hearing was held in Emmett's case, and this time attorney Fritch was there to move—hopelessly—to quash the complaints filed against his notorious client. The state called four witnesses, enough to establish a prima facie case, and Fritch declined to cross-examine, presumably choosing not to reveal whatever meagre defense he might have had. Emmett would remain in jail, said the court, and it set a March seventh trial date.

The March trial, held in Independence, played to a packed house, including many Coffeyville citizens who drove up to relive that ugly October morning. On the first day of trial, Emmett, still on crutches, did not disappoint them. He pleaded "not guilty" to murder, consistent with his story from the beginning, that Bob had killed both Cubine and Baldwin and that Emmett had shot nobody during the raid.

But the next day, Emmett suddenly entered a plea of guilty to second-degree murder of George Cubine. According to the *Star and Kansan*, "strong influences were brought to bear on Emmett to induce him to plead guilty." Apparently his brother Ben was one of those "strong influences." Emmett at first offered to plead guilty to manslaughter, but quickly learned that the court would not accept a plea to such a relatively minor offense. Emmett's lawyer, according to Emmett at least, told him that he was "reasonably certain I would get close to the minimum sentence, perhaps ten to fifteen years."

As it turned out, "reasonably certain" was not nearly good enough. Emmett was sentenced to spend the rest of his life in prison, surprising nobody very much but Emmett, who apparently thought he had reached a better bargain with the state. Most accounts say Emmett got life, and that is what the official judgment says, although the prosecutor, Judge J. R. Charlton, afterward remembered the sentence as twenty-five years.[42]

The *Coffeyville Journal* reported the results of Emmett's trial on March 10, saying Emmett "cried like a baby" when he heard the sentence: "He claimed that the sentence was unjust, that he was not guilty of murder and had only pleaded guilty to save his friends the expense of fighting the case."[43] Afterward Emmett claimed that his lawyer had told him he had made a "bargain" with the judge, but there is no proof whatever of any agreement between the court and the defense.

And so Emmett was shipped off to prison at Lansing, Kansas. Callahan lost no time in loading Emmett on the Missouri Pacific with a substantial escort, and Emmett rattled off north to prison "as fast as steam could carry him."

One writer says that Emmett was and remained under sentence of death, because the Kansas law of the day had an odd provision that permitted the death penalty for murder, but prohibited execution of the sentence until both a year elapsed and the governor ordered the execution carried out. That might well be, if a prisoner was indeed sentenced to death, but Emmett was not.

And so the years went by, and Emmett continued to serve his sentence. He spent a long time in prison, where he learned rudimentary tailoring and rose to run the shop where new convicts were literally "fitted with stripes." He was not a disciplinary problem, and in 1907 was granted an extraordinary four-month parole to have his old wounds treated.

In Topeka for treatment, Emmett talked freely about his outlaw days, perhaps in a calculated effort to pave the way for permanent release. Although he steadfastly denied that he had killed anybody during the raid, he otherwise spoke only of his present contrition and reformed attitude. His message was pretty much the same no matter to whom he talked, like this comment to a Kansas historian who met him in a Topeka restaurant while he was out of prison for medical treatment:

I was guilty because I was with the crowd that planned the crime and murdered the citizens. I was with the gang because I loved my brother Bob.... I might have gotten away, I think, but I could not bear the thought of leaving him there weltering in his blood.... I guess it was a good thing that I was shot and sent to prison, for I have learned a lesson, and that is that crime does not pay.[44]

Emmett's message may or may not have come from the heart—he was always glib where his own welfare was concerned. Though he certainly had more than enough time to ponder on the evil consequences of following the owlhoot trail, he also had time to perfect his contrition speech. In any case, he apparently said what the Kansas governor wanted to hear, for not long after his sojourn in Topeka that august official granted Emmett an unconditional pardon. No doubt the fact that Emmett returned on his own from his medical treatment helped convince the state that he had learned his lesson.

A curious document also may have played some role in Emmett's release. This writing purported to be a letter written by Emmett before the raid, and was addressed to Adeline. In it, he tried to enlist her help in stopping the attack on Coffeyville. Newspaper accounts said the letter helped move the governor to issue Emmett's pardon, and perhaps it did. Headed "Ind. Ter,. October 1, 1892," the letter was printed in the *Oklahoma City Times* of April 17, 1908.

Dear Mother. Get somebody to see Bob at once. He has planned to rob two banks in _____ on the 5th. Am with him now, but he will not listen to me. If he pulls off this job, I will have to go with him. Grat is in it too, and I won't let them think I am a quitter, so will go with them, unless somebody talks them out of it. It's going to be close to where we used to live. If Will is in Kingfisher, send him. He knows where we are. Yours, E.[45]

The *Times* went on to say that Adeline sent Bill Dalton—then "practicing law in Kingfisher"—galloping madly off to find his brothers and save the day. Bill, as the story goes, of course arrived too late. The same newspaper story said Adeline confided in U.S. Deputy Marshal William Grimes, who "dispatched couriers" to what he thought was the Daltons' camp, also without success.

Grimes, incidentally, seems to have been a bit of a blowhard, who was later fired for taking undeserved credit for Dalton-chasing. One may doubt that Grimes sent "couriers" posting after the Daltons, even if he said he did. Any legitimate lawman would have led a posse after the gang.

The whole incident of the letter to mama has a certain odor about it. There was plenty of time to produce the letter for Emmett's trial, but it did not appear. It is also hard to imagine a letter getting from the gang's last hideout to Adeline's rural Kingfisher home in time for anybody to react, especially if the note had really been written on October 1.

Moreover, neither Adeline nor Bill Dalton, he of the big mouth, mentioned anything about the letter during their stay in Coffeyville. Finally, and most damning, if Bill Dalton spurred over hill and dale to head off his brothers, how could he possibly find out that his siblings had come to grief, return to Kingfisher, collect Adeline, and get back to Coffeyville just two days after the raid? Whether the letter was contrived or not, Emmett was out of prison.

The governor's clemency was not popular in Coffeyville. One tale, that the "citizens of Coffeyville presented a petition to the governor for his pardon," is plainly in error.[46] There was no reason anybody in Coffeyville would feel very friendly toward Emmett, let alone work to get him out of prison; not that soon, anyway. The memories of that terrible day fifteen years before must still have been fresh in the hearts of the friends and relatives of the dead defenders. Indeed, in 1903 the History of Montgomery County had reported tersely that "no governor has yet dared to brave the indignation of the friends of the victims of the raid by granting [parole]."[47]

Whether Coffeyville's people liked it or not, Emmett breathed free air again, and this time he stayed out of jail. He married Julia Johnson, described in dozens of accounts as his "childhood sweetheart," who, legend says, faithfully waited for him to complete his sentence. They tied the knot in Bartlesville, Oklahoma, on September 1, 1908. Emmett wrote afterward that Julia was his "inspiration" while he did time, and that she had patiently waited for him for fifteen years.[48]

Emmett and Julia were married, all right, but it is far from certain that they were sweet on each other as kids. Julia figures prominently in Emmett's *When the Daltons Rode* but does not appear in *Beyond the Law*, his first book. And Julia was surely not the virginal, faithful childhood love Emmett's book made her out to be. By the time they were wed, Julia could call herself Julia Johnson Gilstrap Lewis, for she had a colorful history.

In *When the Daltons Rode*, Emmett describes how he fell for Julia in the spring of 1887, the pretty story in which he rode his pony past a country church and heard organ music of the sort the angels must play. Investigating, he discovered Julia, sweet sixteen, seated at the organ making the world a brighter place. It's a fine story, especially if you ignore the evidence of Julia's granddaughter that Julia couldn't play a lick on any instrument.[49]

There's a lot more about Julia in Emmett's second book, all kinds of romantic tales about her riding through the night to warn Emmett about an approaching party of lawmen. That tale makes exciting reading, but it's hard to square with Emmett's later assertions that Julia knew nothing of his dastardly occupation until he was shot up at Coffeyville.

And then there's the story of "Their Last Meeting," which Emmett places very shortly before the Coffeyville raid. How he left her side at the Johnson home, near Vinita, and got to Tulsa in time to ride north is unexplained. Even harder to explain is how Emmett could visit Julia at her parents' home when both her mother and father had been dead for over a year. Love found a way, apparently.

Later on, Emmett's step-granddaughter said flatly that Emmett and Julia were never sweethearts at the time of the raid.

Instead, they met after Emmett was released from prison. Julia would never, the granddaughter said, have married somebody else had she been "so sweet on Emmett."[50]

Anyhow, Julia had been married at least twice before, the first time to one Bob Gilstrap, said to have been a half-blood Cherokee. That was in 1887, and two years later, on Christmas Eve, Gilstrap got himself killed in a shoot-out with a man called Leno. After Gilstrap was killed, Julia was alone—with her daughter Jennie Gilstrap—until the fall of 1902.

In that year, instead of waiting patiently for Emmett to finish his term, she married one Ernest (or Earnest) Lewis. Julia doesn't seem to have had much judgment in men. Ernest turned out to be that same "Killer" Lewis who rode with the storied lady bandit Tom King (who may have been fabulous Flo Quick, too).

Lewis spent some time in prison along the way, then ended up in Bartlesville, where he ran what was genteelly and euphemistically called a beer parlor. Killer lasted until November of 1907 when he took on the law in his own saloon and the law won. In one version Lewis died of the bullets of a lawdog with the engaging handle of Pussyfoot Johnson. In another, Lewis opened up on one peace officer without warning, killing him. A second officer, named Keeler, turned out to be tougher and faster than Lewis was. Whoever plugged Lewis, Julia was a widow again.

Julia may even have been married—or been semipermanently attached—a third time before she wed Emmett. There is a persistent story that she wed an Indian named Whiteturkey somewhere along the way. A pioneer neighbor of Julia's, north of Tulsa, indeed refers to her as "Julia Gilstrap-Whiteturkey, who later married Ernest Lewis and is now Mrs. Emmett Dalton."[51]

Julia was apparently a woman of some spirit—"feisty," folks would have called her in those days. She reportedly took umbrage over a newspaper story about Lewis, written after his death. Where other widows might have succumbed to the vapors or written a peevish letter to the paper, Julia was moved to pursue the editor through the streets with a horsewhip. Feisty indeed.[52]

After Emmett got out of the pen and he and Julia married, they lived for a time in Bartlesville. One writer says Emmett later lived in Tulsa for a while, where he was a "special officer" appointed to "handle the hardest of the hardcases."[53] The couple moved to California in about 1918. For a while Emmett was part of the burgeoning movie industry. He and former Coffeyville photographer John Tackett produced a potboiler about the outlaw days called, predictably, *Beyond the Law*. Emmett even starred in the film, which turned out to be a nonstarter. After that, Emmett dabbled in the construction business, apparently with more success.

On one occasion, Emmett even entertained thoughts of re-entering the United States marshal service. Heck Thomas's daughter wrote that Emmett once called on her father in Lawton, soliciting the old lawman's support. Predictably, Heck refused. He was so opposed to Emmett's putting on a badge that he went a step further, putting his opposition in a letter to the marshal in Muskogee. There would be no federal star for Emmett.[54]

Emmett visited Coffeyville in 1931, long after the citizens' bitter animosity had died away to a dull ache. Julia came with him, and Emmett at last had a headstone carved and set up for Bob, Grat, and the friendless Powers. The pipe to which they had tethered their horses all those years before, used as a grave marker when the three were buried, was also left in place at the head of the graves. It is still there.

Emmett was sixty when he came to visit, and mellow with the years. He spent some time with a *Kansas City Star* reporter, walking over the scene of the fight. The result was some truly fulsome prose, the most modest of which was purported to be a quote from outlaw Henry Starr, who called Emmett "the nerviest, gamest, loyalest long rider of the whole wild bunch."[55]

The story introduced Julia with a drippy quote from *Evangeline*, all about "ye who believe in the beauty and strength of woman's devotion," and a rehash of the tale about faithful Julia waiting for her man. Also included was a reprise of the sad farewell. Emmett told the reporter he remembered "how pretty she looked.... I sat with my rifle across my knees while she played a tune or two on the organ."[56]

Best of all, Emmett delivered himself of a paean of praise for the Condon contingent of bandits, a contribution to the misinforming of an entire generation. "In all my life I have never known an exhibition of chilled steel nerve such as Grat Dalton, Powers and Broadwell gave there, waiting, watching the minute hand of the big clock on the wall creep slowly around, counting the seconds, while the town armed itself and began bombarding the bank."[57] This in spite of the fact that dull-witted Grat and his henchmen could *not* have watched the "big clock on the wall," or they would have known Ball was lying to them.

Emmett and the reporter also went out to Elmwood Cemetery, where they visited the last resting place of Frank Dalton and walked over to the graves of Bob, Grat, and Powers. There Emmett offered one his familiar speeches on the hard lessons of the raid and a life of wrongdoing. "I challenge the world to produce the history of an outlaw who ever got anything out of it except *that* [pointing to the graves], or else huddled in a prison cell.... [T]he biggest fool on earth is the one who thinks that he can beat the law, that crime can be made to pay. It never paid and never will, and that's the one big lesson of the Coffeyville raid."[58] Or something like that. Anyhow, that's what the paper said he said back in 1931, and it sure made good copy and highly edifying reading.

Emmett apparently made this speech every time he got somebody to listen to it. In late April, 1931, probably on the same trip, he pontificated for the *Dallas Times-Herald*, which called him a "prominent Hollywood realtor," and duly reported his pious remarks. "In our ignorance we thought we were justified in our outlawry. I know now we were fools."[59] Emmett was not, however, so sanctimonious that he missed a chance to excuse the brothers' criminal career. They had begun following the owlhoot trail, he said, because of "a crooked deal in a faro game," the hoary old excuse for the Santa Rosa holdup.

After the Coffeyville visit, Emmett and Julia went back to California. In the autumn of 1935, they entertained a visitor in the little bungalow on Prince Street in Hollywood. Their caller was none other than Charley Gump, the Coffeyville drayman, who still carried the scar he had got from Bob's Winchester slug all those years before. This time the meeting was all peace and pleasant conversation. As the *Los Angeles Evening Herald* reported, Gump stayed to partake of "the tasty roast prepared by Mrs. Dalton, who has been married to the 'grandest man in the world' for the past twenty-seven years."[60] Gump, full of tasty roast and mellow with years, opined for the press that he didn't really think Bob meant to kill him, but just to "disable me by shooting me through the hand," a mighty charitable and unlikely conclusion. He also told the reporters that Emmett "is now one of our best citizens," before he departed into the sunset.[61]

In later years Emmett began to decline. He had at least one stroke, and his health failed him badly. As some sort of compensation, he seems to have found religion at the last, even if it was religion of a peculiar sort. He was baptized in the tabernacle of Aimee Semple McPherson in the summer of 1936.

Toward the end Emmett was a "shaking shrunken wreck," a shadow of the husky bandit of so many long years before. And on July 13, 1937, Emmett was dead. He died with his boots off, in, of all places, Hollywood. His body was cremated, and the remains were probably buried in the family plot at Kingfisher, though there are a couple of stories that he was buried with his brothers in Coffeyville.

The Kingfisher burial apparently took place in darkness, for the family wanted no resurgence of the old publicity.[62] Emmett's sister Leona—an honest and much respected lady—seems to have handled arrangements for the clandestine burial. One story says she and Alva Mauck, a Kingfisher undertaker, planted what was left of Emmett with an ordinary posthole digger.[63] There is a stone to Emmett's memory in the family plot today.

Julia lived on until 1943. She died in Fresno, California, at seventy-three, and was buried in the family plot in Dewey, Oklahoma. She apparently had married again, this time a man named Johnson, who survived her.

It is somehow fitting that Emmett died in Hollywood, which would later successfully distort the story of Coffeyville out of all resemblance to what really happened. Broderick Crawford, Brian Donlevy, and Randolph Scott started it all back in 1940, with *When the Daltons Rode*. The Daltons rode again five years later (sure enough, *The Daltons Ride Again*), with Lon Chaney, Jr., and Milburn Stone (Doc, in "Gunsmoke"), who deserved better.

In 1975 Richard Widmark starred in *The Last Day*, and television chipped in in 1979 with Jack Palance and Dale Robertson, in a thoroughly forgettable drama called "Last Ride of the Dalton Gang." Meanwhile—in 1957—Hollywood had produced a dreadful turkey called *The Dalton Girls*, about which the less said, the better.

I remember the early movies. Those were the days of two features (the main film and the "B" movie), a newsreel, a cartoon, a serial and previews, all for fifteen cents. As a kid, I loved the films about the noble outlaw, but I sure didn't learn much about history. Somehow, one always left the theatre sympathizing with the robbers, who usually had been driven to a life of crime.

Maybe that's the trouble with too much fantasy. You lose track of what's important. You forget that the Daltons and the hoodlums like them contributed nothing to the building of America. You have to grow up before you realize these United States were born of ordinary, hardworking, law-abiding people, the sort of men who fought and died at Coffeyville because they didn't like criminals pushing them around.

God rest them. They built a wonderful nation.

8

THE SIXTH MAN, AND OTHER MYTHOLOGY

RIVERS OF INK have been lavished on the question of "the sixth man," the whole perplexing notion that there were not five Dalton raiders, but six. There are those who are convinced that Bob Dalton did indeed take along a sixth gunman, who for some reason was late for the party. Some writers have critically examined the evidence on the question. Others have concluded, without particular investigation, that there was a sixth man, as did one scholarly researcher who simply repeated a line from a contemporary news story: "It is supposed the sixth man was too well known to risk coming into the heart of the town."[1]

For these "sixth man" theorists, the question then becomes who the mystery bandit might have been. Lots of people have been nominated for the honor, including Emmett Dalton's future wife, the storied Julia Johnson.[2] Other writers have concluded, on sound evidence, that only five men rode into Coffeyville that sweet October morning.

As we have seen, Captain Elliott's newspaper story of the holdup says that two separate sets of Coffeyville citizens—the Hollingsworths and the Seldomridges—saw six riders entering town before the raid. And Elliott himself, writing two days after the

raid, probably reflected contemporary Coffeyville opinion when
he wrote matter-of-factly,

> It is pretty well settled that there were six men in the gang when
> they entered town. It is supposed that the sixth one was too well
> known to risk coming into the heart of the city, and that he kept off
> some distance and watched the horses. . . . It is presumed that one
> of the parties either backed out as they were about to enter town
> or else diverged his course into a cross street and made a circuit
> through the south west portion of the city in order to reach the
> plaza from the south and aid in stampeding the citizens from that
> point in case of attack.[3]

First impressions are often most accurate, so Elliott's early
story is worth considering. It has become fashionable to decry the
existence of the sixth man as pure romantic myth, but I'm not so
sure.

The reference to six bandits did not appear in Elliott's little
book, published later, but no reason was given for leaving out any
reference to an extra rider. The omission is tantalizing, and because
it was unexplained it added further mystery to the question of the
sixth man. Otherwise, nobody in town ever reported seeing more
than five bandits, with one exception. This was Tom Babb, one
of the Condon Bank staff, who much later told a reporter he had
seen a sixth bandit escape.

There is no confirmation of Babb's statement, but neither
was there any reason for this solid citizen to invent a mythical
rider. Perhaps Babb saw a rider galloping away from the plaza and
simply assumed the man belonged to the Dalton gang. Or perhaps
he *did* see the sixth man.

Just possibly he saw Bitter Creek Newcomb, for one story
has Bitter Creek entering town from the south to provide fire
support for the main bandit force. If Bitter Creek was with the

band, and he did enter Coffeyville that way, he would have been clearly visible from the windows of the Condon Bank, looking south across the plaza. And that was where Tom Babb was, before and during the raid. However, as we'll see, that is not where Babb says he saw the mysterious sixth rider.

One very knowledgeable writer suggests that Babb's memory might have been "clouded by time."[4] And this may indeed be the explanation, since the interview in which Babb mentioned the sixth man took place when he was seventy-eight, fifty-eight years after the raid. Still, Babb was then president of the Fredonia Bank, not normally the sort of position stockholders award to senile people.

The biggest obstacle to accepting Babb's story of the sixth man is the inherent improbability of the rest of Babb's story. For Babb says he left the bank, sprinting *through the cross fire between Isham's and the alley*, in time to run the length of Ninth Street to Maple, turn back north, and see the sixth bandit galloping madly west out of the alley until he turned south and disappeared a block west of Maple. "He was lying down flat on his saddle, and that horse of his was going as fast as he could go."[5]

Then, Babb says, he witnessed the destruction of the gang in the alley from what amounted to point-blank range, and was "right next to" John Kloehr when the liveryman cut down two of the bandits. He says he and others watched Carey Seaman aim at Emmett Dalton—and hesitate. Recognizing Emmett, Babb and the others shouted at the barber to shoot, but Seaman coolly held his fire until he was sure his target was one of the raiders.

It could have happened that way. Babb was no doubt young and eager and full of adrenaline. And, as he said all those years later, "I could run pretty fast in those days." Still, it's hard to imagine him dashing through the barrage from Isham's, then running a block and a half in time to see the sixth man escape, with time left to move still further east, all quickly enough to get close to

John Kloehr before the firing ended. And if anybody saw Babb's astonishing dash, nobody thought enough about it to mention it.

More likely his memories expanded with the years, perhaps from the natural desire to be more a part of a great event than he actually was. We'll never know. At the least, however, Babb's statement adds some weight to the possibility that perhaps there was a sixth bandit. As we'll see, there are a few other bits of evidence that point in the same direction.

On the other hand, supporting the "five riders" theory is the conclusion of a Coffeyville posse which, sniffing the country to the south of town, came upon the camp from which the gang had staged their raid. Members of the posse said there were "only five places where horses had fed."

Nearly everybody has a theory. One of the most popular is the belief that Bill Doolin was included in the raid—in spite of Emmett's assertion that Bob dispensed with the "reckless" Doolin's services before the gang left Oklahoma. One of the most positive of the Doolin theorists was Fred Sutton, a frontiersman who embellished his account of the raid with extensive, entertaining, and probably fanciful dialog among members of the gang. Sutton's tale went like this.

Doolin, says Sutton, was included in the plans for Coffeyville, but his horse went lame the night before the attack. "The band rode on," says Sutton, leaving Doolin to steal a horse and follow.[6] Sutton says Doolin told him the details years later, as the outlaw languished in the Guthrie jail. Pushing his stolen horse—a "thoroughbred," of course—hard toward Coffeyville, Doolin met a single horseman riding flat out away from the town. The horseman halted next to Doolin and spoke in high excitement: "Have you met any bandits down this road?" Doolin cleverly said he hadn't, and the man went on.

They came this way. The Dalton gang rode into town this morning, three went into one bank, two into another, got twenty thousand from one and eleven thousand dollars from the other, and when they come out it looked like the whole town had rallied against them. It was a battle! The Daltons killed four, and four of them were killed. One was shot full of lead and they've got him in jail. They say some escaped and they're making up a posse. They sent me down this road to warn everybody.

Doolin said he answered innocently, thus: "Holy smoke! I'll just wheel around right here and go on ahead of you down this road and carry the news. Mine is a faster horse than yours."[7]

Thereafter, writes Sutton, Doolin galloped like Paul Revere, pretending to give the alarm and eluding capture thereby. Sutton ends with this absurdity. "And he galloped on, never stopping until he reached a friendly camp west of Tulsa."

If that ain't a heap of horsefeathers, as polite westerners used to say. That would have had to be some horse, thoroughbred or not. The distance from Coffeyville to "west of Tulsa" could not have been less than a hundred miles, some of it very tough going. It would tax Pegasus to run all that way; the "never stopping" part is just plain moonshine.

It is, however, persistent moonshine, repeated over and over again. Richard S. Graves, in a curious little book called *Oklahoma Outlaws*, recites the tale under the stirring heading "Bill Doolin's Wild Ride." Doolin's pony, Graves wrote, went lame, and the outlaw went far off course to get a horse on which he could depend. "It was planned," said Graves, "to have three men enter each bank."[8]

Arriving at the rendezvous point, however, Doolin found the rest of the gang already gone. The tale gallops on—"Doolin rode slowly in the direction of Coffeyville, but something seemed to hold him back."[9] Then follows the episode of the excited citizen, riding hard to raise the countryside against the invaders. Realizing his danger, Doolin turned back, and here Graves rose to really admirable flights of fancy, which one may call the "flying wraith" account. "Doolin started on a ride that has ever since been the admiration of horsemen in the Southwest. . . . Doolin stopped only to give the horse breathing spells and crossed the Territory like a flying wraith, flitting by ranch and farm in the night like a ghostly rider saddled upon the wind."[10]

Disregarding the hyperbole, there is another reason to take Graves's narrative with more than a grain of salt. The book was produced as part of the hype for a "photo-drama" called "The Passing of the Oklahoma Outlaws," narrated by Bill Tilghman. The little book was hawked at theatres where the drama was shown. *Oklahoma Outlaws* also contains, as sober fact, the marvelous fairytale of the "Rose of Cimarron," the Ingalls girl who performed prodigious feats to arm and rescue her lover—none other than Bitter Creek Newcomb—during a wild battle with lawmen in the fall of 1893. So much for *Oklahoma Outlaws*.

Marshal Nix, in his later days, also adopted the wonderfully poetic phrase about the "flying wraith . . . a ghostly rider saddled upon the wind!" He had Doolin riding up to Coffeyville with the rest of the gang, and not only that, but "Doolin rode beside young Bob, serving as a sort of first lieutenant and offering such suggestions and warnings as an older man could give to daring and rash youth."[11]

Nix wrote that Doolin's horse "wrenched a foot," during the night before the raid. Doolin dropped back during the morning ride to catch a new mount, saying "I'll not be more'n fifteen or twenty minutes behind you boys." In Nix's account the rest of the gang waited briefly for Doolin, and then rode on into town without him.

Still another tale has Doolin turning his lame horse away the night before the raid, to obtain a new mount from "the house of a friend far off the road to Coffeyville."[12] Bill was late getting to the rendezvous, so the raid went on without him. The horse Doolin got from his friend was of course a thoroughbred, on which he fled south when the raid went sour. This writer also rhapsodizes about Doolin's mighty ride to safety, a monumental trip during which the outlaw and his tireless steed "crossed the territory like a flash, flitting by ranches and farms in the night like a ghostly rider saddled upon the wind."[13] Wonderfully evocative words, those, but it sure seems we've heard them before somewhere.

For whatever it's worth, Doolin himself said he was the sixth rider. He made the statement to several lawmen—including Bill Tilghman—at Guthrie after his capture in 1896. He confirmed that he had met a rider streaking out of Coffeyville with news of the robbery, waited until the man had ridden on, then hit the road for safety. Resting himself and his horse twice, he reached a safe haven down in Hell's Fringe, the no-man's-land along the border between the Indian and Oklahoma territories.[14]

The theory that Doolin was the sixth man has also been repeated elsewhere, even in one of Glenn Shirley's earlier books, although that excellent historian discarded the legend in his later writing. Setting aside the nonsense of a steady hundred-mile gallop, however, it is still possible that Doolin *was* the "sixth man."

To make this assumption, you have to disregard Emmett's account of the raid—but then, Emmett is wrong about lots of other things. And Emmett may have had a very good reason for denying that Doolin rode up to Coffeyville with his brothers. The wounded Dalton told his story first just after the raid, when he was in custody, and might have lied to shield any gang member who had gotten clear of Coffeyville. After Doolin's death, one may theorize, Emmett simply stuck to his original story.

Even if you are not eager to believe Doolin, Wells Fargo agent Fred Dodge's book also lends some support to the theory that Doolin was the sixth man. If Dodge's informant was correct, and if Dodge accurately remembered what the informant told him, Doolin was with the party as it began to travel north. And if the part about Dengue fever is also correct, it could account for Doolin's absence from the fight in Coffeyville.

Dodge had no reason to invent an informant, nor had he reason to create from whole cloth the information about Doolin. Illness, rather than a lame horse, would be a more compelling reason for Doolin to fall behind. Horses were plentiful around Coffeyville; stealing a decent pony surely would not have taken long. Had Bob Dalton decided six men were necessary to crack the two banks, he would presumably have waited a few minutes while one of his best fighting men got another mount.

On the other hand, Heck Thomas did not mention the Dodge informant's story of Bill Doolin and the fever attack. Instead, Thomas said, "We located their hide-out on October 3, got full information that *five* men still composed the gang" (emphasis mine).[15]

It's a little hard to believe that Dodge did not tell Thomas about Doolin's presence with the gang, if that is what the informant actually said to Dodge. While Dodge might have promised his informant anonymity, he is unlikely to have promised not to pass his information on to other lawmen. Since possemen chasing the Daltons rode always in harm's way, it would be natural to tell your partner that the odds had changed a bit, that you were probably following six outlaws rather than five.

Still, it is possible that Doolin was part of the gang, that he was not disabled by fever, that he did have a lame horse, and that Bob thought Doolin could catch another animal and overtake his comrades more quickly than he did. If Doolin's horse went lame close to Coffeyville, at least this would account for the fact that the citizens who first met the gang saw six bandits, and later witnesses spotted only five. This was author Harry Drago's thesis. "Bill Doolin's horse had gone lame and he had turned back to put his rope on a goodlooking sorrel gelding he had noticed grazing in a pasture beside the road. He exchanged mounts and was racing back to catch up with Bob and the others when he encountered an excited horseman."[16]

But if switching horses was as simple as all that, surely the rest of the gang would have waited for their sixth gun before entering the banks. And if Doolin "raced" to catch up, he would certainly have arrived in town, at latest, while the fighting was still on. He would have reached downtown Coffeyville at least in time to try to help his comrades fight their way out of that terrible alley.

In no case would Doolin still have been on the road, far enough away from Coffeyville not to hear the firing. If he was the sixth rider that the Seldomridges and Hollingsworths saw not far from town, he fell out of the band close enough to Coffeyville to hear the gunfire when it began—and ended. He could not have been so far from the banks that he had to learn of the debacle from a hard-riding messenger, a horseman who had already had time to learn all the details of the fight including how many dollars were stolen, and to saddle up and ride clear out of Coffeyville.

If Doolin was along on the raid, he was left out of the fight for some reason more complicated and time-consuming than a lame horse. Something more delayed him than roping a sorrel "in a pasture beside the road." Assuming he was there, the most logical assumption is that Dodge's informant was right—Doolin was ill with fever, and dropped out just outside the city.

While Doolin is the leading candidate for the dubious honor of being the sixth man, he is not without competitors. One is our old partner Bitter Creek Newcomb, whom Colonel Hanes nominates as sixth man, albeit on no apparent evidence. As the tale is related in *Bill Doolin, Outlaw O.T.*, Newcomb was to enter the First National along with Bob and Emmett. For some reason unexplained, the story goes, Bob later ordered Bitter Creek to ride into Coffeyville from the south. In case of trouble, he would then be able "to support the gang from a different quarter."[17]

Hanes then says that Bitter Creek was late getting into town, for "some difficulty he encountered and never fully explained." He limbered up his Winchester and fired a few rounds in support of his beleaguered comrades, but once he saw the game was up for the rest of the gang, Bitter Creek sensibly rode hard for the south. In Hanes's book Newcomb's horse, Old Ben, is the hero of the epic ride to Ingalls, although Hanes does not say Old Ben galloped all the way.

This tale is substantially harder to swallow than accepting Doolin as the sixth man. There is no apparent reason for Bob suddenly to order Bitter Creek to do something other than what he had originally been assigned to do. Moreover, if Newcomb could be spared from the First National, he would have been far better employed holding horses or providing a base of fire for the rest of the gang in case of trouble. It would be easy to discard the Newcomb theory entirely, were it not for the statement by Condon employee Tom Babb, which does place a sixth bandit in the area south of the bank.

As with Doolin, there is no reason for Emmett not to have mentioned Bitter Creek's presence at Coffeyville, at least not in his books. Perhaps he would have protected Newcomb when he talked to the law just after the Coffeyville fight. Later, however, there was no need to protect Bitter Creek, then long passed to his reward. However inflated and misleading some of Emmett's statements in his books might be, he would gain nothing by omitting mention of a sixth man, except consistency with his statement to the law and the press just after the raid.

Another contemporary candidate for sixth man, and the earliest, was one Allie—or Ally, or Aly—Ogee. He was named in early newspaper accounts of the raid as the escaped bandit. Other papers announced that Ogee was wounded and that a posse was chasing him. One even stated solemnly that Ogee had been killed and his body recovered. Indeed, during the days just after the raid, the press abounded with stories of "six bandits" and the escaped Ogee. He even appeared as the sixth man in a Coffeyville paper called the *News-Broad-Ax*, which should have known better.

So persistent were the reports of Ogee's involvement that he felt moved to announce publicly that he was both innocent and breathing normally. He wrote to the Coffeyville *Journal* shortly after the raid to say that he was not only alive but alive in Wichita, where he had been at work in Dold's Packing House at the time of the raid. People who knew Ogee also wrote letters to the paper, confirming his innocence.

According to a newspaper report two days after the raid, Emmett flatly denied that there had been more than five bandits. Somebody apparently asked him whether the mysterious Allie Ogee had been part of the gang. Emmett is quoted as answering, "Five were all there were of us. I have not seen Allie Ogee for two years."[18]

But there are logical reasons to be a little dubious of Emmett's tale. First off, Emmett was either vague or just plain wrong about a lot of things. Second, and more important, it is logical that he would cover for an escaped comrade in the days just after the raid. He would be especially likely to do so if the sixth man were Bill Doolin, sick with dengue fever and perhaps holed up somewhere close to Coffeyville and unable to run.

A case can also be made for brother Bill Dalton as the sixth rider. Remember the tale of the "stop-us-before-we-sin" letter Emmett is supposed to have written to Adeline. Suppose for a moment that the letter was *not* an invention dreamed up in later years to get Emmett out of durance vile. If Bill Dalton did ride to intercept the gang, and did arrive in time, he might well have agreed to go along on the raid. And if Babb's story is correct, and Bill ran out on his brothers, Emmett would surely deny his presence, out of family pride.

Bill did not, after all, have any great scruple about stealing from other people, and he is said to have had an almost pathological hatred of banks and bankers. Unfortunately, except for the mysterious letter, there's not a bit of evidence to support the theory that he was also in on the raid. But it's a tempting explanation of the sixth man controversy.

One other piece of evidence weighs heavily against any theory about both Doolin and Bill Dalton as the sixth bandit. Manhunter Chris Madsen, many years later, told author Frank Latta this story; if it's true, neither Doolin nor Bill Dalton could have been anywhere close to Coffeyville at the time of the raid.[19]

Madsen was in Guthrie when the Coffeyville fight broke out. Shortly after Madsen learned of the fight by telegraph, Bill Dalton called on him to ask whether the telegram was genuine. Madsen said it was and Dalton, apparently unconcerned, asked Madsen to wire the Coffeyville mayor to ask whether he and Adeline would be welcome to visit the wounded Emmett. Madsen sent the wire, and Coffeyville responded that Bill and Adeline could see Emmett if they wired ahead.

There was more. "As I learned later," said Madsen, Dalton and another "lookout" were waiting outside Guthrie with remounts for the outlaws fleeing from Coffeyville. With Bill and his companion, Madsen said, was none other than Bill Doolin. Perhaps Chris Madsen no longer remembered clearly when he made this statement. Perhaps he embroidered the truth. But if he didn't, the fabulous sixth rider was some other man. Or maybe, as some writers have suggested, it was a woman.

Some of the women attached to western outlaws were simply girlfriends and wives who carried messages and provided information, food, and more intimate comforts to their fugitive lovers. Some were no more than groupies, like "Little Britches" and "Cowboy Annie," who hung out with the Doolin gang and got a vacation in the federal reformatory for their pains. Many were wonderfully faithful, through terrible hardships and privations and long separations. Bill Doolin's wife was one of these, a loyal woman who loved deeply indeed, if not very wisely.

There were surely female outlaws sprinkled through western history, too. The much-Hollywooded Belle Starr is probably the best-known example, although Belle, "the bandit queen," didn't much resemble the movies' dashing beauty who rode and fought like a man. Reasonably comely in her youth, Belle—Myra Maybelle was her given name—developed into a less than ravishing woman who wasn't much of a bandit, let alone a queen. Though she was hardly the "female Jesse James" the movies made her out to be, she was a convicted horsethief, at least. Over the years she consorted with all manner of frontier hard-cases, and in fact married three of them.

Others, however, were a more serious proposition. One of these was the redoubtable Florence Quick, a remarkable woman who rose to be, as Glenn Shirley called her, "the most elusive horse thief operating in Oklahoma during the period [the 1890s]."[20] Flo was a product of Johnson County, Missouri, a bright girl who got bored with school, ran off with a wastrel called Mundis, and thereafter drifted from man to man, stealing horses all the while.

A reporter for the *Wichita Daily Eagle* waxed eloquent over Florence: "[I]f she was a man she would be a fine type of cavalier. She is an elegant rider, very daring. She has a fine suit of hair as black as a raven's wing and eyes like sloes that would tempt a Knight of St. John.... [H]er figure is faultless."[21]

While "hair black as a raven's wing" and "eyes like sloes" may have been hyperbole, we are left with the impression that Flo was a looker by the standards of the day. It is therefore no wonder that a couple of Flo's jailbreaks were made possible by her carefully displayed physical charms. In one case, in fact, the jailer went with her: "an elopement," the newspaper noted, "and not an escape."

Flo ended up unofficially attached to one Killer Lewis, later husband to Julia Johnson, who in turn later became Mrs. Emmett Dalton. Flo and Killer cavorted about Guthrie in 1892, the year of the Coffeyville raid. When not making whoopee in Guthrie, Lewis was a thoroughly unpleasant hombre who robbed and shot people for a living. Flo broke Lewis out of jail at least once, and accompanied him on a variety of more or less successful criminal adventures. One of them is worth repeating. If nothing else, the tale gives some of the flavor of the fin de siècle frontier.

Lewis and Flo decided to rob a train. They chose to attack the Santa Fe, between Red Rock and Wharton. For some reason they enlisted the dubious aid of one Manvel, a virtual moron, who equipped himself with dynamite, assorted pistols, a rifle, and a Knights of Pythias sword. He then hid himself and all this hardware in a closet on the train. At the appointed spot on the line, he sprang from the closet, clanking with weapons, and forced the conductor to halt the train.

So far, so good. But as Manvel herded the conductor off the train, he got all tangled up with his own monstrous sword and fell in a heap. Before Manvel could rise, the conductor whopped him with his own rifle and some helpful passengers piled on and trussed up the bewildered desperado with the train's bell cord. Lewis and Flo, waiting nearby, wisely departed for safer climes and the railroad, for once, emerged unscathed and victorious.

Manvel was carted off to an Illinois asylum, and in time the law caught up with Lewis. He did some penitentiary time, then took up running a saloon in Bartlesville, Oklahoma. There, as we've seen, he caught terminal lead poisoning at the hands of the law. Flo, who began to call herself Tom King, went merrily on with her criminal career, lifting the likely pony, doing a little occasional whoring, escaping from jail three or more times.

Heck Thomas had jailed her on at least two of those occasions, and had no illusions about keeping her behind bars. Flo was frank about her carnal agility. Once when Thomas and Chris Madsen were carting her off to jail in a wagon, Flo asked: "What's the name of the jailer where you're taking me?"

In his broad Danish accent, Madsen answered "Vy do you vant to know?"

"Because," said Flo, "every jailer in Oklahoma has his price. If I know which one this is, I'll know his."[22]

After an 1894 arrest, she was again released. One account says she was released on bail and promptly made herself scarce prior to trial. Another says she won her freedom because she was obviously pregnant. Or perhaps she was allowed bail because nobody wanted her to deliver while languishing in the calabozo.

Chris Madsen said Flo/Tom was "a heavy drinker and a dope fiend. It was the dope that killed her.... [S]he caused me more trouble than all the other women I ever had anything to do with." He arrested Flo several times, and on just one of those occasions Madsen had enough of Flo to last a healthy man a whole lifetime. It happened when he took her to Oklahoma City for trial, a wagon trip that took an entire afternoon. "She cursed and swore at me and called me all the vile and obscene names in existence.... [S]he didn't stop more than ten minutes all the way. When we got there she was so hoarse she couldn't talk."[23]

Flo (or Eugenia Moore) was a real person, even if she wasn't the sixth man. She was small and attractive, and she could be a real charmer, so maybe she *was* a sweetheart of Bob Dalton, or perhaps she was only a friend. They had their picture taken together in 1889 in Vinita, then in Indian Territory, unless you accept another theory that the picture wasn't Eugenia at all but really Emmett's future wife, Julia. More of this anon.

"Eyewitness" and some other sources say Flo died early of cancer, before the Coffeyville raid, a tragedy that hardened Bob's heart and inspired him to further evil deeds.[24] As we've seen, Emmett has the news reaching Bob just before the gang rides north to Kansas. The word comes in a letter from Silver City, and Bob responds by throwing Flo's picture into the campfire, or simply tearing it up, muttering dramatically, "Now I will make them understand that 'Hell on earth' is a reality"[25]—whoever he meant by "them."

Preece calls Flo Quick "Bob Dalton's Bandit Bride," and repeats all the marvelous stories of her intelligence work for the gang. He says Flo called herself Daisy Bryant. Homer Croy, who also concludes that Flo really was the formidable Tom King, says she later got out of the bandit business, married and "settled down to a humdrum life."[26] Still another tale has Flo "forming her own gang" after the Coffeyville disaster, and quickly coming to grief: "Before long, Flo joined Bob in death. This boldest of the West's lady outlaws went out, like Bob, boots down and sixgun smoking."[27]

Flo—or Tom King—was quite a character, and the West was a little less wild when she finished her earthly race. Just where this happened, like so much about Flo, is not clear. We've heard the one about her starting her own gang and going out in a blaze of gunfire. A different tale has her killed at Wichita in 1893, in the wake of a holdup gone sour.[28] Still another version of her end was related by Heck Thomas, who said she was shot in the course of a holdup near Tombstone, Arizona.[29]

A Texas writer named Mark Pannill has concocted an intricate theory to account for the sixth rider. To add spice to the abiding mystery, in his analysis Doolin, or Bitter Creek Newcomb, or Allie Ogee, or whoever, has been transmogrified into none other than Julia Johnson, the woman who married Emmett in 1908 after his release from prison.[30]

Just how Pannill reaches this conclusion remains something of a mystery even after you read his little pamphlet. Pannill claims that Eugenia Moore was really Flo Quick, but not, somewhat confusingly, the real-life Flo, alias Tom King. And then he says that Emmett called the lady Quick because he wanted to hide the fact that his wife of later years—Julia—rode along on the raid.

The assertion does not stand up even to cursory examination, although it gets high marks for ingenuity. It centers around the well-known Vinita photograph of Bob Dalton, reproduced here. He is seated, hatless, and a woman stands beside him, her hands on his shoulder. Various theories identify her as Eugenia Moore, one calls her Daisy Bryant, and still others hypothesize that the woman in the photo is Flo Quick, alias the redoubtable Tom King.

Pannill says the photograph is of Julia Johnson, and he may be correct. He apparently had some photo analysis done, which confirmed that the woman's facial characteristics more closely resemble Julia than Flo. There has also been a suggestion that the woman in the photo might be Julia's sister, Lucy, who closely resembled her. After his reasonable hypothesis about the identity of the woman in the picture, however, Pannill goes into an involved analysis to explain why Emmett would have accepted the woman in the picture as Flo Quick, when in fact she was his own wife. And here the fabric of his theory really comes unraveled.

For Pannill embarks on an unlikely tale about Emmett— up in Lansing Prison—probably meeting a prisoner named Quick while he was confined. He then draws a lengthy comparison between the two men to prove that Emmett invented an outlaw woman based in part on the physical dimensions of Quick. Bear with us here, for Pannill's weird theory gets ever more convoluted and fanciful.

The theory involves, among other things, adding Quick's and Emmett's ages and dividing by two to get Eugenia Moore's age in 1893. The same process—this time averaging the two men's heights—produces the height of Eugenia Moore. Pannill even "averages" the colors of the two men's hair to establish Eugenia's. And so on. The whole theory and its fantastic "proof" are profoundly unconvincing. The only good thing you can say about either theory or proof is that they are certainly fun to read.

There are also some other nominees for sixth man, though none of them seems to be a serious contender. One of them was the younger brother of John Sontag of the Evans-Sontag gang in California. Another is a mysterious outlaw called Buckskin Ike, rumored to have ridden with the Daltons in earlier days. And then there is George (or maybe Caleb) Padgett, a yarn spinner of the "I bin everwhar" persuasion. According to Padgett, he was running whiskey in the Cherokee Nation in 1891 and joined up with the Daltons. He was the appointed horse holder in Coffeyville, he says, and fled for his life when the raid began to come apart.[31]

And in 1951 a Sullivan, Indiana man, Clint Riggs, wrote to the *Coffeyville Journal* with what he said was a statement from one Caleb Padgett, who had died in 1938. Padgett's family, said Riggs, knew of his involvement in the raid, and had asked Riggs not to reveal it until enough years had passed for the information no longer to embarrass them. Riggs wrote that Padgett had fled from Coffeyville as Tom Babb said the sixth bandit had done.[32] It is, of course, just possible that Padgett was the man Babb saw, if Padgett was there at all. It seems to me that both Doolin and Bitter Creek and even Bill Dalton are better candidates, but we'll never know.

In his famous newspaper story on the raid, Elliott did refer to the four local citizens who said they had seen six riders entering town. Elliott did not elaborate, however, and may have doubted the accuracy of their observation at the time. It is a fair assumption that Elliott, a prominent Coffeyville citizen, was at least acquainted with the Seldomridge and Hollingsworth families. Elliott never mentions more than five bandits in his little book about the raid, even though he describes the sighting of the gang by members of both families in his newspaper article. Careful journalist that he was, it is probable that Elliott spoke to both families in the interim and got their stories firsthand. It may well be that both the Seldomridges and Hollingsworths later told Elliott they might have been mistaken.

It is also logical that even a reasonable possibility there was a sixth bandit would have been mentioned in Elliott's narrative. As we have seen, Coffeyville spent many uneasy days after the shoot-out. The citizens remained armed, watchful, and ready for an attack by the remains of the Dalton gang or their sympathizers. Not only that, but the raid had been an epochal event in the small town. Every detail of the fight would have been hashed and rehashed by the townspeople and the press—yet after the first few days there is no further mention whatever in the Coffeyville press of "the one that got away."

I am therefore inclined to believe that the sixth man may never have existed. And yet, and yet—what about the evidence of Tom Babb? What of the unrefuted statements of four sturdy, stone-cold-sober citizens, who flatly said there were six men riding into Coffeyville that bracing autumn morning, and Dodge's story of what his informant told him about Doolin's attack of fever.

And there is one more tantalizing tidbit. In 1973, an interview was taped with Violet Brown Koehler, an elderly woman who had been a small child at the time of the raid. Talking of the end of the raid, she said, "Finally they got on their horses ... those that were left. Several of 'em of course, were killed there, as well as several of the town's people. And they got on their horses and left."[33] Sadly, the interviewer did not follow up on this fascinating statement, and now the chance is gone forever.

The other longstanding mystery of the raid is the persistent theory that the citizens had been warned of the gang's approach, or at least told that the city's banks might be targeted by the Daltons. The tale crops up again and again in stories about the Dalton gang and in accounts by old-timers who lived in Indian Territory at the time of the raid.[34] Even O. Henry perpetuated the tale in "Holding Up a Train." It has also been roundly condemned as pure invention, but it will not go away.

The rumor that the town had been warned, if rumor it was, was abroad as early as the Friday after the raid, for Elliott angrily attacked it in his long article in that day's paper. "The story that the citizens were anticipating a visit from the Dalton gang is simply a canard of the worst kind, and is a reflection upon the courage and promptness to act on the part of our people. They had no idea of receiving a visit from the Daltons at the time."[35]

On the face of it, the theory that the town was forewarned is nonsense. There is no question that nobody was armed in Coffeyville that Wednesday morning, not even Connelly, the city marshal. Still, one source of the warning story seems to have been none other than Deputy Marshal Chris Madsen, manhunter extraordinary, and it is hard to discount entirely anything said by such a solid man.

For what it may be worth, here is the tale of the warning. Its main source is Frank Latta's *Dalton Gang Days*, which relates a story told to Latta by George A. Yoes back in 1942. Yoes repeated his account in an interview with Latta two years later. At the time of the Coffeyville raid, Yoes was a deputy marshal, the son of Jacob Yoes, then United States Marshal in Fort Smith. Here is what he said: "I am the only man living who knows just how they got put out of business. I have never before told anyone about it, but here is the story."[36]

George Yoes told Latta that an outlaw, jailed at Fort Smith at the time of the raid, warned him and his father that the Daltons would hit two banks, either in Coffeyville or in Van Buren, Arkansas. The Yoes responded by arming the Van Buren merchants and passing warnings to the banks at Coffeyville.

Harold Preece, a prolific writer on the Dalton gang, asserted that "a minor lone rider, an acquaintance of Bob's, had tipped off the marshals at Guthrie, and they'd notified the town authorities."[37] Preece does not indicate whence this information came. And, in a 1960 magazine article, Preece said the law was "tipped off through still another informer who'd listened to Emmett."[38] Perhaps Preece's informant was the inmate of the Fort Smith jail to whom Yoes referred; perhaps not. Maybe there never was such an informant at all. Presumably the account came to Preece from somewhere, and was not invented. Thus, while Preece's assertion does not prove that the town was warned, it does imply that there may be a grain of truth somewhere in the tale.

If Yoes's story were the only source on the warning, it might be chalked up to the maunderings of an old man with a balky memory. None other than Chris Madsen, however, confirmed the story in a letter written to Latta after Yoes gave his own account. As Madsen reported it, Marshal Jacob Yoes gave notice to the marshal at Guthrie, Oklahoma, that either Coffeyville or Van Buren was the gang's next target. Madsen did not say whether anybody tipped off the banks, but said that he "notified the deputies near the Oklahoma and Kansas borders to be prepared to take the field at once if ordered by wire. As some of the deputies were too talkative, I did not let them know what information we had from Mr. Yoes. . . . [W]e kept our office open day and night, waiting for news."[39]

An old-time Indian Territory marshal—C. B. Rhodes—also wrote, much later, that Marshal Yoes had been tipped off about a raid. But Rhodes said Yoes was told only that "outlaws," unnamed, intended to hit the Van Buren bank. Yoes reacted, and "secretly bought twelve Winchesters and placed them in the hands of the men he knew to be the bravest citizens in Van Buren. . . . It was said that bank robberies and other crimes on the Coffeyville and Indian Territory lines were pulled off instead."[40] Significantly, Rhodes's narrative says absolutely nothing about a warning to Coffeyville, and Rhodes said he got his information from George Yoes himself.

Another source says that "Dodge and Thomas" learned from an informant that the Daltons were going to hit "the Santa Fe again, or perhaps a bank in one of the northeastern towns, Muskogee or Vinita, or maybe across the Kansas line at Coffeyville." The tipster also knew that if Coffeyville were the target, the bandits intended to strike both banks. According to this tale, Dodge then placed his posse near the Santa Fe tracks, where it could respond to an emergency on the line or in any of the three towns. The same writer then goes into considerable detail about preparations in Coffeyville. There was, he says, "a meeting of town officials," and "a plan . . . whereby the two banks could be defended by volunteers at a few minutes' notice." Moreover, says the same narrative, "Arrangements were made to store weapons at the Isham Brothers & Mansour Hardware next door to the First National."[41]

This rather ignores the fact that hardware stores, then and later, carried firearms as part of their stock. No special "arrangements" were necessary. The source of this tale probably invented at least some of it, for the atmosphere in Coffeyville and the behavior of its citizens show pretty clearly that the town expected October 5 to be a routine, peaceful day like other days.

In his own account, Fred Dodge wrote only that he and Heck Thomas reasoned that the gang "had been unlucky on the Railroads and might try a Bank." Accordingly, Dodge sent a messenger to find a telegraph on the railroad. Because the posse was then about equidistant from Vinita, Muskogee, and Coffeyville, he told the messenger to warn the Wells Fargo offices in all three towns. Reliable Heck Thomas did not mention the warnings, although presumably he would have known about them if they were given. And, assuming that a messenger was indeed sent to give the alarm, there is no evidence that he ever did so. Cox, the Pacific Express man in Coffeyville, was part of the fight against the Daltons. It is logical that his Wells Fargo counterpart would have warned him of coming trouble, but there is nothing to show that Cox, apparently unarmed on the day of the raid, had any forewarning of the attack.

Remember the legend that Bob had visited Coffeyville just before the raid looking for whiskey, and that his visit "got back to the marshals through somebody or other." The sequel to that fable is that Marshal Yoes "shipped some rifles" to Coffeyville and the town otherwise got itself prepared. That is why, the story goes, Emmett Dalton thought "it looked like everybody in Coffeyville was carrying a gun."[42] One writer told the story this way: "[R]umors swept Coffeyville to the effect that the Daltons were coming to rob the banks. All but a frightened few of the town's citizens were getting set for the kill, making preparations to manhandle the West's worst desperados."[43] The same source even repeats threats and boasts, supposedly made by various of the town's citizens, about shooting up the gang.

I don't think so. As we know, nobody in Coffeyville ever mentioned expecting anything more exciting than a pleasant autumn day of business as usual, much less a bandit raid. Whatever news Yoes may have gotten from his stoolpigeon, whatever wires he and Madsen may have sent, whatever news Dodge's man may or may not have dispatched, it seems pretty clear that nobody in Coffeyville was warned that the town might be the target of the most notorious outlaws then in the badlands to the south.

Most significantly, nobody in Coffeyville was armed when the raiders struck. So much, therefore, for the idea that the citizens were expecting trouble of this most unpleasant and lethal variety. Even Marshal Connelly was without so much as a revolver. Had there been the slightest warning of an outlaw raid, however remote the chance, it is inconceivable that Connelly would have been out in the street unarmed. Not a soul had a weapon handy except George Cubine, who apparently had a rifle in his uncle's shop only by happenstance.

It is theoretically possible that Connelly received some news of the possibility of a Dalton raid and simply discounted it. That notion, however, is inconsistent with what we know of Connelly. He was a good officer, a conscientious man, and a solid citizen of Coffeyville. It is also inconsistent with the times, for the

Dalton gang had struck repeatedly up and down the railroads, and nobody knew where they might appear again.

Professor Lue Barndollar of Coffeyville, in her excellent little book *What Really Happened On October 5, 1892*, discounts the whole idea of forewarning as a fable. She astutely appraises Yoes's account, and is probably right about the whole episode of the warning: "I tend to be suspicious when a person says he or she is the only person living who knows some particular information."[44] So do I. Nevertheless, it is hard to discount entirely the same tale told both by Yoes—a good officer, by all accounts—and by the formidable Chris Madsen. There is, however, a theory by which the Yoes story can be accepted as true, and which at the same time accounts for the hiatus of fifty-two years in telling the story publicly. And this is it, simple and straightforward:

Maybe there actually was some warning from an informant somewhere, but the alert was never passed on to the people who needed to hear it. Let us assume that Jacob Yoes did wire Guthrie, as Madsen says he did. Let us also assume that Yoes's son George helped arm the Van Buren merchants but only *thought* that somebody had warned the Coffeyville banks. He could logically make that false assumption, particularly if he knew his father had telegraphed the Guthrie marshal's office.

Madsen, for his part, agrees that news of the impending holdup did reach Guthrie, and that office alerted deputies along the border to stand by for action. Madsen may have assumed, as the younger Yoes did, that Fort Smith had notified the endangered banks. That precaution would have seemed elementary to an experienced lawman—so elementary that he might have made the fatal mistake of assuming that Yoes had passed on his warning to the towns in the eye of the storm.

The failing, then, might lie in the marshal's office in Guthrie. "Lord, another Dalton scare," some minion might have said, "We'll alert the deputies. Surely Fort Smith has told the banks." And if something that simple happened at Guthrie, and the message got lost, delayed, or misplaced as a result, would anybody have been eager to talk about the failure after all the killing in Coffeyville? However dedicated employees in the marshal's office might have been, it is mostly unlikely that anybody would stand up and say, "Well, we should have warned the banks, or Fort Smith should have. I guess between us we got four good citizens killed."

Probably the story of the warning is pure myth after all, as Professor Barndollar and most other writers conclude. I am not quite willing to write the tale off entirely, as long as there is some tenable explanation of why nobody came forward with the story for over half a century. And I think there is such a possible reason, as set out above: nobody, no matter how honest, would want to admit to having failed to save men from dying.

And nobody will ever know for sure.

AFTERWORD

And that is the tale of the Coffeyville raid. Along the way I may very well have quoted the wrong people, drawn the wrong conclusions, and chosen the wrong accounts of the raid on which to rely. It's easy to take a false trail when you write about the bad old outlaw days, for tall tales are many and the truth is forever elusive.

The best advice I can give readers is to doubt everything about the Dalton mythology . . . and to enjoy it all. All of the tales are entertaining, even the silliness about succulent girl outlaws and nonstop hundred-mile gallops. It is all the stuff of the American legend, and it is rousing stuff indeed.

I have not tried to send any messages, unless you count my intention to portray the Dalton gang as the unromantic hoodlums they really were. J. B. Kloehr, grandson of the reluctant hero of the raid, put it as well as anybody can: "I think they were just desperate, ruthless . . . no good. You can't go out and kill people like they did and commit as many crimes as they did and be held up in any respect as a hero. . . . I don't think there's any way you can ever glorify that."[1]

One thing is certain about the story of the Coffeyville fight. When you read about the citizen defenders of the town, you read about the very best of America. They were the kind of people whose descendants went on to tame a continent, destroy an assortment of tyrants, find a cure for polio, bring down an Evil Empire, transplant hearts, and put a man on the moon.

Moral lessons are best reserved for Sunday sermons, so I'll try not to preach too obviously in these last few lines. But there is one plain and useful lesson to be drawn from the Coffeyville fight: ordinary people, even without a leader or a plan, can act together to protect what's good, if they are tough enough and brave enough. The citizens of Coffeyville were.

Some will say that sort of self-sufficiency and courage were virtues of the last century, of unsophisticated mid-America, of the frontier; people today don't want to "get involved." But I'm not so sure. I'm not sure neighborhoods and residential streets and small towns are not capable of the same bright spirit today.

From the impressions I've gained of the people of present-day Coffeyville, I'm inclined to believe they would do today exactly what their forefathers did more than a century ago. I think they would band together again; I think they'd fight to protect their town from hoodlums bent on terrorizing it.

Would we?

NOTES

PREFACE

1. *Daily Oklahoman*, April 23, 1939.
2. *Coffeyville Journal*, October 2, 1991.
3. *Coffeyville Journal*, commemorative edition (a reprint of the Oct. 5, 1892 front page plus other information on the raid and the town).

CHAPTER ONE

1. Albert D. Richardson, *Some Portions of His Narrative Concerning Kansas* [pages are unnumbered].
2. Bruce Catton, *This Hallowed Ground*, 4–5.
3. Richardson, *Some Portions of His Narrative*.
4. WPA Writers' Project, *Kansas: A Guide to the Sunflower State*, 193.
5. *Ford County Globe*, January 21, 1879. Quoted in Nyle H. Miller and Joseph W. Snell, *Great Gunfighters of the Kansas Cowtowns*, 12.
6. *Coffeyville Journal*, historical edition, March 1893.
7. Ibid.
8. Ibid.
9. Frank Eaton, *Pistol Pete*, 29.
10. Margaret Whittemore, *Historic Kansas*, 106–108.
11. Lew W. Duncan, *History of Montgomery County*, 129.
12. Ibid.

CHAPTER TWO

1. C. B. Rhodes ms., ch. 51, Rhodes Collection.

2. Homer Croy, *He Hanged Them High*, 10.

3. Harry Drago, *Road Agents and Train Robbers*, 227.

4. Croy, *He Hanged Them High*, 5.

5. WPA Writers' Project, *Indian-Pioneer Papers*, interview with Ellis Hammett, September 2, 1937.

6. Glenn Shirley, *Belle Starr and Her Times*, 69–70.

7. Glenn Shirley, *Law West of Fort Smith*, 105.

8. Glenn Shirley, *Six-Gun and Silver Star*, 21.

9. See generally, R. L. Wilson, *Winchester: An American Legend*.

10. Charles T. Haven and Frank A. Belden, *A History of the Colt Revolver, 1836 to 1940*, 145 ff.; James E. Serven, *Colt Firearms 1836–1954*, 228–29.

11. Haven and Belden, *A History of the Colt Revolver*, 150; Serven, *Colt Firearms*, 229. And see George Markham, *Guns of the Wild West*, 66.

12. See generally, Eugene Cunningham, *Triggernometry*, 414 ff.

CHAPTER THREE

1. *Kansas City Star*, May 10, 1931.

2. Emmett Dalton, *Beyond the Law*, 127. Hereafter cited without author's name.

3. Ibid., 128.

4. Ibid.

5. Shirley, *Six-Gun and Silver Star*, 44, Emmett's confession.

6. Leon Claire Metz, *The Shooters*, 65.

7. *Indian-Pioneer Papers*, interview of Minnie Uto, n.d.

8. *Coffeyville Journal*, commemorative edition, "Bandits Not First of Family Buried Here." David Stewart Elliott, *Last Raid of the Daltons*, foreword.

9. *Indian-Pioneer Papers*, interview with Rhoda Morris, February 23, 1938.

10. Evan G. Barnard, *A Rider of the Cherokee Strip*, 198.

11. *Indian Pioneer Papers*, Morris interview.

12. *Indian-Pioneer Papers*, interview with Bob Payne, March 18, 1938.

13. *Indian-Pioneer Papers*, Uto interview.

14. *Indian-Pioneer Papers*, interview with Susan Morrison, February 14, 1938.

15. Duncan, *History of Montgomery County*, 70.

16. Nancy Clemens, *American Bandits*, 47.

17. Glenn Shirley, *Heck Thomas, Frontier Marshal*, 95–97.

18. J. A. Newsom, *Life and Practice of the Wild & Modern Indian*.

19. Harold Preece, *The Dalton Gang*, 16, 41.

20. *Coffeyville Journal*, August 16, 1888.

21. Preece, *The Dalton Gang*, 56.

22. Metz, *The Shooters*, 68.

23. *Indian-Pioneer Papers*, interview with Ninnian Tannehill, April 22, 1938.

24. Glenn Shirley, *West of Hell's Fringe*, 43.

25. *Indian-Pioneer Papers*, Payne interview.

26. St. Louis *Daily Globe-Democrat*, October 16, 1892.

27. *Indian-Pioneer Papers*, interview with Orrington "Red" Lucas, May 20, 1937.

28. Nancy Samuelson, *The Dalton Gang Story: Lawmen to Outlaws*, 56.

29. Ibid.

30. *Indian Pioneer-Papers*, Lucas interview.

31. Ibid.

32. Harold Preece, "Bob Dalton's Bandit Bride."

33. Shirley, *West of Hell's Fringe*, 40.

34. *Indian Pioneer Papers*, interview with Frank M. Carr, September 10, 1937.

35. *Indian-Pioneer Papers*, interview with Orrington "Red" Lucas, December 29, 1937.

36. *Indian-Pioneer Papers*, Carr interview.

37. Preece, *The Dalton Gang*, 16.

38. Samuelson, *The Dalton Gang Story*, 100.

39. *Indian-Pioneer Papers*, interview with Jim Williams, August 20, 1937.

40. Glenn Shirley, *Gunfight at Ingalls*, 33. *Indian-Pioneer Papers*, Williams interview.

41. On Charley Bryant, see Preece, *The Dalton Gang*, 104; Richard Patterson, *The Train Robbery Era*, 152; and Shirley, *West of Hell's Fringe*, 42.

42. *Indian-Pioneer Papers*, Williams interview.

43. Thomas A. McNeal, *When Kansas Was Young*, 272.

44. Thomas Beer, *The Mauve Decade*, 68.

45. Preece, *The Dalton Gang*, 68 ff.

46. *Beyond the Law*, 30; and Emmett Dalton, *When the Daltons Rode*, 67 (hereafter cited without author's name).

47. *Beyond the Law*, 91.

48. Ibid., 31 ff. See also *When the Daltons Rode*.

49. *Beyond the Law*, 32.

50. Patterson, *Train Robbery*, 150–151.

51. Burton Rascoe, introducing *The Dalton Brothers, by an Eyewitness* (hereafter cited under "Eyewitness"), 24.

52. Shirley, *West of Hell's Fringe*, 48. Preece, *The Dalton Gang*, 113. Evett Dumas Nix, *Oklahombres, Particularly Some of the Wilder Ones*, 38.

53. Preece, *The Dalton Gang*, 118.

54. Harold Preece, "Adeline Dalton, Outlaw Mother."

55. Patterson, *Train Robbery*, 151.

56. Nix, *Oklahombres*, 40–41. Patterson, *Train Robbery*, 152.

57. Preece, *The Dalton Gang*, 134.

58. Ibid., 155.

59. Paul I. Wellman, *A Dynasty of Western Outlaws*, 168.

60. Shirley, *West of Hell's Fringe*, 70, and note 8 to chap. 5.

61. *Indian-Pioneer Papers*, interview with Charles Ferchau, August 27, 1937.

62. *When the Daltons Rode*, 147.

63. Shirley, *West of Hell's Fringe*, 78.

64. Nix, *Oklahombres*, 39.

65. Preece, *The Dalton Gang*, 168.

66. Harold Preece, "The Real Emmett Dalton."

67. Samuelson, *The Dalton Gang Story: Lawmen to Outlaws*, 153–54.

68. Preece, *The Dalton Gang*, 180.

69. Shirley, *Heck Thomas*, 162.

70. Preece, *The Dalton Gang*, 180 ff.

71. *Indian-Pioneer Papers*, interview with Herbert W. Hicks, March 30, 1937.

72. Shirley, *West of Hell's Fringe*, 84; Preece, *The Dalton Gang*, 191–92.

73. *Indian-Pioneer Papers*, interview with H. E. Ridenhour, April 14, 1937.

74. *Indian-Pioneer Papers*, Ridenhour interview; interview with Mrs. U.S. Dixon, January 18, 1938.

75. *Indian-Pioneer Papers*, Dixon interview.

76. *Beyond the Law*, 121.

77. Harry Drago, *Outlaws on Horseback*, 219. Drago says the same thing in *Road Agents and Train Robbers*, 217, without the "cowardly."

78. "Eyewitness," *The Dalton Brothers*, 158; Arthur H. Lamb, *Tragedies of the Osage Hills*, 34.

79. Nix, *Oklahombres*, 44.

80. Shirley, *Six-Gun and Silver Star*, 43–44, Emmett Dalton's "confession" to Deputy Marshal Ransom Payne.

81. *Beyond the Law*, 137.

82. Preece, "The Real Emmett Dalton."

83. Bailey Hanes, *Bill Doolin, Outlaw O.T.*, xiii.

84. Fred Dodge, *Under Cover for Wells Fargo*, 122.

85. Shirley, *Heck Thomas*, 164.

86. McNeal, *When Kansas Was Young*, 273.

87. Shirley, *Six-Gun and Silver Star*, 44.

88. "Eyewitness," *The Dalton Brothers*, 172.

89. Ibid., 173.

90. Preece, *The Dalton Gang*, 207–208.

91. "Eyewitness," *The Dalton Brothers*, 175. The *Kansas City Times* of October 6, 1892 used virtually the same language, leading one to suspect that "Eyewitness" might have been that paper's correspondent.

92. *Coffeyville Journal*, centennial edition, September 30, 1992, reminiscences of Ida Gibbs-Jones, forty years after.

93. Shirley, *Six-Gun And Silver Star*, 44.

94. *When the Daltons Rode*, 232.

95. Shirley, *West of Hell's Fringe*, 94.

96. *When the Daltons Rode*, 218.

97. Ibid., 158.

98. Ibid., 221.

99. *Beyond the Law*, 129.

100. *When the Daltons Rode*, at 222.

101. Frank Latta, *Dalton Gang Days*.

102. *Beyond the Law*, 130 ff.

103. *Indian-Pioneer Papers*, Carr interview.

104. *Indian-Pioneer Papers*, interview with Claude Timmons, June 28, 1937.

105. Dodge, *Under Cover for Wells Fargo*, 127.

106. Shirley, *Heck Thomas*, 167.

107. Ibid., 168.

108. Bailey Hanes, "Bloodbath at Coffeyville," *Westerner*, January–February 1972.

109. Latta, *Dalton Gang Days*, 208. *When the Daltons Rode*, 236.

110. *Wichita Morning News*, October 10, 1952; reprinted in the *Coffeyville Journal*, September 30, 1992.

111. *Beyond the Law*, 139.

112. Latta, *Dalton Gang Days*, repeated in the *Coffeyville Journal*, October 1–2, 1993.

CHAPTER FOUR

1. C. B. Rhodes ms., ch. 57, Rhodes Collection.

2. Coffeyville at 100, *A History of Coffeyville*, 24.

3. Elliott, *Last Raid of the Daltons*, 58.

4. Ibid., 57; *Coffeyville Journal*, commemorative edition.

5. Drago, *Road Agents and Train Robbers*, at 219.

6. Clemens, *American Bandits*, 49.

7.   Nix, *Oklahombres*, 48. Paul Wellman calls these protuberances "bearskin-covered saddlebags"; the long coats, says Wellman, were to cover the bandits' six-guns (*A Dynasty of Western Outlaws*, 174–75). Clemens, *American Bandits*, 49.

8.   *When the Daltons Rode*, 237.

9.   McNeal, *When Kansas Was Young*, 273.

10.   Latta, *Dalton Gang Days*, 210.

11.   *Beyond the Law*, 141–42; *When the Daltons Rode*, 240. Gump is also mentioned as giving the alarm in David Dary, *True Tales of Old-Time Kansas*. One can guess that Emmett is the authority for Dary's statement.

12.   Latta, *Dalton Gang Days*, 221–22.

13.   A Cubine family story, given to the author courtesy of Jackie Isham Barrett, Coffeyville.

14.   Elliott, *Last Raid of the Daltons*, 30.

15.   Latta, *Dalton Gang Days*, 213.

16.   *When the Daltons Rode*, 243.

17.   Elliott, *Last Raid of the Daltons*, 31.

18.   *Coffeyville Journal*, commemorative edition.

19.   Ibid.

20.   Drago, *Road Agents and Train Robbers*, 220.

CHAPTER FIVE

1.   *Beyond the Law*, 143–44.

2.   Duncan, *History of Montgomery County*, 26.

3.   *Kansas City Star*, May 10, 1931.

4.   Ida Gibbs-Jones, in the *Journal* centennial edition.

5.   Harry Drago incorrectly says it was a pistol, *Outlaws on Horseback*, 226–27.

6.   Wellman, *Dynasty of American Outlaws*, 182.

7.   *Beyond the Law*, 145.

8.   Harry Drago, *Outlaws on Horseback*, 226–27.

9.   Wellman, *Dynasty of American Outlaws*, 181.

10.   The Defenders' Museum, Coffeyville, tells the story and displays the spanner, a picture of Dietz, and the roll of paper, complete with hole.

11.   Elliott, *Last Raid of the Daltons*, 31.

12.   *When the Daltons Rode*, 247.

13.   Wellman, *Dynasty of American Outlaws*, 180.

14.   *Coffeyville Journal*, commemorative edition.

15.   Thomas Beer, *The Mauve Decade*, 67–68.

16.   Clemens, *American Bandits*, 49.

17. *Coffeyville Journal*, commemorative edition.
18. *Kansas City Star*, May 10, 1931.
19. Metz, *The Shooters*, 73.
20. Ida Gibbs-Jones, in the *Journal* centennial edition.
21. Jay R. Nash, *Bloodletters and Badmen*, 148. Ed Bartholomew, *Biographical Album of Western Gunfighters*, ("Ayres, the fifth citizen to die").
22. Wellman, *Dynasty of American Outlaws*, 182.
23. Drago, *Outlaws on Horseback*, 226–27.
24. Nash, *Bloodletters and Badmen*, 149. This book is a mine of misinformation, apparently written to thrill rather than to inform. It also has McKenna owning a stable, turns Kloehr's rifle into a shotgun, has Powers "firing his sixguns," and says young Baldwin was "killed instantly," all wrong, all in less than a page.
25. Hanes, "Bloodbath at Coffeyville," 37.
26. "Eyewitness," *The Dalton Brothers*, 222–23.
27. *Beyond the Law*, 146.
28. Ibid., 151.
29. Ibid., 152.
30. Ibid.
31. Ibid.
32. Beer, *The Mauve Decade*, 69.
33. Ibid.
34. *Beyond the Law*, 150.

CHAPTER SIX

1. Duncan, *History of Montgomery County*, 209 ff.
2. Ibid.
3. *Coffeyville Journal*, October, 7, 1892.
4. *Coffeyville Journal*, commemorative edition, obituaries.
5. Jim Hoy, "The Coffeyville Boot."
6. *Coffeyville Journal*, commemorative edition.
7. *Coffeyville Journal*, October 5, 1988. J. B. Kloehr, interview with the author, October 1993.
8. *Coffeyville Journal*, October 14, 1892.

CHAPTER SEVEN

1. *Kansas City Times*, October 7, 1892.
2. Homer Croy, *Last of the Great Outlaws*, 233.
3. Preece, *The Dalton Gang*, 255–56.
4. *Coffeyville Journal*, commemorative edition.

5. *St. Louis Globe-Democrat*, October 17, 1892.

6. *Coffeyville Journal*, October 14, 1892.

7. *Globe-Democrat*, October 17, 1892. Commentary from the Minneapolis, Louisville, Philadelphia, and Pittsburgh press is from a contemporary newspaper account in the author's possession.

8. *Coffeyville Journal*, October 28, 1892.

9. Ibid.

10. Ibid.

11. V. V. Masterson, *The Katy Railroad and the Last Frontier*, 257.

12. Preece, *The Dalton Gang*, 270.

13. *Coffeyville Journal*, October 14, 1892.

14. Shirley, *West of Hell's Fringe*, 243. By contrast, Harold Preece says Bill was cordial to everybody. He probably means that Bill was on good behavior when he first came to town (*The Dalton Gang*, 271).

15. Shirley, *Heck Thomas*, 170.

16. Ibid.

17. Drago, *Road Agents and Train Robbers*, 225.

18. Lue Barndollar, *What Really Happened*, 67. Samuelson, *The Dalton Gang Story: Lawmen to Outlaws*, 127.

19. *Coffeyville Journal*, commemorative edition.

20. Shirley, *West of Hell's Fringe*, 104.

21. Beth Thomas Meeks, *Heck Thomas, My Papa*, 27–28.

22. Dodge, *Undercover for Wells Fargo*, 228–30.

23. Ibid.

24. Ibid.

25. Ibid.

26. Ibid.

27. *Coffeyville Journal*, November 4, 1892. Barndollar, *What Really Happened*, 64.

28. Barndollar, *What Really Happened*, 64.

29. *Coffeyville Journal*, September 30, 1992.

30. Shirley, *Heck Thomas*, 175.

31. Ibid.

32. Shirley, *West of Hell's Fringe*, 118.

33. *Indian-Pioneer Papers*, Lucas interview, December 29, 1937.

34. Meeks, *Heck Thomas, My Papa*, 30.

35. *Indian-Pioneer Papers*, interview with Neal Higgins, August 15, 1937.

36. *Indian Pioneer Papers*, interview with William Ballard, July 20, 1937; Williams interview.

37. Dary, *True Tales of Old-Time Kansas*, 122.

38. Barnard, *A Rider of the Cherokee Strip*, 198.

39. Harry V. Johnston, *My Home on the Range*, 67–68.

40. *Coffeyville Journal*, December 9, 1892.

41. *Coffeyville Journal*, December 23, 1892.

42. *Indian-Pioneer Papers*, interview with Judge J. R. Charlton, November 17, 1937.

43. Coffeyville *Journal*, March 10, 1893.

44. McNeal, *When Kansas Was Young*, 275.

45. Samuelson, *The Dalton Gang Story: Lawmen to Outlaws*, 153.

46. J. Marvin Hunter and N. H. Rose, *Album of Gunfighters*. The text of this book may not be entirely reliable, but the pictures are excellent. It is highly recommended for this reason.

47. Duncan, *History of Montgomery County*, 40–41.

48. *When The Daltons Rode*, 275.

49. Samuelson, *The Dalton Gang Story: Lawmen to Outlaws*, 155.

50. Hazel Chapman, Skiatook, Oklahoma, *Coffeyville Journal*, October 2, 1991.

51. *Indian-Pioneer Papers*, interview with Elsie Brook, July 12, 1937.

52. Samuelson, *The Dalton Gang Story: Lawmen to Outlaws*, 158.

53. Preece, *The Dalton Gang*, 282–83.

54. Meeks, *Heck Thomas, My Papa*, 71.

55. *Kansas City Star*, May 10, 1931.

56. Ibid.

57. Ibid.

58. To reporter A. B. Macdonald, quoted in Dary, *True Tales of Old-Time Kansas*, 121.

59. *Dallas Times-Herald*, April 26, 1931.

60. *Los Angeles Evening Herald and Express*, October 7, 1935. Quoted in C. B. Rhodes ms., Rhodes Collection.

61. Ibid.

62. Samuelson, *The Dalton Gang Story: Lawmen to Outlaws*, at 160. Both Preece, (*The Dalton Gang*, 287) and Latta, (*Dalton Gang Days*, 229) say Emmett's ashes ended up in Coffeyville.

63. *Coffeyville Journal*, October 16, 1993.

CHAPTER EIGHT

1. Olita Fowler, *An Historical Sketch of Coffeyville*, master's thesis for Kansas State Teachers College, 1938.

2. Preece, *The Dalton Gang*, 115–16.
3. *Coffeyville Journal*, October 7, 1892.
4. Barndollar, *What Really Happened*, 35.
5. *Coffeyville Journal*, centennial edition, reprinting an article from the *Journal*, October 5, 1950.
6. Fred Sutton, *Hands Up!*, 188 ff.
7. Ibid., 189–90.
8. Richard S. Graves, *Oklahoma Outlaws*, 53 ff.
9. Ibid., 54.
10. Ibid., 55.
11. Nix, *Oklahombres*, 45.
12. Lamb, *Tragedies of the Osage Hills*, 38.
13. Ibid., 39.
14. Shirley, *Six-Gun and Silver Star*, 59.
15. Shirley, *Heck Thomas*, 167.
16. Drago, *Road Agents and Train Robbers*, 220.
17. Hanes, *Bill Doolin, Outlaw O.T.*, 57.
18. Preece, *The Dalton Gang*.
19. Latta, *Dalton Gang Days*.
20. Shirley, *West of Hell's Fringe*, 242–43.
21. Ibid., 243.
22. Shirley, *Heck Thomas*, 186.
23. Latta, *Dalton Gang Days*, 193.
24. Nash, *Bloodletters and Badmen*, 147.
25. *Beyond the Law*, 126.
26. Homer Croy, *Trigger Marshal*, 161.
27. Preece, *The Dalton Gang*, 267–75. This is a tantalizing reference, information which Preece says he had from Flo's cousin. Unfortunately, he gives no details. See also "Bob Dalton's Bandit Bride," *Real West*, March 1965, 10 ff.
28. Preece, *The Dalton Gang*, 237.
29. Shirley, *Heck Thomas*, 187. Latta agrees: *Dalton Gang Days*, 202.
30. Mark Pannill, *The Sixth Man: Who Was She?*
31. Preece, *The Dalton Gang*, 303.
32. *Coffeyville Journal*, October 3, 1990. The author could find nobody in Coffeyville who knows what happened to either letter or statement.
33. *Coffeyville Journal* centennial edition, from a 1973 interview of Violet Brown Koehler, done by Lloyd LeRoy Thompson, curator of the Brown Mansion in Coffeyville.
34. *Indian-Pioneer Papers*, Ridenhour interview.

35. *Coffeyville Journal*, commemorative edition.
36. Latta, *Dalton Gang Days*, 224.
37. Preece, "Adeline Dalton, Outlaw Mother."
38. Preece, "The Real Emmett Dalton."
39. Latta, *Dalton Gang Days*, 225–26.
40. Rhodes ms., ch. 48, Rhodes Collection.
41. Patterson, *The Train Robbery Era*, 56.
42. Preece, *The Dalton Gang*, 207–8.
43. Ibid., 209.
44. Barndollar, *What Really Happened*, 49.

AFTERWORD

1. *Coffeyville Journal*, October 5, 1988. Kloehr told the author substantially the same thing in October, 1993.

BIBLIOGRAPHY

BOOKS

Adams, Ramon. *Sixguns and Saddle Leather: A Bibliography of Books and Pamphlets on Western Outlaws and Gunmen.* Norman: University of Oklahoma Press, 1969.

Barnard, Evan G. *A Rider of the Cherokee Strip.* New York: Houghton Mifflin, 1936.

Barndollar, Lue Diver. *What Really Happened on October 5, 1892.* Coffeyville, Kans.: Coffeyville Historical Society, 1992.

Bartholomew, Ed E. *Biographical Album of Western Gunfighters.* Houston: Frontier Press, 1958.

Beer, Thomas. *The Mauve Decade.* New York: Knopf, 1926.

Catton, Bruce. *This Hallowed Ground.* New York: Doubleday, 1955.

Clemens, Nancy. *American Bandits.* Girard, Kans.: Haldeman-Julius Publications, 1938.

Coffeyville at 100, Inc. *A History of Coffeyville.* Coffeyville, Kans.: Coffeyville Journal Press, 1969.

Croy, Homer. *He Hanged Them High.* New York: Duell, Sloan & Pierce, 1952.

———. *Last of the Great Outlaws.* New York: Duell, Sloan & Pierce, 1956.

———. *Trigger Marshal.* New York: Duell, Sloan & Pierce, 1958.

Cunningham, Eugene. *Triggernometry.* Caldwell, Idaho: Caxton, 1989.

Dalton, Emmett. *Beyond the Law.* Coffeyville, Kans.: Coffeyville Historical Society, n.d.

———. *When the Daltons Rode.* Doubleday, Doran, 1931.

Dary, David. *True Tales of Old-Time Kansas.* Lawrence: Kansas Press, 1984.

Dodge, Fred. *Under Cover for Wells Fargo*. Boston: Houghton Mifflin, 1969.

Drago, Harry. *Outlaws on Horseback*. New York: Dodd, Mead, 1964.

———. *Road Agents and Train Robbers*. New York: Dodd, Mead, 1973.

———. *Wild, Wooly and Wicked*. New York: Potter, 1960.

Drake, Charles C. *"Who's Who?" A History of Kansas and Montgomery County*. Coffeyville, Kans.: Coffeyville Journal Press, 1943.

Duncan, Lew W. *History of Montgomery County, Kansas*. Iola, Kans.: Iola Register, 1903.

Eaton, Frank. *Pistol Pete: Veteran of the Old West*. Boston: Little, Brown, 1952.

Elliott, David Stewart. *Last Raid of the Daltons*. Coffeyville, Kans.: Coffeyville Journal, n.d.

Elliott, David Stewart, and Ed Bartholomew. *The Dalton Gang and the Coffeyville Raid*. Fort Davis, Tex.: Frontier Book Co., 1968.

"Eyewitness." *The Dalton Brothers*. New York: Frederick Fell, 1954.

Gard, Wayne. *The Chisholm Trail*. Norman: University of Oklahoma Press, 1954.

Graves, Richard S. *Oklahoma Outlaws*. Oklahoma City: State Printing and Publishing Company, 1915.

Hanes, Bailey. *Bill Doolin, Outlaw O.T.* Norman: University of Oklahoma Press, 1968.

Harkey, Dee. *Mean As Hell*. Albuquerque: University of New Mexico Press, 1948.

Harmon, S. W., *Hell on the Border*. Fort Smith: Hell on the Border Pub. Co., 1953.

Haven, Charles T., and Frank A. Belden. *A History of the Colt Revolver, 1836 to 1940*. New York: Bonanza Books, 1940.

Howes, Charles C. *This Place Called Kansas*. Norman: University of Oklahoma Press, 1984.

Hunter, J. Marvin, and N. H. Rose. *Album of Gunfighters*. Bandera, Tex., 1951.

Johnston, Harry V. *My Home on the Range*. St. Paul, Minn.: Webb, 1942.

Lamb, Arthur H. *Tragedies of the Osage Hills*. Pawhuska, Okla.: Osage Printery, n.d.

Latta, Frank. *Dalton Gang Days*. Santa Cruz, Calif.: Bear State Books, 1976.

Markham, George. *Guns of the Wild West*. Bath, U.K.: Arms & Armour Press, 1993.

Martin, Nelda W. *The End of the Old West*.

Masterson, V. V. *The Katy Railroad and the Last Frontier*. Columbia: Missouri Press, 1988.

McNeal, Thomas A. *When Kansas Was Young*. New York: Macmillan, 1922.

Meeks, Beth T. *Heck Thomas, My Papa*. Norman: Levite of Apache, 1988.

Metz, Leon Claire. *The Shooters*. El Paso, Tex.: Mangan Books, 1976.

Miller, Nyle H. and Joseph W. Snell. *Great Gunfighters of the Kansas Cowtowns, 1867–1886,* Lincoln: University of Nebraska Press, 1967.

Nash, Jay. *Bloodletters and Badmen.* New York: Evans, 1973.

Newsom, J. A. *Life and Practice of the Wild & Modern Indian.* Oklahoma City: Harlow Publishing Co., 1923.

Nix, Evett Dumas. *Oklahombres, Particularly Some of the Wilder Ones.* St. Louis, Mo.: Eden Publishing House, 1929.

O'Neal, Bill. *Encyclopedia of Western Gun-Fighters.* Norman: University of Oklahoma Press, 1979.

Pannill, Mark. *The Sixth Man: Who Was She?* Waxahachie, Tex.: Vincon, 1988.

Patterson, Richard. *The Train Robbery Era.* Boulder, Colo.: Pruett Publishing Co., 1991.

———. *Train Robbery : The Birth, Flowering and Decline of a Notorious Western Enterprise.* Boulder, Colo.: Johnson Books, 1981.

Preece, Harold. *The Dalton Gang: End of an Outlaw Era.* New York: Hastings House, 1963.

Prentis, Noble L. *A History of Kansas.* Winfield, Kans.: E. P. Greer, 1899.

Richardson, Albert D. *Some Portions of His Narrative Concerning Kansas.* Coffeyville, Kans.: Zauberberg Press, 1958.

Samuelson, Nancy. *The Dalton Gang Family.* Mead, Kans.: Back Room Printing, 1989.

———. *The Dalton Gang Story: Lawmen to Outlaws.* Eastford, Conn.: Shooting Star Press, 1992.

Serven, James E. *Colt Firearms 1836–1954.* Santa Ana, Calif.: Serven, 1954.

Shirley, Glenn. *Belle Starr and Her Times.* Norman: University of Oklahoma Press, 1990.

———. *Gunfight at Ingalls.* Stillwater, Okla.: Barbed Wire Press, 1990.

———. *Heck Thomas, Frontier Marshal.* Norman: University of Oklahoma Press, 1981.

———. *Law West of Fort Smith.* Lincoln: University of Nebraska Press, 1968.

———. *Six Gun and Silver Star.* Albuquerque: University of New Mexico Press, 1953.

———. *Toughest of them All.* Albuquerque: University of New Mexico Press, 1953.

———. *West of Hell's Fringe.* Norman: University of Oklahoma Press, 1978.

Steele, Phillip. *In Search of the Daltons.* Springdale, Ark.: Frontier Press, 1985.

Sutton, Fred. *Hands Up!* Indianapolis: Bobbs-Merrill, 1927.

Waters, William. *A Gallery of Western Badmen.* Covington, Ky.: Americana, 1954.

Wellman, Paul I. *A Dynasty of Western Outlaws*. Garden City, N.Y.: Doubleday, 1961.

Whittemore, Margaret. *Historic Kansas*. Lawrence: Kansas Press, 1954.

Wilson, R. L. *Winchester: An American Legend*. New York: Random House, 1991.

WPA Writers' Project. *Kansas: A Guide to the Sunflower State*. New York: Viking, 1939.

Yost, Nellie I. *Medicine Lodge*. Chicago: Sage Books, 1970.

ARTICLES

Finney, Frank F., Sr. "Progress in the Civilization of the Osage, and Their Government." *Chronicles of Oklahoma* 40, No. 1 (Spring 1962).

Hanes, Bailey. "Bloodbath at Coffeyville," *Westerner*, January–February 1972.

Hoy, Jim. "The Coffeyville Boot," *Persimmon Hill*, Spring 1991.

Preece, Harold. "Bob Dalton's Bandit Bride," *Real West*, March 1965.

————. "Adeline Dalton, Outlaw Mother," *Real West*, September 1965.

————. "The Real Emmett Dalton," *Real West*, March 1960.

MANUSCRIPTS

Cranor, Ruby. "A True Biography of Julia Johnson Dalton," Public Library, Bartlesville, Okla.

Fowler, Olita. *An Historical Sketch of Coffeyville*, master's thesis for Kansas State Teachers' College, 1938. Coffeyville Public Library, Coffeyville.

Rhodes, C. B.. Rhodes Collection, University of Oklahoma Western History Library, Norman.

WPA Writers' Project. *Indian-Pioneer Papers*, University of Oklahoma Western History Library, Norman. Interviews with:

Ballard, William
Brook, Elsie
Carr, Frank M.
Charlton, Judge J. R.
Davis, William Floyd
Dixon, Mrs. U. S.
Ferchau, Charles
Hammett, Ellis
Hicks, Herbert W.
Higgins, Neal
Knight, Laura
Lucas, Orrington
Morris, Rhoda

Morrison, Susan
Payne, Bob
Ridenhour, H. E.
Steep, Andrew J.
Tannehill, Ninnian
Timmons, Claude
Walker, Agnes
Williams, Jim
Wyatt, Marion G.
Uto, Minnie

LETTERS

A. Connor to the author, October 1993.
B. Mundhenk to the author, October 1993.
J. I. Barrett to the author, October 1993.
A. Winkler to the author, October 1993.

INTERVIEWS

J. R. Kloehr, October 1993.
Jackie Isham Barrett, October 1993.

NEWSPAPERS

Coffeyville Journal
Daily Oklahoman (Oklahoma City).
Dallas Times-Herald
Ford County Globe
Kansas City Star
Kingfisher Free Press
Los Angeles Evening Herald and Express

INDEX

Abilene, Kans., 7

Adair, Iowa, train holdup at, 27

Adair, I.T., 49, 65–66, 70

Adams Grain Company (Coffeyville), 94

Adamson and Wells Brothers (Coffeyville merchants), 16

Alila, Calif., holdup at, 44, 54–55, 59, 168

Ammunition, 29

Anderson, William ("Bloody Bill") (bushwhacker), 7

Arkansas River, 48

"Arkansas Tom." *See* Daugherty, Roy

Atchison, David, Senator, 5

Auction, of Daltons' effects, 170–71

Ayers, Bert (Coffeyville banker), during robbery, 102–105, 116

Ayers, Tom (Coffeyville banker), 17; during robbery, 102–105, 116; shot, 125, 126, 146, 155

Babb, Thomas C. (Coffeyville banker), during robbery, 98–102, 134, 184–86, 201

Baker University, 142

Baldwin, Lucius M., 98, 121, 140, 142

Ball, Charles M. (Coffeyville banker), during robbery, 98–102, 120, 147, 152

Barndollar, J. J., 16

Barndollar, Lue (professor), 206, 208

Barndollar Brothers (dry goods, Coffeyville), 16, 74, 89, 97, 118, 171

Bartlesville, Okla., 176

Bar X Bar ranch, 47

Baxter Springs, Kans. cow town, 10, 51

Beecher, Henry Ward, 4

Beecher's Bibles (Sharps rifles), 4

Beeson, Chalk, Sheriff, 164

Bender (outlaw family), 12–13

Benson, Frank, 73

Biddison (Coffeyville lawyer), 126

Bisley Colt, 31, 76

Black Dog band (of Osage tribe), 15

Blake, William ("Tulsa Jack"), 165; killed, 166

Blakely (Coffeyville cigar maker), 81

Blue Duck (I.T. outlaw), 23
Boothby, Jim, 103
Boswell's Hardware (Coffeyville), 89,
    96, 123, 125, 132
Brewster, J. H., 102
Broadwell, George, 158
Broadwell, Richard L. ("Dick"), 50; in
    Condon Bank, 98–102, 118,
    124; dead outside town, 133,
    147, 151, 158; at Leliaetta, 57,
    61, 69, 70, 71, 78, 88, 91, 98;
    runs from Condon, 125,
    wounded, 119, 126
Brooks, "Bully," attacks Senator
    Sumner, 5
Brown, Charles (Coffeyville
    shoemaker), 123; killed by Bob,
    123, 140
Bryant, Black-Faced Charley, 32, 49,
    51, 53, 56; killed by Ed Short,
    57, 62
Bryant, Daisy, 53, 58; Flo Quick as,
    198, 199
Buck, Rufus (I.T. outlaw), 24
Buckeye Street (Coffeyville), 86
Buckskin Ike (I.T. outlaw), as 6th
    man, 200
Buford's Men, 4
Burlington, Kans., 142
Burton, Amos, 75
Butler, Andrew, Senator, 5

Caldwell, Kans., 7
California Creek, 79, 80
Callahan, John, Sheriff, 155, 170, 171
Candy Creek, 78
Caney, Kans., bank robbery at, 163,
    164

Canty, Ben (Silver City, N.Mex.
    lawman), 52, 76
Carpenter, Charles T. (Coffeyville
    banker), during robbery, 98–102,
    120
Cass County, Mo., 36, 37
"Cat wagons" (mobile brothels), 46
Chapman, Ed., 78
Charlton, J. R., Judge, 172
Cherokee Bill (I.T. outlaw), 24
Cherokee Strip, 75
Chisholm Trail, 10
Christie, Ned (Cherokee outlaw), 22
Churches, Coffeyville, 15
Cimarron, Rose of, 62, 188
Cimarron River, 47, 48, 49, 55
Circus, in Coffeyville, 73
Claremore, Oklahoma Territory, 64
Claymore, Kans., 18
Clifton, Charles ("Dan," "Dynamite
    Dick"), 165; killed, 166
Cochran, Alex, shot by Bob Dalton,
    42–43
Coffey, Col. James A., 15
Coffeyville Defenders' Museum, 134
Coffeyville Journal, 16, 42, 136, 137
Colt revolvers, 29–33, 32, 76
Condon, C. M. (Coffeyville banker),
    17
Condon Bank (Coffeyville), 72, 73,
    74, 89, 90, 91, 92, 93, 95; robbery
    of, 98–102, 116, 123, 124, 147
Connelly, Charles T. (city marshal),
    122, 123; Civil War service, 143,
    149; killed by Grat, 127–28, 133,
    135, 137; and "warning," 205
Consolidated Oil Company,
    Coffeyville, 94
Cook, Bill (I.T. outlaw), 24

Cooper Creek, 51
"Cowboy Annie" (Doolin gang groupie), 194
Cox, C. S., 117, 204
Cubine, George, 96, 103, 117; killed by Bob, 123, 137, 141, 171, 205
Cubine's Boot & Shoe (Coffeyville), 89

Dale, Frank, District Judge, 165
Dalton, Adeline Younger, 36, 40, 56, 77; in Coffeyville, 155, 156; and divorce, 136; letter to sons, 174–75, 193
Dalton, Ben, 38, 44, 56
Dalton, Bill, 39, 46, 55; in Coffeyville, 155–57, 162; with Doolin gang, 163, 167; holdups and death, 168–69, as 6th man, 193–94
Dalton, Bob, 33; Coffeyville plans, 34, 39, 41, 43; dying words, 131, 151, 191; in First National, 102–105; history, 46–47, 51, 54, 56; at Leliaetta, 58, 60, 64, 72, 76, 77, 78, 80, 81, 84, 85, 92, 96; shoots Ayers, 125, 129; shoots Gump, 119, 121, 122; kills Cubine and Brown, 123; tries to shoot Kloehr, 130
Dalton, Emmett ("Em"), 34, 36, 39, 41, 43; dies, 180, 191; in First National, 102–105, 117, 121, 122, 129; history, 47–48, 51, 53, 54, 56; at Leliaetta, 58, 60, 62, 66, 69, 72, 74, 75, 76, 77, 78, 79, 80, 81, 84, 92, 96; married, 178; shot by Seamen, 131, 133, 149, 154, 159; tried and convicted, 171–73, 174

Dalton, Frank, 21; killed, 40; as marshal, 39–40
Dalton, Grat, 39, 40, 41, 45; in Condon Bank, 98–102, 117, 120, 124; history, 47, 54, 60, 63, 64, 76, 77, 78, 84, 85, 91; killed by Kloehr, 128, 151; kills Connelly, 127; runs from Condon, 125; wounded, 126
Dalton, Grattan. See Dalton, Grat
Dalton, Henry, 38
Dalton, James Lewis (Lewis) (father), 36, 37; dies, 38; and divorce, 136
Dalton, Littleton, 38, 77
Dalton, Mason Frakes. See Dalton, Bill
Dalton, Robert Reddick. See Dalton, Bob
Dalton, William Marion. See Dalton, Bill
Dalton family history, 36–40
Daugherty, Roy ("Arkansas Tom"), 165, 166
Davis (Coffeyville farmer), 80
Davis, Ollie (Coffeyville prostitute), 10–11
Davis Blacksmith Shop (Coffeyville), 90, 91
"Death Alley," 91, 125, 137, 149, 154
Delonadale, pistol-whipped by Grat Dalton, 45
Dengue fever, and Bill Doolin, 79, 189
Deringer, Henry (pocket-pistol maker), 28
Dietz, Lewis, 97; wounded, 120, 147
Dodge, Fred, 61, 63, 70, 71, 72, 79, 158, 159, 161, 162, 163, 189–90, 204

Dodge City, Kans., 6; life in, 8, 16
Doolin, Bill (I.T. outlaw), 36, 46; at
    Caney, Kans., 163, 164; and
    dengue fever, 79; history of, 48;
    killed by Thomas, 167; at
    Leliaetta, 57, 61, 69, 70; as 6th
    man, 186–91, 194
Duemcke, Herman, 127
Dunn, Rosa. See Cimarron, Rose of
Dynamite, at Isham's, 130
Dynamite Dick. See Clifton, Charles
Dynamite Jack (I.T. outlaw), 25

Easton, Kans., murder at, 6
Elgin, Kans., 167
Elk, Okla., Bill Dalton killed at, 169
Elliott, David Stewart, 37, 85, 96,
    103, 120, 123, 129, 133, 135,
    137, 149, 153, 155, 184, 200, 202
Elmwood Cemetery (Coffeyville),
    158, 179
El Reno, Oklahoma Territory, 67
Elsworth, Kans., 7
Epworth League, 143
Evans, Tom. See Bill Powers

Falk, Minnie, 117
Farmer's Home hotel (Coffeyville),
    68, 72, 129, 150
Films, of Dalton gang, 181
First National Bank of Coffeyville,
    17, 80, 89, 91, 95; robbery of,
    102–105, 117, 122, 141, 191
Fishback's pool hall (Adair), 65
Fitzpatrick, W. S., U.S.
    Commissioner, 45
Flynn, Pete (early Coffeyville
    marshal), 11
Fort Gibson, I.T., 19

Fresno, Calif., 54
Frey, J. J., 154
Fritch, F. J., 171
Frontier Model revolvers. See Colt
    revolvers

Gad's Hill, Mo., James-Younger
    holdup at, 27
Gibbs, Ida, 73, 74, 118
Gilbert, William (Coffeyville
    resident), 85, 86
Gilstrap, Bob, 177
Goff, W. L., Doctor (killed at Adair),
    66, 67, 71
Goldsby, Crawford. See Cherokee Bill
Grimes, William, Deputy U.S.
    Marshal, 174–75
Gump, Charles, 95, 96, 116, 118, 147,
    180
Guthrie, Oklahoma Territory, 45, 58,
    164, 167, 195, 206

Halsel, Oscar, 48
Hames, J. R., 116
"Hanging Judge." See Parker, Isaac
Hart, Loss, Deputy U.S. Marshal, kills
    Bill Dalton, 169
Harte, Bret, 137
Hays, Kans., 7
Heard, Mary, 48
Hell's Fringe, 189
Hickory Creek, 80
Hicks, Herber, 64
Hollingsworth, C. L., 102
Hollingsworth, R. H., 86, 87, 183, 200
Hueston, Tom, 164
Huff, Katie, marries John Kloehr, 145
Hutchins, J. R., Deputy U.S. Marshal,
    24

Hutchinson, Kans., 50

Independence, Kans., 143
Indian Territory, 19, 44
Ingalls, Oklahoma Territory, 49, 69, 165, 166
Iron Mountain railroad. See Kansas & Arkansas Valley
Isham, Henry (Coffeyville merchant), 97, 125, 146
Isham, J. T. (Coffeyville merchant), 16
Isham's hardware (Coffeyville), 89, 96, 117, 123, 124, 125, 132, 146, 204

James, Frank, 152
James brothers, 27
Jennings, Al, 166
Johnson, Julia, 62, 76, 80, 156, 175; marries Emmett, 176–78, 195, 198
Johnson, Pussyfoot, 177
Jones, Andy, 73, 74
July, Jim, 24

Kansas and Arkansas Valley Railroad, 10
Kansas-Nebraska Bill of 1854, 4
Kanza Indians, 3
Katy. See Missouri, Kansas & Texas Railroad
King, Tom (female horse thief), 53, 58, 177, 198, 199
Kingfisher, Oklahoma Territory, 51, 55, 59, 60, 77; Emmett buried at, 180
Kingfisher Creek, 51
Kloehr, J. B., 208

Kloehr, John J., 95, 127; kills Grat, 128, 130, 144, 145, 159–61, 170
Kloehr Brothers livery & hotel business, 16, 90, 94
Knotts, A. W., 102
Koehler, Violet Brown (Coffeyville citizen), 201

Labor Party, bomb plot by, 18
Lang, William H., 116
Lang & Lape Furniture & Undertaking (Coffeyville), 116
Lansing, Kans., prison at, 173
Lawrence, Kans., 5, 6
Leavenworth, Fort, 6
Leavenworth, Kans., 37
Leavenworth, Lawrence and Galveston Railroad, 10, 15
LeFlore, Charley, 65, 66, 70
Leliaetta, I.T., 57, 64, 69, 70
Levan, John, 98
Lewis, Earnest ("Killer"), and Julia Johnson, 177, 195
Liberty, Kans., 9
Lighthorse, 22
"Little Britches" (Doolin gang groupie), 194
Locust Hill, I.T., 37, 38
Long, Jack, 103, 122, 124, 125
Long-Bell Lumber Company (Coffeyville), 88, 90, 128
Longview, Tex., holdup at, 168
Lucas, Orrington ("Red"), 45–46
Lynch mob, and Emmett Dalton, 150

McCluskie, Mike, in Newton, Kans., gunfight, 8–9
McCoy's Hardware (Coffeyville), 90

McElhanie, Bill ("Narrow-Gauge Kid"), 52, 54
McKenna, Aleck, 95, 96
McKenna & Adamson's dry goods (Coffeyville), 94, 95
McPherson, Aimee Semple, 180
Madsen, Chris, Deputy U.S. Marshal, 23, 63, 165, 194, 196–97, 202, 203, 206
Maledon, George (hangman at Fort Smith), 19–20
Manvel (cretin outlaw), 196
Marais des Cygnes River, 5, 6
Marshals, U.S. Deputy, for Parker court, 21
Mashed-O Ranch, 72, 77–78
Mauser, self-loading pistol, 30
Medicine Lodge, Kans., 9; Carry Nation in, 16
Mennonites, 14
Methodist Episcopal Church, 140, 142
Mid-Continent Field (Kans. gas field), 17
"Minnie" (Bob Dalton's alleged girlfriend), 42
Missouri, Kansas & Texas Railroad, 10; holdups on, 26, 52, 57
Missouri Compromise, 3
Missouri Pacific Railroad, 10, 143
Modern Woodmen of America, 142, 143
Montgomery, Charlie (killed by Bob Dalton), 41
Montgomery, Gen. Richard, 15
Montgomery County, Kans., 37
Moore, Eugenia, 52, 53, 58, 76, 80, 197, 199
Moran, J. P. ("Pat"), 94, 95

Morgan, Jess, 103
Morphine, use of in I.T., 21
Movies, of Dalton gang, 181
Munn, Charles, 90, 91
Muskogee, I.T., 19, 204

"Narrow Gauge Kid." See McElhanie, Bill
Nation, Carry, 16
Ned's Fort Mountain (Christie home), 22
Newcomb, George ("Bitter Creek"), 49, 51, 56, 61, 69, 70; at Caney, Kans., 163, 164; killed, 166; as 6th man, 184, 191, 192
New Model Army. See Colt revolvers
Newspapers, typical contents of, 138
Newton, Kans., gunfight in, 8
Nix, Evett, Marshal, 68, 86–87, 188

Ogee, Allie, 192–93
Oklahoma City, Oklahoma Territory, 77, 197
Onion Creek, 15, 80, 81, 85
Opera House, Coffeyville, 90
Opium, use of in I.T., 21
Orlando, Oklahoma Territory, 55, 164
Osage cattle trail, 10
Osage Hills, 67, 75
Osage Indians, 3, 15
Osage police, 44; Bob Dalton as "chief" of, 43
Osawatomie, Kans., 5

Padgett, Caleb (George), as 6th man, 200
Parker, Isaac (judge at Fort Smith), 19; at Parker, Kans., 15, 18; tries Belle Starr, 24, 39, 56

Parsons, Kans., 154, 163
Paso Robles, Calif., 54
Peacemaker. *See* Colt revolvers
Peffer, W. A., 12; as vigilante, 13
Pegg's Prairie, 78
Perana (patent medicine), 21
Perkins, Luther, 99
Perry, Okla., 56
Picker, George, 125, 126
Pierce, Charley ("Cockeye Charley"),
    50; at Adair, 65, 70; killed, 166;
    at Leliaetta, 57, 61
Powell, Susan (early Coffeyville
    settler), 15
Power, William Tod (or St.). *See*
    Powers, Bill
Powers, Bill, 48; in Condon Bank,
    98–102, 119, 124; dead in alley,
    133, 151, 158; at Leliaetta, 57,
    61, 69, 71, 78, 85, 88, 91; runs
    from Condon, 125; wounded,
    126
Pryor Creek, I.T., 64

Quantrill, William, 6, 7, 41, 51
Quick, Flo, 46, 53, 56, 58, 62, 63, 76,
    177, 195; and Killer Lewis, 196,
    197–98, 199

Radcliff, George W., 54
Raidler, William F. ("Little Bill"),
    164, 167
Rammel Brothers drugstore
    (Coffeyville), 89, 103, 122, 140
Read, Haz, 98
Read Brothers (Coffeyville
    merchants), 12, 98, 121
Red Hot Street (Coffeyville red light
    district), 10, 16

Red Rock station, I.T. train holdup at,
    61
Reed, Jim (I.T. outlaw), 23
Remington firearms, 29
Reynolds, T. Arthur, 98; wounded,
    119, 124, 145, 147
Rhodes, C. B., 203
Rhodes, Eugene Manlove, shelters
    Doolin, 167
Riggs, Clint, 200
Rogers, Bob (I.T. outlaw), 24–25;
    killed near Coffeyville, 25
Rogers, Will, visits Coffeyville, 16
Ross, E. G., Senator, 16
Ross's Paper, 16

Sac and Fox Agency, 79
Sacred Heart, I.T., 168
Santa Rosa, N.Mex., 53
Savage (Coffeyville farmer), 80
Scott, Louis (early Coffeyville
    settler), 14, 15
Seamen, Carey, 127; shoots Emmett,
    131, 147, 185
Seldomridge, J. L., 87, 183, 200
Seldomridge, John M., 87, 183, 200
Seymour, Ind., first peacetime train
    holdup at, 27
Shawnee cattle trail, 10
Shepard, W. H. (Coffeyville banker),
    during robbery, 103–105, 116
Shields, "Satan," 26
Shirley, Myra Belle. *See* Starr, Belle
Short, Ed, Deputy U.S. Marshal,
    killed, 57
Sibert, John, 122
Silver City (N.Mex. mining town),
    52, 53

Simpson, Jerimiah ("Sockless Jerry") (Kansas politician), 153
"Six-Shooter Jack" (I.T. outlaw), 50
Skiatook, I.T., 78
Slaughter, C. C. (Texas cattleman), 49
"Slaughter's Kid." *See* Newcomb, George
Slosson's drugstore (Coffeyville), 73, 94, 95, 116, 126, 149
Smith, Charles, 95
Smith and Wesson revolvers, 31
Smith's Barber Shop (Coffeyville), 89, 95
Sontag, John, brother as 6th man, 200
Southern Hotel, 144
Southern Pacific Railroad, 54
Southwest City, Mo., 67
Spanish-American War, 137
Spears, Jim (John Kloehr), 159
Spearville, Kans., 164
Spencer, Al (train robber), 26
Starmer, William, 55–56
Starr, Belle, 23–24, 58
Starr, Henry, 178
Starr, Sam, 23
Starr, Tom, 23
Stevens Switch, South Coffeyville, 10
Stillwater, Oklahoma Territory, 164
Sumner, Charles (Massachusetts senator), 5
Sutton, Fred, 186
Swisher Brothers Machine Shop (Coffeyville), 127

Tackett, John, 178
Thomas, Heck, Deputy U.S. Marshal: on Bob Dalton's shooting, 46; kills Doolin, 167, 190, 204; at

Red Rock, 61, 71, 72, 79, 157, 158, 159, 161, 162, 165; wounds Christie, 22, 23
Three Guardsmen, 36
Tilghman, Bill, Deputy U.S. Marshal, 23, 167, 188
Timmons, Claude, 78
Tulare County, Calif., 54, 55
Tulsa, I.T., 77
"Tulsa Jack." *See* Blake, William
Turkey Red wheat, 13–14
Turkey Track cattle ranch, 48
Twin Mounds, Daltons fight posse at, 55

Ullom's Restaurant (Coffeyville), 90
Uncapher, Joe, 99, 126

Van Buren, Ark., 202, 206
Verdigris City, Kans., 18
Verdigris River, 13, 14, 18
Vinita, I.T., 37, 65, 72, 197, 204
Visalia, Calif., 54, 59

Wagoner, I.T., train holdup at, 57, 69
Waightman, George ("Red Buck") (I.T. outlaw), 164; killed, 166
Walker, Annie (Baxter Springs madam), 51
Walker, Marshal R. L., 44
Warkentin, Bernard, 13
Waukomis, Oklahoma Territory, Black-Faced Charley killed at, 57
Webley (British Bulldog revolver), 31, 84, 134
Wells, Bob, 129
Wells, Walter H., Doctor, 150, 151, 154, 170

West, Richard ("Little Dick"), 165;
    killed, 166
Westport Landing, Mo., 36
Westralia, Kans., 18
Wharton, I.T., 56, 57, 58, 71, 162
Whipple, Eva, 155
White, Talbot, 71
Wichita, Kans., 7
Williams, Parker, 97, 118, 119
Winchester rifles, 28–29, 30, 76
Wilcox, H. A., 158
Wilcox, J. H., 99

Yantis, Oliver ("Ol' ") (I.T. outlaw),
    163, 164
Yoes, George A., 202, 206
Yoes, Jacob, U.S. Marshal, 45, 202,
    203
Yokum, Bob (I.T. outlaw), 50
Youngblood, T. S., Doctor, wounded
    at Adair, 66
Younger, Cole, and Belle Starr, 23,
    152
Younger, John, 45
Younger's Bend, 23